Liberation Theology

The Political Expression of Religion

Ricardo Planas

Sheed & Ward

Sheed & Ward™ is a service of National Catholic Reporter Publishing, Inc.

Library of Congress Catalog Card Number: 86-61356

ISBN: 0-934134-99-5

Published by:

Sheed & Ward
115 E. Armour Blvd. P.O. Box 414292
Kansas City, MO 64141-0281

To order, call: (800) 821-7926

CONTENTS

FOREWORD

Liberation theology is probably the most important development in Christian theology in this century. It is ecumenical and spans many cultures, though rooted more particularly in the Latin American culture and in the Catholic context. Concerned with the most troubling issues of the contemporary world, liberation theology necessarily has far-flung political implications. Yet to this time there has been very little written about this theological movement from a political point of view, at least as far as more careful analysis is concerned. There has been, instead, a good deal of uninformed condemnation of liberation theology both as a theological school and in terms of its political impact. This theology and its authors have been accused of some strange aberrations from morality and common sense without any substantive demonstration that they indeed hold these positions. For this reason one can but welcome a careful, scholarly effort to analyze the phenomenon of liberation theology in its political aspects.

There are other reasons for regarding this book as a truly significant contribution. The impetus for liberation theology and its verification lie in those conditions of the Third World cultures of our time which we find it difficult to appreciate and understand from the vantage point of our First World comfort and security. Yet the issues which this theology raises are issues which concern us all directly. It is not surprising that there should have been considerable resistance to the questions and proposals raised by these authors, but it is also both necessary and urgent that the more reflective sections of the North American people should be invited to make the effort to understand the implications for our own culture and society. Ricardo Planas in this book attempts just such an introduction of North American readers into the reality and importance of the issues raised in liberation theology.

This is a serious book which invites serious reading and honest, far-reaching reflection. It is not written to entertain, nor even simply to instruct, but rather to challenge by the systematic analysis of what is really at stake in this theological movement. At a time when American citizens are confronted with increasing responsibility for interventions made on their behalf by their government in the affairs and the fate of many Third World nations, this book and the scholarship which it represents are most timely. One can but hope that it will find a wide and receptive readership.

Monika K. Hellwig

"No force is greater as an idea whose time has come."
(attributed to T. de Chardin)

An error cannot subsist without lacking a nucleus of truth in it. Hence, when dealing openly with the error, . . . a question must undoubtedly always be kept present: what truth is hidden beneath the error and how can it be recovered fully from the error?
(attributed to Cardinal Joseph Ratzinger)

PREFACE

This work does not do credit to the ideas of those involved in the liberation theology movement. It is easy to critique the writings of men without having to become involved in their daily struggles for freedom and justice. My sole purpose, however, is to present liberation theology from the standpoint of political analysis to an audience that appears too remote from the conditions that gave birth to the liberation movement. My objective has been to evaluate the views that constitute what is called "liberation theology," to contribute to a better understanding of the complexity that surrounds it. It is precisely this complexity that prevents one from making light pronouncements in favor or against those involved in the liberation movement and their ideas.

I am indebted to several persons who have contributed to the writing of this manuscript: Prof. Charles Elliott, George Washington University, who suggested the topic and sustained my effort, providing incisive criticism throughout the work; Prof. Carl Linden, also from George Washington University, from whom I learned an appreciation for political theory; Prof. Monika Hellwig, Georgetown University, for reading the manuscript and for encouraging me to publish it; my good friend Pablo Paz y Miño, whose ideas and support facilitated this endeavor. I owe special mention to my dear wife, Nancy, for editing parts of the manuscript and for her companionship.

Finally, I have chosen to dedicate this work to my sons, Richard David and Michael Sean, for they gave me the strength to complete the work. Above all, I owe a great deal to my A.C.U. community, where I learned about religion and politics and the ideals which enabled me to pursue this topic. To these ideals — spirituality, the application of knowledge to improve society, and service to those in need — I dedicate this work.

Ricardo Planas
Washington, D.C.

INTRODUCTION

Politics and theology meet and find common expression through the cultural channel of religion. Religion can legitimize a government, provide cohesiveness among social groups, and add stability within the body politic. On the other hand, religion can become a disruptive force in society if attempts are made to suppress it, or if it takes a strong stand against political and social institutions. Events in recent years in Poland and in some countries in the Middle East and Latin America show the impact religious beliefs and institutions can have in political affairs. A religious issue or incident may suddenly erupt into a source of domestic conflict, and eventually spill across national boundaries and affect the politics of other nations.

From the perspective of understanding political phenomena, religion is not merely a personal or private matter. Religion is the cultural expression of a faith or set of beliefs shared by many. At times religious behavior takes the form of the private prayer, or it may be characterized by the gathering at the temple. Moreover, religion makes demands upon the faithful to act overtly in accordance with shared beliefs. The close relationship between religious beliefs and overt behavior (ethics and morality) survives and nurtures itself within a value-oriented environment such as the home, religious school, or church. But in many cases, the true believer makes moral and ethical claims upon society on behalf of one's faith. A person strives to make the cultural environment conform with the values that one upholds, values which have social and political implications. In this sense, religion competes for allegiance with social and political doctrines.[1]

Both religion and politics have the potential to arouse passions and to motivate people to action. Religion touches the ultimate, and for many the most sacred, aspects of human existence — God, love, sin, salvation. Politics, in its "struggles for power," processes of "allocating values," and messianic attempts to transform society, affects the personal or vested interests of all. However, when religion is assigned a political role, either to challenge or to help preserve the status quo, it acquires a dynamic force that can reach the individual at the collective level and move the person to varying degrees of action. Within this context it is not surprising that combining these two social elements elicits highly emotional and subjective rhetoric and controversy.

The spirit-matter tension in Christian theology, and the issues that liberation theology deals with create a situation that easily lends itself to partisan attitudes. Thus, critics may condemn priests who are actively involved in challenging the political status quo, claiming that their attitude reflects a loss of faith. Others in favor of liberation theology perceive these religious men as "living their faith in the context of the struggle for liberation."[2] This does not necessarily suggest that value preferences are distorting the truth in this case, but instead it is important to realize how the cultural conditioning of religious views affect the perception of reality, to the extent that both observations may be correct, each on its own merits. The faith that some critics argue has been lost, refers to the traditional view that the priest's role takes place in the parish, spiritually nourishing his flock, celebrating the sacraments, and seeking the salvation of souls. For the priest to "go astray" from this traditional role is for many a sign of weakening, or loss of faith. For those who side with liberation theology, faith is not absolutely tied to a set of practices or specific tasks. In the constant search for the will of God, faith may at times impose a different set of priorities, the refusal of which may denote its lifelessness. Such conflicts reflect the controversy surrounding the liberation movement.

Hence, part of the conventional wisdom may see liberation theology as a political substitute for religion, as a Marxist attempt to spread class strife and foster revolution and socialism under the disguise of social justice, and also as a sort of "fifth column" within the Church. Others may feel that liberation theology, in its present form, constitutes the only path to salvation and Christian political liberation.[3]

This work will seek to show that liberation theology arises mainly as a reaction against traditional religious views, and a different theological approach, as well as being a Third World response to the social and political conditions prevailing in Latin America. In addition, it will show that both the theory and the praxis in liberation are influenced by authentic religious values, even when they operate within a loose Marxist framework which serves, functionally, as a catalyst to religious and social ideas oriented toward structural and personal change. This work will attempt to explain how liberation theology has forced the Chruch to come to terms with the temporal world in a more extensive and committed manner than the one previously espoused in 1965 by the Second Vatican Council. In effect, the Latin American Church cannot be properly understood without taking into consideration the ideas of liberation theology. Today, the Church is moving toward a cautious incorporation of these ideas. This in turn may lead to a change in the social and political expectations, values, and attitudes of people in the region that will transform the political panorama in Latin America, if the pastoral aspects of the theology are implemented.

Liberation theology brings forth a strong socio-political orientation that is central to both its theory and its praxis. This aspect has been largely ignored, probably because liberation authors are constantly intertwining the religious with the political. It is not an easy task to unravel the two, and to "decipher" the political content of what are basically theological and politically mediated works. Hence the purpose of the study is to penetrate the theological jargon and the religious connection, and to extract the political dimension in liberation. However, to focus strictly on the political issues and concepts, isolating them from the theological and the religious, would prevent the reader from attaining the original purpose of the study: an understanding of liberation theology. To completely divorce these elements would be virtually impossible since the theological component serves as the theoretical basis of the political and religious praxis. The latter cannot be comprehended without the former.

This study, then, will show how the theological and the political aspects relate to each other. It will discuss the political rationale of liberation theology; its political objectives; its theory-praxis nexus; and its approach to social and political change. In addition, the work will analyze the theology's major political tenets and specific concepts such as liberation, class struggle, the praxis, violence, dependency, revolution, socialism, social change, and the Christian and Marxist ideas. Finally, it will assess the impact the movement may have in Latin American politics and the implications it carries for American foreign policy. The study focuses on the primary sources of liberation theology, the ideas of the authors themselves: Gustavo Gutiérrez, Segundo Galilea, Hugo Assman, Juan Luis Segundo, Ignacio Ellacuría, Enrique Dussel, Raúl Vidales, Pablo Richard, Ronaldo Muñoz, Jon Sobrino, Leonardo Boff, and others.[4]

What is Liberation Theology?

A proper understanding of liberation as a theological reaction should be sought in terms of a traditional viewpoint that stresses the separation of religion and politics (the result in part of the spirit-matter dichotomy in cultural life), and the opposite stand, that which views religion and faith as having a sociopolitical dimension. According to the former, liberation theology implies political action and deals with economic realities, issues regarded as banal when compared to things of the spirit and of God. Thus, what is freedom from oppression and misery compared to freedom in God and freedom from sin? What is living in poverty compared to living in God's grace, and the riches of the spirit? This view does not regard politics in itself as immoral. Though politics often involves vested interests, power, ambition, deception, and ruthlessness, this view alleges that such is the human condition. The honest and moral politician may see politics as a noble instrument. His faith, however, is something personal. His relationship with God is private, and God's values are held independently of whatever political values he represents.

Furthermore, although he regards the political as moral, he cannot perceive politics as being as sublime as the spiritual, for the Kingdom of God is not of "this world." Hence, this view leads to the creation of two kingdoms on earth. This dictates the separation and distinction of the political and religious realms, the former being temporal, characterized by material activity, and the latter being spiritual, in which one enjoys one's personal relationship with God.

The other parallel view states that religion does in fact have a place in politics. But when religion is seen as espousing revolution against the traditional values represented by Western liberalism, and does so within a Marxist framework, one begins to think in terms of the wolf dressed in sheep's clothing, infiltrating the children of God in order to subdue them. At stake here is nothing less than individual freedom, the family, private property, and of course, God. It is then that the political aspect is de-emphasized with the allegation that one cannot pursue redemption on earth, that happiness and fulfillment can only be found in God's kingdom at the end of history, and that material conditions are important but no one can regard them as absolute.

Liberation theology is the attempt to break with both of these views. From its standpoint it is the irruption of God's kingdom in history that gives life on earth its significance. Hence, it is concrete man and woman — not their souls or their bodies, but the human person as a material entity with a spiritual dimension — that is important. Thus, the dignity of the human being fashioned in God's image is at the crux of liberation theology. If God saw that what He created was good, then the continuation of that Creation and its progress are part of His plan. That plan requires that the people liberate themselves from sin as well as from the effects of sin, and from conditions of servitude. In liberation theology the suffering that one must bear in the course of life is not only passive. A great deal of it is the result of a person's love of God and the commandment to love one's neighbor, which forces a person to witness one's faith by helping those in distress and by transforming the world so that it conforms to God's plan on earth. For the believer, God's call to subdue the earth means to change it so that it becomes a worthy temporal habitat for all the children of God.

Human suffering owes its presence to the evil within each person. Such evil is reflected in social conditions, in issues and problems that are manifested politically, economically, and culturally through systems and structures. Hence, the struggle against sin and in favor of justice requires political action. In a way, liberation theology is a religious ideology, i.e., a conception of Christianity that propels those involved toward a goal that is distinctively Christian: liberation — a goal that is temporal and eschatological at the same time, for it relates to the kingdom on earth and to salvation. It does this by stressing an attitude that seeks to put into practice God's commandment to love one's neighbor in a situation of poverty and injustice.

The Marxist input arises primarily as the medium for the critique of religious and social reality. In liberation theology it is not Marxism that fosters revolution. On the contrary, Christianity does that. Revolution is neither a Marxist invention, nor do Marxists have a monopoly in it. The role of Marxism in liberation theology is to allow the believer to look at faith from a different perspective and to uncover certain incongruities that exist between reality and gospel values. Given the Marxist orientation toward material reality, toward praxis and social change and against capitalism, it has served liberation theology as a means to question the historical realization of a spiritualized religion and an unjust economic and political system in Latin America. This does not mean that liberation theology accepts Marxist atheism, but neither does it affirm that all involved in the movement have accepted Marxism critically, or deny that some have tended to link Marxist concepts to faith and salvation in a dogmatic fashion.

From a political standpoint, liberation theology analyzes present conditions with the aid of social scientific methodologies, in an attempt to understand the social aspects of sin. At this level the terminology is understandably more political, and some of the concepts used are less theological. Given the complexity of the problems that affect the poor today and the political nature of these problems, Christian love requires, in many instances, political involvement as its ultimate expression. Gustavo Gutiérrez, a pioneer in liberation theology, sees this as a logical conclusion: "When I discovered that poverty was something to be fought against, that poverty was structural, that poor people were a class, it became crystal clear that in order to serve the poor one had to move into political action."[5] Liberation theology, then, constitutes a struggle to liberate the poor from their condition. The vehicle or instrument to attain liberation is political action. Faith and religious values are the source of motivation. And, a combination of Christian and Marxist ideas serve as the frame of reference used to analyze and evaluate reality.

As a praxis, liberation theology is oriented toward the transformation of reality. It questions the political status quo and the religious culture, announces new social goals to be sought, provides ideological guidelines for political action, gives an element of human hope, and motivates human behavior. It also attempts to develop pastoral programs for spiritual and political action, and deals with consciousness-raising activities through the creation of ecclesiastical communities at the grassroots level.

Nonetheless, the movement suffers serious shortcomings. Theoretically, there are too many authors presently engaged in the unsystematic development of a wide variety of themes. This inherent chaos makes the theology difficult to follow and to understand. There is a lack of rigor in conceptualization and analysis on the part of the writers, which accounts for its ambiguities and vagueness. Also, there are inconsistencies in the analysis of reality, in part due to a reliance on Marxism without the previous revision of its categories. Furthermore, one can sense in some instances high levels of frustration in the rhetoric, and as a result, an eagerness to dive into ideological waters with little or no exploration, and without much concern for long-run consequences. Finally, from the standpoint of the layperson, the theology is excessively and unnecessarily abstract.

On the other hand, the critics who are in a position to evaluate this movement are often not helpful. The tendency is to regard liberation theology as a homogeneous movement, to reduce it to a few themes, or to identify it with two or three authors, and pass judgments for or against it based on limited information or prejudice. Some who favor and welcome the liberation movement for its political postures may tend to view it positively and endorse it without serious analysis. In a sense they act as apologists for the liberation process. Others, identifying those aspects they find unorthodox or unpalatable with their own ideas, may reject the movement altogether. Some critics have realized the diversity within liberation theology and have spoken of several theologies, unfortunately giving the impression that each one stands by itself as a finished product with its own author.[6]

A more realistic assessment lies somewhere between these two views. One can imagine for a moment a large intellectual canvas in which students from two distinct schools paint their ideas with an originality that characterizes their individual interests, yet they are influenced by common values and similar experiences. The commonality of their task presupposes that similar colors will be used, although the way they are combined will be different. Some of their lines and traces will converge, while others will not. This is to say that there will be areas of agreement, but differences of opinion unavoidably will emerge.

A distinctive feature that characterizes liberation theology is that this approach is the result of a "collective awakening" among hundreds of lay Christian activists, priests, and some Catholic bishops who decided to assume a more radical posture with regard to poverty and oppression in Latin America. Prior to the Medellín Episcopal Conference in 1968 (referred to hereafter as Medellín), seen by may as the real beginning of liberation theology, many priests, laypersons, and bishops already had begun to express themselves publicly in liberation terminology.[7] Hence liberation theology cannot properly be identified with any particular writer, any more than it can be subsumed under the category of a specific ideology or reduced to one set of issues while ignoring others.

The considerable overlapping of issues among the writers, and the diversity of opinions of each one within a common framework, makes liberation theology a pluralistic movement, though one developing within a core of basic principles, values, and methodology. One assumes that in order to make some sense of this theology it would be important to identify the major tendencies or currents that operate within it. Attempts have been made by theologians and critics alike to develop a typology, according to praxis or motivational concerns, of the participants in liberation.[8] Neither appears to be operational. To begin with, probably few writers or activists would want to identify themselves with some of the categories, or would refuse being assigned to one whose characteristics they most likely will question. Another problem is that writers and activists can be in agreement with one another on some themes, yet differ strongly on others. That is, they criss-cross with one another on the issues in terms of degrees and positions.

The fact that liberation tendencies among its contributors defy functional classification, however, is not an obstacle that detracts from an understanding of the movement. To delineate even further the boundaries of liberation theology, the following formulation is proposed: liberation theology is a religious/political movement that operates on two levels that are connected, namely the theoretical (more closely associated with the theology, though it may include political research and theory) and the praxiological (which is identified with action on the religious and political planes). Some members within the movement would certainly object to this categorization. Segundo Galilea, a liberation theologian, prefers to call liberation theology that material which is the product of scientific research and has deep theological or pastoral basis. He would distinguish it from sociopolitical manifestos, and declarations that are "spontaneous impressions and judgments . . . from involved and committed Christians."[9]

Such a distinction may have theological validity, but it would be difficult to sustain from a liberation standpoint. Stressing such differences leads to the question of whether liberation theology refers to the writings or to the "acting" aspect of theology. The writers, Galilea included, invariably would answer that the emphasis is on action — the praxis — while theology is secondary.[10] Without the praxis, the primary objective of the theology, to change reality, cannot be attained. The result would be a devitalized and purely theoretical faith. Without the theory, on the other hand, the action would lose its own feedback and eventually its effectiveness. In the end, the issue seems less significant, for in the eyes of the theologians the formulation of an action-oriented theory is in itself a form of praxis.

Furthermore, the theory has to be actualized in praxis through committed individuals who choose to participate in the liberation process. Hence there is a close relationship between those who share and identify with the spirit of liberation theology and who are willing to act accordingly, and those who have undertaken the responsibility of giving intellectual and theoretical shape to the feelings, the ideas, and the aspirations of liberation. Throughout the study the former are referred to as "activists," and the latter as "theologians" or "writers".[11] The work will continue to focus on the painting in the imaginary model, which means that it will stress the themes in liberation theology while regarding the theologians and the activists as secondary. In other words, it will be more concerned with what is being said than with who is saying it.

A last point here has to do with the Scriptures, on which theology depends and is based. The task is not to question the former in terms of its origins, nor to accept its validity through personal faith as a prerequisite to approach the theme. Instead, the Scriptures are regarded here as a historical document, on the same level as the Constitution or a particular philosophy, which can be subjected to a political and a sociological critique. This means that personal faith is not required to be able to understand liberation theology.

NOTES

[1]Modern and classical liberalism make valuational claims upon government and civil society, with a strength of conviction that resembles secular religions. For different viewpoints on this issue see, M. Stanton Evans, *The Liberal Establishment* (New York: The Devin-Adair Co., 1965); Robert Paul Wolff, *The Poverty of Liberalism* (Boston: Beacon Press, 1968); Frederick Watkins, *The Political Tradition of the West — A Study in the Development of Modern Liberalism* (Cambridge, Mass.: Harvard University Press, 1948).

[2]Derek Winter, *Hope in Captivity: The Prophetic Church in Latin America* (London: Epworth Press, 1977).

[3]These views find expression in Quentin L. Quade, who writes that "liberation theology and its cousins are not religion but politics, a series of programs for the economic and political redemption of society," in a work he edited, *The Pope and Revolution,* foreword by Richard John Neuhaus (Washington, D.C.: Ethics and Public Policy Center, 1982), p. 11. Also, see Miguel Poradowski, "Puebla y la Revolución Marxista en América Latina," in *VERBO* (nov.-dic. 1979): 1149-1171;

and Christians for Socialism, "Final Document of the Convention," in John Eagleson, ed., *Christians for Socialism,* trans. John Drury (Maryknoll, New York: Orbis Books, 1975), pp. 160-175.

[4]The pioneer work is that of Gustavo Gutiérrez, *Teología de la Liberación.* Other notable efforts include: Leonardo Boff, *Teología Desde el Cautiverio* (Bogotá: Indo-American Press Service, 1975); Hugo Assman, *Theology for a Nomad Church,* Introd. by Frederick Herzog, trans. Paul Burns (Maryknoll, New York: Orbis Books, 1975); Segundo, *The Liberation of Theology;* Enrique Dussell, *Ethics and the Theology of Liberation,* trans. Bernard F. McWilliams, C.SS.R. (Maryknoll, New York: Orbis Books, 1978); Pablo Richard, *La Iglesia Latinoamericana Entre el Temor y la Esperanza* (Bogotá: Indo-American Press Service, 1981); Segundo Galilea y Raúl Vidales, *Cristología y Pastoral Popular* (Bogotá: Ediciones Paulinas, 1974); Convención del Escorial, 1972, *Fe Cristiana y Cambio Social en América Latina* (Salamanca, España: Ediciones Sígueme, 1973); Ignacio Ellacuría, *Freedom Made Flesh,* trans. John Drury (Maryknoll, New York: Orbis Books, 1976); CELAM, *Diálogos;* John Eagleson, ed., Christians for Socialism Movement in Latin America, *Christians and Socialism,* trans. John Drury (Maryknoll, New York: Orbis Books, 1975); *Signos de Liberación:* Post-conciliar documents of the Latin American Church, 1969-1973 (Lima: Centro de Estudios y Publicaciones, 1973); *Signos de Lucha y Esperanza:* Post-conciliar documents of the Latin American Church, 1973-1978 (Lima: Centro de Estudios y Publicaciones, 1978); Encuentro Latinoamericano de Teología, *Liberación y Cautiverio* (Mexico, D.F.: n.p. agosto, 1975); Ronaldo Muñoz, *Solidaridad Liberadora — Misión Eclesial* (Bogotá: Indo- American Press Service, 1977). In addition, there are numerous articles in Spanish taken from journals such as *Diakonia, Christus, ECA, Mensaje,* and *SIC.*

[5]*Theology in the Americas,* slightly edited, taken from Robert McAfee Brown, *Theology in a New Key: Responding to Liberation Themes* (Philadelphia: The Westminster Press, 1978), p. 42.

[6]Cardinal Alfonso López Trujillo acknowledges several liberation theologies. Nevertheless, he tends to group them altogether, reduces them to key issues, and attacks them as one. See his "Las Teologías de la Liberación en América Latina," in CELAM, *Liberación: Diálogos en el CELAM* (Bogotá: CELAM, 1974), pp. 27-67 passim.

[7]Comisión Episcopal de Acción Social, *Signos de Renovación* (Lima: Editorial Universitaria S.A., 1969). This book is a re-compilation of documents of the Latin American Church published after the Second Vatican Council and prior to the Medellín conference.

[8]Pablo Richard, a liberation theologian from Chile, creates a detailed typology on the basis of a concrete socio-political option (political current) or the absence of that option (social current), in "El Rol Político e Histórico de la Iglesia," *Nueva Sociedad* 36 (mayo-junio 1978): 22-23. Segundo Galilea, another liberation theologian, suggests distinguishing between those who engage in theological reflection as the result of their "preoccupation with faith and evangelization," and those who are comittted to a political ideology, in his *Teología de la Liberacion*

Después de Puebla, Segunda Edición (Bogotá: Indo-American Press Service, 1979), p. 14. Also, former Archbishop López Trujillo distinguishes between the "religious" current represented in the sin-conversion dialectical relationship, and the "socio-political," with emphasis on the politico-conflictive relationship, in "Las Teologías de la Liberación," in *Diálogos,* p. 45.

[9]Segundo Galilea, "Liberation Theology and New Tasks Facing Christians," in Rosino Gibellini, ed., *Frontiers of Theology in Latin America,* tran. John Drury (Maryknoll, New York: Orbis Books, 1979), p. 166.

[10]The theologians do not imply that theology is unimportant. The message they want to bring forth is to insist that theology should not stop at theoretical knowledge. It must lead to action. An understanding of reality should point to and motivate its transformation, be it through conversion or through structural changes. Theology is also important as a corrective of the praxis. See Gustavo Gutiérrez, *Teología de la Liberación* (Salamanca, España: Ediciones Sígueme, 1972), pp. 34-38. Also, Juan Luis Segundo, *The Liberation of Theology,* trans. John Drury (Maryknoll, New York: Orbis Books, 1979). pp. 75-90.

[11]The term "theologian" is used loosely in this work. It refers to those who are theologians by training and to writers who are involved in developing liberation themes. They are distinguished from the social scientists who provide research material to the theologians.

1.
THE CITY OF GOD AND THE CITY OF MAN

Liberation theology arises as a religious response to a problem that is both religious and political: the condition of the poor in Latin America. The movement appears as the manifestation of one of the most conflictive issues in Christianity, which after nearly two thousand years continues to elude a definitive solution: the proper role of the Church vis-á-vis the world. Moreover, it is a reflection of a deeper conflict within the essence of Christianity itself, a struggle between the two commandments upon which the Law and all the prophets' teachings are based: love of God and love of neighbor.

The issue presents a crucial dilemma for the Church. The institution cannot avoid the tension between its zealous duty to worship and to make known its spiritual teacher — the vertical orientation — and the impulse to attend the temporal needs of God's children — the horizontal dimension. From a historical perspective this tension reveals a constant search for a correct course.

Church documents indicate that the eschatological nature of the institution is accountable for the tension between the temporal and the eternal cities. That is, Jesus founded the Church and assigned it the mission to spread the news about a transhistorical salvation, that unfolds, nonetheless, in this life, and to help build a kingdom on earth that finds its consummation only at the end of times.[1] There are reasons that give credence to this tension. One has to do with the burden the Church carries as a result of having to fulfill these responsibilities. The Church, however, traditionally has perceived these duties from a dualistic standpoint. As a consequence, the Church has continued to do what other religions, including pagan ones, had done before: to make a distinction between the things of God and the things of man, thereby creating a corresponding hierarchical separation between the "sacred" and the "profane."

The kingdom of heaven versus earthly life dilemma has been further reinforced by a profound piety best revealed in the words of St. Augustine: "You have made us for Yourself, and our hearts are restless till they rest in You."[2] This type of devotion to God was to influence both religion and theology for centuries to come. Indeed, this piety was developing a frame of mind that, affected by a cultural dualism, would facilitate and encourage humanity's primary orientation toward the world to come, and away from earthly realities.

To a large extent the religious attitudes of believers and the disposition of the Church toward the world have been the result of cultural responses to the Christian event. This is to say that these attitudes were the product of feelings, social and religious needs, values, and the level of understanding believers had about the Christian message. Faith was subjected to cultural forces, as it is with any other social phenomena. By the time Christianity had spread throughout the Roman empire the Church, in effect, had inadvertently objectified social and cultural reality by establishing a hierarchy of values upon society. The tension betwen the "here" and the "hereafter" in Christianity was a reflection of, and at the same time conditioned, the conflict described in the Gospel as being more akin to our journey on earth, and the one which Christ emphasized: the struggle between good and evil. It should not come as a surprise then, that such an important issue has been traditionally viewed within the context of the heaven-earth dialectics.

The Origin of Cultural Christianity

The heaven-earth conflict in Christianity emerges under the influence of the dualism that prevailed before and during Jesus' lifetime. The official doctrine of the Church has traditionally rejected any type of Manichean dualism as a means to explain good and evil. It has viewed the world as God's creation, hence as good. It has accepted St. Paul's views on the sacredness of the body as the temple of the Holy Spirit, to be resurrected after death. The Church also realized that the world and matter are not intrinsically evil, since God became flesh in the form of his son Jesus, who willingly lived in this world and showed concern for those who suffered physical ailments. However, through religion — the cultural expression of faith — dualism had been inserted into the Christian message, thereby affecting its interpretation.

Due to its nature, religion introduces a new dimension in human life along with a series of categories and terms. The concepts of God, the afterlife, and eternity confront us and our finitude. Religion deems God superior to us because of the mystery surrounding God's existence as a reality and not as a product of the imagination. Thus, the sacred refers to "that which transcends human reason. . . . Conversely, the profane is all that which remains enclosed in the categories of rationality, of causality or utility, whatever man (sic) can define, master or subdue."[3]

In the Roman pagan culture the "sacred" is associated with religion, with the gods, while the "profane" is identified with the secular or non-religious.[4] In the Old and New Testaments, however, the profane has to do not so much with the "non-sacred" or secular, as with the evil of sin. An outright rejection of God, pride, and egotism characterize the profane. Hence, in the Christian faith the sacred is identified with the "good" and the profane with "evil."[5] But dualism, as means of explanation, denotes the presence of two concepts, usually seen as opposites, each of which accounts for specific outcomes in the real world. Thus, the Christian religious culture began to rank the concepts of the "sacred" and the "profane" according to value, importance, or dignity. As a result, the profane was identified in the pagan sense. The secular or non-religous became not only inferior to the sacred, but it was associated with evil as well.

At the same time, a cultural, i.e., literal, interpretation of the Scriptures, particularly the New Testament, create the following conflicts while dealing with the good-evil dichotomy: flesh-matter-body versus spirit-soul, and world-Satan versus heaven-God's kingdom.[6] In addition, Jesus is presented as the only path of salvation. Those who enter the kingdom achieve eternal happiness, while the ones who consciously chose not to believe are damned forever. The readings also reflect a decisive preference for the spirit (God's kingdom). Thus, sin is identified with the flesh; matter prevents the enhancement of the spirit, which is the giver of life, the body can be "mutilated" and mortified to save the soul, and the world, associated with Satan, stands in opposition to the kingdom which is not of "this world."

Theologians, however, have learned that some things mentioned in the Scriptures cannot be taken literally, that the evangelists quoted Jesus using hyperbole, probably to stress the important aspects of his message. Nonetheless, the issue has to do not with orthodoxy but with the way in which the Church and its believers act, with the manner in which the Christian message was perceived, understood, affected by the culture, and how it manifested itself through religious practices. During the second and third centuries the Church was being institutionalized, and a process of cultural syncretism had begun to take place combining philosophic dualism, pagan religious attitudes, and Christian beliefs. This religious culture gave way to the Christian religion of the Middle Ages. This whole process shall be referred to as "cultural Christianity."

The new religion spread rather swiftly during the first four centuries, especially in light of strong opposition from government and the pagan religion within the Roman Empire, the existence of Judaism, and the continuous threat of doctrinal divisions. The values that Christianity brought forward — equality, universality (a faith open to all), compassion, brotherhood, hope, forgiveness, and peace — found receptivity in a world characterized by the "moral vacuum of a dying paganism, the coldness of stoicism and the corruption of Epicureanism, brutality, cruelty, oppression, and sexual chaos."[7] By the fourth century Christianity began to reflect a clearer picture of how it viewed the world. In this and the next sections, the religious tradition of the medieval period, or what has been referred to as cultural Christianity, will be characterized. This approach does not do justice to the complexity of the age, but that is the limitation of any generalizations. Mindful, however, of the sin of historical simplification, these sections will seek to highlight and comment on those features that are relevant to the topic.

The Christian religion was characterized by its emphasis on the transcendent end of eschatology, both in the individualistic and social senses. That is, the guiding values of the time were the heavenly kingdom, salvation of the soul, and the worship of God. Faith was not primarily oriented toward life on earth, but toward the life to come. This is not to say that Christians did not work for a living, that they withdrew from society *en masse,* or failed in their moral obligations.[8] Individual morality (the values of charity, kindliness, compassion, justice) was exercised as taught in the gospel and preached by the apostles and their followers. Church morality even had what many regarded as a positive social impact by helping to suppress violence, restoring dignity to sex, to marriage, and to women; it strengthened the family, denounced infanticide, and though it "accepted slavery as part of the law of war, she did more than any other institution of the time to mitigate the evils of servitude."[9]

The things of the "hereafter," however, were the focus of attention for Christians and the Church, more than what is referred to as the secular aspects of the temporal realm. The world to come served as the rationale for social and political involvement, and even conditioned many religious practices to the extent that a sense of spiritual individualism began to creep into the attitude of many Christians.

The Church for its part had to spend much of its time on the defensive, consolidating its authority, formulating a doctrine while defending it from a multitude of creeds, and attempting to remain faithful to its founder despite being persecuted for sedition against the Roman Empire. Two principles evolve here that would become basic guiding criteria for Church policy in centuries to come: the safeguarding of orthodoxy, and the survival of the institution. The attacks against the Church would contribute over the years to an excessively dogmatic stance and mistrust of the world, and to a penchant for associating with temporal leaders to insure survival.

The Church's "other-worldliness" began to form in the early centuries, and eventually would shape the medieval culture. The perceived importance of Christ's message of salvation and an increasing awareness of Christianity's ultimate destiny, led religion to assume a concern for the world, conceived as the altar of God where His creatures, through their behavior as prescribed by the Church, would render homage. At the same time, there was an indifferent and contemptuous attitude toward the secular aspects of the temporal city. The "sacred" category was assigned to matters relating to the deity, hence when compared to things sacred the secular became profane and greatly inferior. Religious practices such as worship, rituals, prayer, contemplation, were perceived as being superior to any earthly concern. It was not so much that the sacred and the spiritual were regarded as higher than the secular, as it was the case that the latter was degraded and held in low esteem.[10] All in all, this was not inherent in the Christian faith, but in its cultural interpretation. Nonetheless, the Church had already embarked on spiritualistic and sacralizing paths, with many effects which lasted well into the sixteenth century, while others are present even today.

The Middle Ages

In regard to religion's view of the world, the period of the Middle Ages is most relevant to the discussion of liberation theology. It provides the type of religious and political culture that would be imported into colonial Latin America. This section will deal with Christianity's task of social reconstruction. By the end of the chapter it will be possible to understand liberation theology in terms of a reaction against such a view.

It would be a serious mistake to assume that medieval Christianity was expressly opposed to focusing on earthly affairs. Throughout this period the Church was consistently involved in temporal matters: politics, the arts, science, education, warfare, finances, etc. Ironically, at the same time a large number of its members were literally withdrawing from secular activities to seek spiritual perfection. Both attitudes were held for religious reasons. What needs to be stressed is that social change or the restoration of the social order did not have then the connotations they have today. At that time what may have been understood by social reconstruction implied individual conversion from a pagan, i.e., irreligious life, to one based on belief, worship, ritualism, and to the extent possible, the application of individual morality.

The issue was not to construct a perfect temporal order, to eradicate poverty, or to bring about drastic changes in social structures. Life was oriented toward God; man was secondary, and at times non-existent in the eyes of the Church. This is not to say that the Church was not concerned about the poor. Its objective was to ameliorate social roots within society. The institution established hospitals, almshouses, leper houses, and schools. Also, contributions to orphanages, dowries to poor girls, and upkeep of parish roads and bridges were expected of good

Christians. Later the Church also contributed to the development of a social conscience by condemning usury and protecting the poor from profiteering.[11]

In the early Middle Ages the institution continued to show the effects of dualism, but in a neo-platonic fashion. St. Augustine, the most influential theologian at the time, set the tone in his writings:

> Those bodies are called spiritual . . . which, being quickened by the Spirit, have the substance, but not the unwieldiness and corruption of the flesh. Man will then be not earthly but heavenly.[12]

> Two cities have been formed by two loves: the earthly by the love of self, even to the contempt of God; the heavenly by the love of God, even to the contempt of self. The former, in a word, glorifies in itself, the latter in the Lord. For the one seeks glory from men; but the greatest glory of the other is God.[13]
>
> . . .
>
> The one consists of those who wish to live after the flesh, the other of those who wish to live after the spirit.[14]

Again, we notice the flesh-spirit, heaven-earth dialectics, except this time they are being introduced into political theology. Even though Augustine, as well as Paul in his epistles, may have had a clear understanding of the terms "flesh" and "earthly," in cultural Christianity these retained their dualistic connotations. The spiritual struggle between God and Satan is accorded a social role. Most of what is material is pagan and thus profane, related to evil, and opposed to God.

By the eleventh century the Christian conception of reality was neatly divided and ranked according to the good-evil categories. The separation of planes between sacred and profane was even more strongly accentuated. All things related to God and his kingdom were considered superior to profane ones. A contemporary scholar of the medieval period, Gerd Tellenbach, has suggested two ideal types that help to describe the different conceptions of the world held by the Church.[15] One, the priestly or sacramental, sees the Church oriented toward the world to convert it and guide it to eternal life. This view reflected the essence of the priest's role, to represent God, and to mediate between God and people. Soon, salvation became the one goal to be sought by believers in the medieval Church; all secular matters were secondary. Since salvation was attainable only through the Church, and was a spiritual function, the popes felt they were responsible for setting the proper temporal order, including appropriate conduct, to insure churchgoers' entrance into the kingdom.[16] The Church progressively took it upon itself to extend authority over the temporal city. At the height of the papacy, Pope Gregory VII provided his own rationale: "The Son of God had given Peter and his successors the power to bind and loose souls, a power . . . which is spiritual and heavenly; how much the more, then, can Peter dispose of what is purely earthly and secular."[17]

Thus, clericalism appears to be predicated on a dualistic conception of the world. This was logical at that time if one considers the ultimate aims of the Church's actions as consistent with its self-ascribed responsibilities and its lack of a conception of a civil society independent of the Church, with only one religious body — Christendom.

The other world view is identified with the monk's conception, which Tellenbach labels the "ascetic." In spiritual life asceticism stands for a renunciation of desires, including material possessions, as means to mortify the flesh in order to achieve moral virtue and a more perfect spiritual union with God. As a by-product of religious dualism, its emphasis, however, is the opposite of the priestly view of individual perfection and personal salvation.[18] Since temptations lie in the outside world, asceticism is practiced by seeking refuge from the world to achieve inner peace and spiritual security. Thus came monasticism, i.e., the actual withdrawal into a monastery where the spiritual life could be cultivated.[19]

It is important to point out that monasticism and asceticism are conditioned approaches to spiritual perfection. Through the former, the individual alters one's social environment so that the new one is more conducive to one's goal. In the latter, one would attempt to change one's attitude and behavior through stimuli response. There was no awareness then, of the scientific insight that external conditioning plays an important role in individual and social behavior. What motivated these men and women was simply an "obvious" choice of values, God and his kingdom, which according to them could only be attained in solitude. Centuries would pass before social philosophers began to reflect on the implications of social change as a means of improving society. Such a view, however, needs to be evaluated within its proper context. Withdrawal from the world, far from being a sign of social irresponsibility, was in tune with the religious culture of the age. It reflected deep devotion and piety, a desire to become as "perfect as the Father" and to seek one's treasure in heaven, as they had understood Jesus to have said. In a society that was characterized by loose morals, the only way to achieve such lofty ideals was to go into partial or permanent retreat.

Medieval hierarchy placed the laity lower in rank than the clergy and the religious orders. Since they were identified with the secular, the laity had to bow to that which is sacred.[20] The only exception was with regard to the secular ruler, the emperor or king, who was often seen as God's representative for both religious and secular matters. The conviction was held within the Church that the ruler's authority came directly from God and ought to be respected even by the Church on matters of temporal concern. Furthermore, the king was seen as helper and protector of the Church and its faith. Thus, for centuries pope and king competed for authority in the world.[21]

In spite of their low station, the laity were an essential part of the Church. It was their presence that gave the clergy their ascribed dignity and their moral responsibility. The laity were in need of conversion, instruction, and guidance when it came to religion. Until recently, they have been a rather passive element in religious matters, much like in a teacher-pupil or doctor-patient relationship. Throughout the Middle Ages they were nurtured by the priestly conception, but educated spiritually under the ascetic tradition. Given the high level of illiteracy and the risk of letting the general public interpret the sacred Scriptures by themselves, the Church had to rely on simple mechanistic approaches, such as imposing worship habits, Church rules, and belief systems. As one author has stated it, for the laity "Christianization means belief in the Church, worship in the Church, conduct prescribed by the Church."[22] Another, in a more critical tone, refers to "churchliness" as Christianity's most distinctive characteristic: "Christian ethics became churchly ethics. An action was good or bad mainly because the Church said so."[23] Such has been the traditional role of the Church, to serve humanity as "mother and teacher" with dedication, if also with exuberant maternalism.

The priestly attitude had a positive if limited moral impact on the laity. It also had the unintended effect of transferring to them its own dualistic view of the world, and in that manner contributed to what may be termed the "Sunday Christian." That is, for the laity, Christianity meant primarily orthodoxy, i.e., having correct beliefs, and ritualism or a series of worship habits that provided believers with a sense of religious identity. Many of them, however, were never able to integrate their faith with the rest of their activities, and in fact were living two lives — one religious and one secular. For them, there was little or no relationship between their religious beliefs and their involvement in secular matters.

The ascetic or monastic influence on the laity was much greater. It reinforced and accentuated the world-heaven, flesh-spirit dichotomies through its piety. If the priestly conception was more involuntary, and hence superficially accepted by the people, monastic piety, being more substantive, reached the innermost feelings of the individual. In the long run, however, these feelings gave way to mechanistic religious practices as well. Some of these detracted from the Church's credibility and dignity, and contributed to divisiveness.[24]

On the other hand, monastic asceticism provided a "strong feeling of the unity of all creatures and a sense of common responsibility with the whole Church before God."[25] It spurred moral movements which counterbalanced the social decay of the times. It provided learned and sensitive men who became spiritual advisers to kings, emperors, and popes. It stimulated some of the greatest literary works of the times, social projects such as welfare systems, and improved agricultural methods.

It is in terms of its religious legacy, nonetheless, that monasticism is most relevant to liberation theology. By placing so much emphasis on personal salvation, the love of God through worship and contemplation, fear of hell, and ascetic practices to achieve domination over the body, monastic piety unconsciously inculcated a strong orientation toward the self and the "hereafter." It is doubtful that the Church was aware of these tendencies. One must bear in mind that although the institution had a strong sense of community, this community was primarily spiritual in character. Thus, there was no contradiction between an individualistic and spiritualistic Christian attitude and a sense of belonging to the Church.

Such a tendency is best reflected in the love of God overshadowing the love of neighbor, and a heedful attitude toward avoiding personal sin without a corresponding interest in the effects of sin on others. The love of God becomes all encompassing and absorbing; sin is to be avoided for spiritual reasons as well as out of fear of eternal damnation. Also, even though monastics devoted themselves to almsgiving and the care of the sick, the hungry, and the needy, they did so to a large extent because it was required by ascetic spirituality. It was not the case that Christian piety was unconcerned about one another. No other social institution or philosophical movement had done so much to sensitize individuals to the needs of others. The issue is that in cultural Christianity the overwhelming attention which the "spiritual" love of God and fear of hell commanded at that time made people appear as pawns of salvation, as impersonal objects rather than children of God.[26]

The purity of intention and good will of ascetic spirituality cannot be denied, but neither can some of its social consequences. One traditional characteristic of cultural Christianity has been its internal conception of freedom without much regard for its external dimension. The concept originates with Paul and its development continued through Augustine until modern times. For Paul, freedom was above all freedom from sin in its internal aspect; that is, sin as the condition that separates human beings from God and enslaves us to our passions. Once liberated from sin, we are free to love and to obey God. To put it in a different perspective, in Paul, the call is to abstain from sin because of the spiritual harm it does to the sinner, while the concern for the injury it causes to the other is secondary. Again, it is not that Paul is insensitive to the human being; it is simply a result of a dualistic God-centered theology.[27]

This trend of thought is in line both with Gospel priorities and Paul's view of reality. If God is superior to us, he deserves to be the primary object of our actions; besides, a transgression against another person is seen above all as a sin against God. Furthermore, since life on earth is transient, suffering is temporary, and bearing it amounts to very little compared to the eternal happiness that is encountered in the kingdom. In effect, the message that cultural Christianity has promulgated is that to sin is much worse than to suffer sin's effects on earth, simply because the one has permanent consequences while the other does not.

It is worth noticing that the authentic Christian part of that message is that suffering does not bring eternal damnation and sin does. The aspect that counsels the believer to endure suffering is culturally conditioned. We can observe the immediate effects of this conception in Paul's treatment of the slavery issue, which has given the impression over the years of his tacit approval.[28]

In Augustine we find the same tendency, now with social and political implications that were to have profound influence in centuries to come. One can safely say that in Augustinian theology social suffering and the material deprivation brought about as a result of political injustice are found to be not only acceptable but in many cases a "test of virtue." So while the evil done by political rulers represents their own eternal condemnation, for those who have to bear injustices these actions are ennobling when accepted in God's spirit.[29] With all the impact it had on medieval Christianity, Augustinian theology is accurately depicted by William Bluhm as being "politically quiet." By this he means that: "there is no demand for good-government crusades, no call for heroic acts of resistance to oppressive rule, no doctrine of political reform whatsoever. . . ."[30] In addition, politics is completely detached from any spiritual transcendence, "and becomes a process for achieving purely material ends."[31] This being so, the Church finds fewer motives to become politically involved from a religious standpoint.

During the Middle Ages the two primary reasons for the institution's involvement in politics were religious, although both were forced by the circumstances: the defense of the faith, and its own security. A third consideration is somewhat less important, but weighed heavily on the minds of the clergy: social stability. In its civilizing role the Church found it necessary to promote social cohesion to insure a proper atmosphere in which to spread the gospel. Also, lest it be accused of sedition and disruption, thus inviting persecution, the Church developed from its beginning a tendency toward the status quo, which it identified with order, even if the type of order would leave much to be desired.

With the advent of ascetic monasticism cultural Christianity confuses austerity and indifference to material possessions with material poverty and deprivation, and these in turn are co-opted by the exaltation of suffering. Although the Church never explicitly stated that wretchedness was exemplary, religious pietism and ascetism made misery and poverty appear as a blessing in disguise or the path to holiness.[32] Altogether, the attitude of the devout Christian was to accept one's condition on earth while one awaited God's promises in the kingdom. Was this type of cultural Chistianity alienating? Did it detract from improving social conditions on earth? Technically, the answer to both questions is affirmative. However, it is doubtful that the questions themselves are historically valid or relevant. It would be improper to evaluate any historical event without considering the cultural standards of the epoch in which it takes place. Historical knowledge presupposes that history is contextually understood. Events take place as a result of decisions and attitudes which in turn are respectively made and shaped on the basis of limited information and awareness, with the intellectual tools existing at the time and within a social context that is *sui generis* from a historical standpoint.

To state that during the reign of the early Church and in the Middle Ages Christianity focused its attention on the spiritual dimension, unconsciously at the expense of temporal affairs, is to affirm a historical fact. To say, however, that Christianity was an alienating element in the culture, hence socially harmful and humanly insensitive because it ignored the ills of this world, is an error in historical methodology, and constitutes an unfair value judgment. The concepts of alienation and social development as we know them today were nonexistent during the early Church period and the Middle Ages. Hence, they are not useful as evaluative criteria.

Religion is the cultural interpretation of faith. It is faith being affected by diverse societal forces, and manifested through human beings who are the product of a culture and of conditioning personal experiences. For early and medieval Christianity, faith meant the revelation to humanity of a transcending God, the good news about salvation. For many it meant the answer to the mystery of final destiny after death, and the ensuing eternal happiness in a heavenly kingdom. The Christian event, God's presence on earth in the person of Jesus Christ, was nothing short of extraordinary for the Church at that time. The proper responses were thought to be gratefulness, humility, and joy manifested in worship rituals, and a personal concern with salvation, which led to withdrawal from the world, indifference to earthly matters, spiritual self-interest, and clericalism.

During these historical periods God was the center of attention, inasmuch as today it is human beings. The religious aim, then, was to build a Christian kingdom, to create the proper environment where God could be justly worshipped and which would be conducive to our salvation. Since human salvation became the overriding priority in the Christian culture, Church interests were bound to be regarded as exceedingly more significant than any temporal matter.

Accordingly, faith and feelings became more important than reason and the mind, since the latter could not comprehend God's mysteries. Thus, theology guided the learning process. In so doing, religion had the semblance of being anti-scientific. In reality, however, there was at the time a total lack of tools and theories that could have oriented the medieval religious mind toward a different task.[33]

Despite the characterization of Christianity as primarily oriented toward the spiritual realm, during the Medieval period the Church was, nonetheless, the most progressive and socially-minded force in the Old World. A contemporary historian assesses its role in the following manner:

> The picture that we form of the medieval Latin

> Church is that of a complex organization doing its best, despite the human frailties of its adherents and its leaders, to establish a moral and social order, amid the wreckage of an old civilization and the passions of an adolescent society. . . . She was, beyond question, the greatest civilizing force in medieval European history.[34]

Because of God, humans were important to the Church, though it was the soul that mattered the most since, being eternal, it was perceived to be under its care. Nonetheless, Christian spirituality, i.e., the understanding that believers have of how the faith should be incorporated in life or the Christian *Weltanschauung,* has stressed that through charity, justice, compassion, and forgiveness one's love for God was manifested. It is in this respect that Christianity played a social role by instilling moral guidelines that could temper human passions such as greed, violence, pride, or lust, which according to Augustinian theology were responsible for the evil in the world.

The Church in Latin America — The Colonial Period

Historians Sheldon and Peggy Liss have remarked that "Spanish-American society essentially attempted to reproduce peninsular life in the New World."[35] This is to say, in effect, that medieval cultural Christianity was exported to colonial Latin America, with all of the features that characterized it in the mother country. By the sixteenth century, when most of Western Europe had moved into the Renaissance, Spain and Portugal had remained medieval. The Reformation not only had caused a schism in the Christian world but also made the Catholic Church assume a more defensive and dogmatic posture vis-á-vis the world. Orthodoxy became the practical criteria of Church membership.

In Spain, the Inquisition was the means by which the State,

with the approval of the Church, attempted to preserve national unity by safeguarding the faith. Spanish Catholicism thus became entrenched, and along with the influence on spirituality of mystics such as Teresa of Avila and John of the Cross, religion was bounded by traditionalism amid the cultural and political changes that were taking place.

Nonetheless, the dogmatic posture did not eclipse a sense of social responsibility on the part of the institution. In the New World Church and State became managing partners, with the former playing a more significant social role:

> Christianity now provided tenets and guides in all social and economic, and political matters. . . . Much of the effectiveness of royal authority stemmed from the use of the Church as an institution of government. . . . The Church was the village center; the priest, often the only official. . . . Many of what are now considered matters of civil jurisdiction were managed by the Church, including public works, welfare activities, hospitals, census-taking, education, medicine, and often what there was of law and order.[36]

The Church had considerable influence in mitigating what otherwise was a situation of oppression and exploitation. On numerous occasions the institution appealed to the Crown on behalf of the native population to prevent abuses by the colonists. Well known for his constant denunciations and his efforts to improve the lot of the Indian peasant is Fray Bartolomé de las Casas, who is regarded by many liberation theologians as a distant precursor of the movement. In most of the region it was the clergy who intervened to put an end to the slave trade and slavery as a system. In addition, the Church was primarily responsible for the education and the health care of the population. Left to itself, and without any opposition to its work, the Church not only had spiritual influence, its primary focus, but was also the only socially progressive force in the region, and the one that did most for the Indians.[37] In Brazil, although colonized by Portugal, Church influence was similar to the rest of the region, so that the religious culture that developed was not significantly different from the Spanish.[38]

In the New World the Church saw its task in the same line as in the Middle Ages: to transform a pagan society into a Christian one and to guide souls into the eternal kingdom. Given similar cultural obstacles, the type of religion that was emerging was highly spiritualistic, strongly emotional, yet superficial. Again, the mixture of paganism and Catholic ritualism prevented the Indians and the creole population (those of European descent who were born in the colonies) from developing the deep understanding of faith that the clergy itself had.

Religion was cultist, processional, and liturgical. Justice and charity were practiced by the Church, but the institution was not able to instill more than social taboos within the population to deter immoral actions. In other words, religion was conditioning social behavior, which from a medieval theistic standpoint was the basis of a Christian society. Considering, however, what it entails to educate in both the religious and civic sense a pagan, illiterate, and barbaric people, being able to create a passive religious culture with social brakes and ethos is in itself a significant achievement.

The Church educated in a paternalistic way, which at that time did not have the pejorative connotation it carries nowadays. The laity were seen as its children, who had to be guided much like sheep are tended by a herdsman.

Overall, the influence of the Church in colonial Latin America was mixed. From a religious standpoint, Christianity was presented largely in terms of piety, with emphasis on ritual, dogma, and obedience to the Church. Faith in its social dimension was more of a deterrent to evil behavior than a positive force of personal action. In that sense one can still say that a religious mentality was being created. People were aware of the presence of the Church in their lives. They were being baptized, and by the end of the seventeenth century they were receiving a very basic, if superficial, level of religious instruction.[39]

Religion was primarily oriented toward the heavenly kingdom. This predominance of the vertical relationship between the individual and God over the horizontal one between individual and individual, in part accounts for the weak influence that the Church had in its social dimension. Again, we see a new society being mirrored after its medieval counterpart. Pagan customs among the Indians resisted the modification of attitudes. An observer of the colonial period has remarked that the encounter of the two cultures gave rise to an external Christian, a participant in Church rituals, sacraments, and processions, with a pagan soul, hence a practitioner of idolatry, polygamy, and drunkenness.[40] Here we see the development of a new pattern that would last until modern times. Established customs became a more powerful element than the assimilation of religious values. Thus, when social changes occurred and ran in opposition to Church values, the latter were individually adjusted to the former, thereby diluting their effectiveness.[41]

Socially and politically, the Church in conjunction with the State could not have applied new systems of government. Neither Spain nor Portugal was prepared to experiment. Monarchical authoritarianism had been the traditional pattern in medieval Europe for both Church and State. Even the enormous influence which the Thomist Jesuit Francisco Suárez is said to have had in the philosophical foundation of Catholic Latin American society, went along the lines of traditional Christian theology despite his theoretical democratic innovations.[42]

In Europe, by the middle of the eighteenth century, the Church's religious view of society and of its role in the world had remained practically unchanged. The anti-religious and anticlerical ideas that began to emerge in the old continent once again pushed Catholicism into a defensive posture. These views reached Hispanic America, and coincided with nationalist sentiments among the creole population. The Church was forced to take a socially conservative turn following the emergence of the newly independent countries.

The Church and the Enlightenment

Liberation theology expresses a high degree of dissatisfaction with traditional theology, including medieval spirituality and the Church's past social orientation in Latin America. But unless an attempt is made to understand the Church's position following the countries' independence from Spain and Portugal, there is a risk of perceiving the institution as giving in to the system, and the liberation movement as a white knight rescuing the faith, or vice versa, conceiving the Church as the representative of the true values of Western civilization, and liberation theology as the personification of Marx and Luther attempting to destroy the faith and the institution. Unfortunately, both misperceptions have occurred within and outside the Church, and have contributed to the failure of establishing a dialogue based on common grounds.

If the Reformation and the Renaissance pierced the veil of medieval Catholicism, the ideas of the Enlightenment drove the Church into a corner. Never before had the institution been assailed so successfully from so many angles. The Enlightenment not only created the separation of Church and State (prior to that the Church insisted only on a distinction, while both cooperated toward similar goals), but conceived the idea of secularism as something fashionable and intellectually proper. Forms of philosophical naturalism, intellectual rationalism, ethical liberalism, and their manifestations through freemasonry and positivism, all of which had expressed strong anti-clerical and in many instances anti-religious views, appeared on the scene and reached the upper and the emerging middle classes.

Through the sciences, philosophy, the arts, and politics the existence of God and/or his providence were questioned, along with the divinity of Jesus Christ. Reason was presented as the sole arbiter of truth. Traditional Church rights were now denied with calls to subject the institution to the civil state. The traditional concept of power stemming from God was rejected. Instead, the State was shown to be the source of all rights, thus claiming absolute sovereignty of the people. Calls were issued for the suppression of religious orders and for the expropriation of Church land. In general, the attack upon Catholicism not only exacerbated the passions of those who undertook it, but also sharpened the wit of others who, like Woolston in England or Voltaire in France, used satire as a deadly philosophical weapon. What had religion — or rather religious people — done to provoke such a harsh reaction? Was not this the same Church that had contributed more than any other institution to tame and civilize people in two worlds on both sides of the Atlantic?

During the Middle Ages, as has been seen, the learning process was heavily influenced by theology. For centuries there was a bias against reason standing by itself. Since Christianity was after all a revealed religion, it was thought that reason not only was unable to penetrate God's mysteries, but that wandering alone could lead people astray, off the path toward salvation. Thus, even after Thomas Aquinas had reconciled reason and faith in the thirteenth century, it was still theologically impossible to conceive of reason as being independent of faith, even without it being opposed to the latter. In this sense, up until then faith continued to supersede reason, and from a cultural standpoint had succeeded in keeping it in check.

The accomplishments of science at the time implied a change of focus toward humanity. In reason the Enlightenment saw the tool that would enable people to master the world and to think and act for themselves socially and politically instead of being guided by the Church. It was a time similar to a technological revolution in which the instruments of religion and faith were discarded as obsolete in favor of the "promising capability" of reason.

In addition, in their zeal to protect the faith from heresy — which could lead the soul to damnation and create social instability — the Church and the State had become intolerant, relying often on persecution and censorship. It is perhaps ironic that Christianity, so mindful throughout the centuries of avoiding chaos that it developed a doctrine of political obedience based on divine designs, was now seen as being responsible for creating the conditions that led to a lack of harmony, and at times to violence. The Church viewed the epoch in terms of people rebelling against God, while the Enlightenment blamed conditions on the irrationality of religion. Diderot, a representative of the movement observed:

> The Christian religion is to my mind the most absurd and atrocious in its dogmas: the most unintelligible, the most metaphysical, the most entangled and obscure, and consequently the most subject to divisions, sects, schisms, heresies; the most mischievous for the public tranquility, the most dangerous to sovereigns by its hierarchic order, its persecutions, its disciplines . . . the most puerile in its morality . . . the most intolerant of all.[43]

Traditional spirituality, which portrayed God as a stern judge and conditioned our behavior by fostering a fear of hell, now created a strong adverse reaction:

> Is there in nature a man so cruel as to wish in cold blood to torment . . . any sentient being whatever? Conclude, O theologians, that according to your own principles your God is infinitely more wicked than the most wicked of men. . . . The priests have made of God such a malicious, ferocious being . . . that

> there are few men in the world who do not wish that God did not exist.[44]

Christian-caused atheism? Unwittingly and inadvertently, yes. In its revolt against cultural Christianity the Enlightenment pitted reason and individuals against faith and God, and Christian dualism had contributed to the conflict. In reality the problem was not with God but with the cultural manifestation of the faith — with religion, and with the Church. In a new era in which people began to experiment with freedom and with their own potential, the individuals of the Enlightenment felt that Christendom was a closed culture, too oppressive to their spirit. Their thirst for knowledge was greater than the religious explanation that theology could provide. Hence, their yearning for freedom of conscience and expression, separation of Church and State, secular education, and their call for the absolute power of the State were seen as controls against the Church's monopoly of knowledge, the power it exercised through the State, and the fanaticism and strife it caused over orthodoxy. Since the State was for practical purposes a theocracy, those who led the attack against the Church knew that by weakening the religious institution they could loosen the power of the monarch.

Convinced of its role on earth, the Church was not able to gauge the social unrest in time, or notice the legitimate — one may even say religious — aspirations of modern men and women, as well as their complaints. Instead, the institution reacted to the negative criticism, the rhetorical condemnations, and the attempts to diminish the influence of religion in society. In the Enlightenment the Church saw an attempt to displace God in favor of ourselves. The Church became apprehensive with the new concept of "right," which cast aside the Christian version of liberty — guided and limited by God — in favor of a human freedom that appears to have no other limits but those set by the masses through politics.

There was concern and distrust on the part of the Church in

leaving society to a new breed of humanity without religious sensitivity. It thereby became a strong opponent of many of today's civil rights for fear that they might give way to a system of values that would oppose God's. It made no sense at that time for the Church to allow freedom of worship if it could result in a person's choice not to believe in any religion. In the separation of Church and State it saw a major threat to Christendom, and to the effectiveness of its mission to guide humanity to the kingdom. The State could become not a partner but a rival with different priorities and goals. Finally, it saw the common good being menaced by the interplay of emotions and passions to which popular democracy could fall prey.[45]

Altogether, the Church had not realized that the new modern philosophy entailed the rejection of natural law, which was — and to an extent still is — the philosophical basis of theology. Without a common language, the Church and the secular world could not communicate with each other. This failure lies as much with the people of the Enlightenment as it does with the Church. The former saw themselves as prophets of a new religion, preaching with the same zealousness as those they accused. They castigated established religion indiscriminately, and in doing so they failed to recognize religion's positive contributions to society.

For its part, the Church was a victim of its devotion and the certitude of its mission. In 1864, it was incomprehensible for Pope Pius IX to accept freedom of conscience in religious or civil matters; he viewed it as something "insane."[46] The Western world had changed, but the Church refused to accept its transformation. From the standpoint of the institution, Western civilization was en route to hell.

Independent Latin America

The ideas of the Enlightenment had a similar impact on the Latin American Church as they had in Western Europe. The unfortunate situation in which the Church found itself dependent upon the Crown for support, lacking a sizeable indigenous clergy, facing the cry for political independence and the intellectual pressures against the faith and its values, made it appear to many as the enemy of freedom and progress. Liberalism, positivism, and masonry had already caused consternation within the Church prior to the wars of independence, creating strong anti-clerical feelings. The same philosophical currents favored self-government. In a way the institution had no reason to oppose independence, had it not been for its fear that those who favored it would try to attack the Church and jeopardize its mission.

From political and economic standpoints there was no question that the Church was a powerful institution. It would not be accurate, though, to view this with cynicism. Barring human weaknesses, the Church was not a private corporation seeking to maximize profits for its own sake or to exercise political power for aggrandizing purposes. True, it was supported by the Crown's army, but without any *caciquismo* or *caudillismo* in mind. Overall, the wealth that the Church had obtained was donated, usually the result of religious customs that dated back to the Middle Ages or because the institution was seen as an able and just administrator. Such also was the basis of its political power. Left to itself, the Church had no rival in its altruistic work. But now a worried clergy saw that, standing alone, the institution would have to protect its rights and the prerogatives that enabled it for so long to perform its religious and social functions. This situation drove the Church into the realm of politics.[47]

The primary concern of the Church following the wars of independence and throughout the first three decades of the twentieth century was to avoid being suppressed. For only through its presence could it insure that God would still have a voice in cultural life. Moreover, one has to consider that the Church has always viewed itself as shouldering the immense responsibility of the salvation of the human soul.[48] Given the severity and tone of the attacks, the institution, in need of political allies, chose the ones with which it had some affinity, plus influence and resources.

The poor, with whom it had identified, were without property and politically disenfranchised, so that their spiritual loyalty to the Church could not play a significant role in the politics. Within the educated and more affluent population two political classes developed: the liberals, who favored independence, were of a bourgeois background and politically and intellectually similar to those who spearheaded the French Revolution, thus largely anti-clerical; and the conservatives, not totally opposed to independence but "who sought security by clinging to time-worn institutions and attitudes," favored old economic and social structures.[49] On its part, the Church truly believed that to avoid chaos while striving for progress, the Catholic tradition of colonial times was essential. It concluded that compared with the future in the hands of liberals, whose materialistic tendencies threatened the spiritual values of Christianity, the past looked even brighter, especially since it had worked quite successfully before.[50] The choice was not difficult. Faced with strong opposition from liberals who wanted to exclude them from most social levels, the clergy found a natural ally within conservative circles.

Once again there is the encounter of two cultures radically opposing each other: an idealistic, religious, paternalistic, and traditional Church versus a pragmatic, secular, and liberal state. In the struggle the Church saw its presence and its credibility considerably diminished in social and political life. As attacks by anti-clerics continued into the century, the hierarchy reacted defensively by leaning on its traditional image of the strong and influential institution of pre-independent days. Insecurity drove it to dwell more on golden times — now "its past was extolled, . . . and prestige became a goal."[51]

The Church in Latin America finally came to terms with the

liberal State in the 1940s and 1950s. This was prompted in part by a degree of tolerance within the Church toward diversity of beliefs. Although not officially sanctioned, pluralism was a reality which the hierarchy had come to accept. Also, the Church opted to maintain its traditional policy of not antagonizing existing regimes to avoid persecution. Finally, a more important consideration was the potential threat of an enemy it considered worse than liberalism: communism. The specter of communism moved liberals into a coalition of interests with the conservatives and the Church. It seems that this was not a difficult move on their part. Despite their progressive ideas, liberals were very much opposed to social and political reforms that could have resulted in loss of economic and political power.[52]

A "Catholic" conservative culture developed in Latin America. Frederick Pike sees this culture interpreting social justice in the medieval sense, as "the expansion of charitable work within a society that will continue to be stratified and largely closed."[53] The secular conservatives are against political pluralism and agrarian reforms. They see private property as derived from "the very nature of things," and from God. The issues they consider religious are education, family life, respect for Church authority, and the problem of communist infiltration. These are all themes that blend well with traditional Catholic values. As Frederic Turner has remarked, both the Church and the conservatives had something to gain from their alliance. The former obtained prestige and protection by joining forces with a source of power; the latter saw their position as legitimized by a moral authority.[54]

Entering into the decade of the 1960s, the Catholic Church in Latin America found itself temporarily secured in a political sense but continued to be unaware of the changing social climate. A series of occurrences jolted it out of its seeming complacency and traditional past, and forced it to take a serious look at itself. The next two chapters will examine those events which contributed to the phenomenon of liberation theology, which more than anything else is responsible for questioning the mission, the theology, and the values of the Latin American Church.

NOTES

[1]Second Vatican Council, *Lumen Gentium,* nos. 48-51. For references to the Council documents we are relying on *The Documents of Vatican II,* gen. ed. Walter M. Abbott, S.J. trans. ed. Very Rev. Msgr. Joseph Gallagher (New York: The American Press, 1966); and for cross-references *The Sixteen Documents of Vatican II,* with commentaries by the Council Fathers, N.C. Trans. (Boston: Daughters of St. Paul, n.d.).

[2]Saint Augustine, *The Confessions* Books I-X, trans. F.J. Sheed (New York: Sheed and Ward, 1942), 1.1.

[3]Bernard Häring, C.S.S.R., *Faith and Morality in the Secular Age* (Garden City, New York: Doubleday and Company, Inc., 1973), p. 75.

[4]In theology the distinction is made between "secularism," which is purposefully anti-religious, and the "secular," which denotes the inherent value of temporal affairs, and its separation from religious authority without necessarily being against religion. Ibid., p. 73.

[5]Ibid., pp. 80-92.

[6]For specific citations, cross references, and theological interpretations on the flesh-matter-body versus spirit-soul, see footnote 1g, pp. 267-269, and footnotes 7d, p. 277; on the world versus God's kingdom, see footnotes 13g, p. 287, and 1b, p. 323, *The Jerusalem Bible,* gen. ed. Alexander Jones, L.S.S., S.T.L., I.C.B. (Garden City, New York: Doubleday and Company, Inc., 1966).

[7]Will Durant, *The Story of Civilization,* vol. 3: *Caesar and Christ* (New York: Simon and Schuster, 1944), p. 602.

[8]There was among the first generation of Christians a true expectation of the parousia which led members in some of the communities to disregard their temporal affairs (2Th 2,3). Also, the Early Middle Ages was characterized by the number of monastic orders that arose partly as a result of Christians seeking a more perfect spiritual relation with Christ, and in order to escape from a world tainted with sin and evil.

[9]Will Durant, *The Story of Civilization,* vol. 4: *The Age of Faith* (New York: Simon and Schuster, 1950), pp. 76-77.

[10]Häring, pp. 92-94.

[11]We owe this important caveat to Jo Ann Hoepner Moran, Associate Professor of Church History at Georgetown University.

[12]Saint Augustine, *The City of God,* trans. Marcus Dods, D.D., with an Introduction by Thomas Merton (New York: The Modern Library, 1950), p. 433.

[13]Ibid., p. 477.

[14]Ibid., p. 441.

[15]As the author explains, the two types are not rigid models; they are used only for explanatory purposes. Gerd Tellenbach, *Church, State and Christian Society at the Time of the Investiture Contest,* trans. with an Introduction by R.F. Bennett (New York: Harper Torchbooks, 1970), p. 55. Earlier he pointed out that "there were plenty of monks who showed sympathy for the world, . . . and conversely secular priests who vied with the most pious of hermits in all the ascetic virtues (p. 51).

[16]Walter Ullman writes: "They (the popes) believed that since the whole universal christianity, . . . was entrusted to them, they had to govern it so as to lead it to its eventual destination." In *Papal Government in the Middle Ages* (London: Methuen & Co. Ltd. 1955), p. 449.

[17]Tellenbach, p. 153.

[18]Ibid., pp. 42-43.

[19]It is worth pointing out that spiritual perfection and salvation were not the only reasons for which monks sought seclusion. R.W. Southern stresses their roles as spiritual soldiers who "prayed for the well-being of the king and kingdom . . ." and fought "with the sword of the spirit against the aery wiles of the devils." The last quote is taken from the Foundation Charter of King Edgar in 966. In R.W. Southern, *Western Society and the Church in the Middle Ages,* The Pelican History of the Church, Gen. ed. Owen Chadwick, Vol. 2 (Harmondsworth, Middlesex, England: Penquin Books Ltd, 1970), pp. 224-225.

[20]It is worth remembering, as Tellenbach points out, that "ecclesiastical laws carried greater weight than secular" (p. 56).

[21]This struggle which took place throughout most of the medieval period is depicted in detail in Ullman.

[22]Gabriel Le Bras, "The Sociology of the Church in the Early Middle Ages," in *Early Medieval Society,* ed. Sylvia L. Thrupp (New York: Appleton-Century-Crofts, 1967), pp. 52-53.

[23]Walter Rauschenbusch, *Christianity and the Social Crisis,* ed. Robert D. Cross (New York: Harper Torchbooks, The University Library, 1964), p. 180.

[24]A strong case can be made of the issue of simony, i.e., the selling of spiritual gifts and Church offices, the selling of indulgences to reduce one's penance in

purgatory, and the corruption of the tithe and proprietary systems finding their origins in a distorted view of monastic pietism.

[25]Tellenbach, p. 78.

[26]St. John of the Cross, perhaps the greatest mystic of all, writing in the sixteenth century.

> "Two contraries cannot coexist in one person; and that darkness, which is affection for the creatures, and light, which is God, are contrary to each other. . . . For all things of earth and heaven, compared with God, are nothing. . . ." "Complete Mortification Necessary for Wisdom," in *An Anthology of Christian Mysticism,* ed. with biographical notes Paul De Jaegher, trans. Donald Attwater and others (Springfield, Illinois: Templegate Publishers, 1977), p. 101.

> "And all of the *goodness* of the creatures of the world, in comparison with the infinite goodness, may be described as wickedness. . . And therefore the soul that sets its heart upon *the good things of the world* is supremely evil in the eyes of God." (Ibid., p. 103, Italics mine)

God speaking to Catherine of Siena in one of her dialogues, in the Fourteenth century: "Divine love cannot suffer to share with any earthly love, and you lack in perfection and transgress My love in the measure that you let temporal things detract from it." (Excerpt from "The Attainment of Perfect Love," in Ibid., p. 61)

Historian Will Durant describes the impact of hell in Medieval Christianity: "Men hoped vaguely for heaven but vividly feared hell. . . . The Catholic, like the early Protestant theology and preaching, felt called upon to stress the terror of hell. . . . Nearly all churches . . . had pictures of the Last Judgment, and these portrayed the tortures of the damned more prominently than the bliss of the saved." (v. 4, p. 733)

[27]Romans 6:12-19; see also cross-reference on footnote 6h, p. 277, *The Jerusalem Bible.*

[28]Along the lines of Paul's theology, he was far from endorsing the system or even being indifferent to it. That he disliked it is seen in his comparison of the system as a transient evil condition with the joy of being free in Jesus Christ. His attitude is more of putting up with the practice, much like he accepts the suffering that God's mission brings upon him. His joy is not over suffering itself though, but of being able to remain true to God in spite of all the suffering.

[29]St. Augustine, *City of God,* p. 112.

[30]William T. Bluhm, *Theories of the Political System* (Englewood Cliffs, New Jersey: Prentice-Hall, Inc., 1965), p. 167.

[31]Ibid., p. 165.

[32]The Lord speaks to his servant Blessed Henry Suso, in the Fourteenth Century:

> "There is nothing more painful than suffering, and nothing more joyful than to have suffered. . . . Suffering gives to the sufferer pain here and joy hereafter. . . . Suffering is ordained that the sufferer may not suffer eternally. Suffering changes an earthly man (sic) into a heavenly man (sic) . . . keeps the soul humble and teaches patience . . . takes away sin, lessens the fire of purgatory, expells temptation, consumes imperfections, and renovates the spirit." (Excerpt from "The Worth of Temporal Trials," in De Jaegher, *Anthology*, pp. 17-19.)

While there may be positive lessons one may draw from suffering, the passive attitude or even spiritual enjoyment that may be derived out of poverty and misery is the cultural aspect of Christianity.

[33]For more detail on this view see Francis Oakley, *The Medieval Experience: Foundations of Western Cultural Singularity* (New York: Charles Scribner's Sons, 1974), pp. 156-170.

[34]Durant, v. 4, p. 818.

[35]Sheldon B. and Peggy K. Liss, eds., *Man, State, and Society in Latin American History* (New York: Praeger Publishers, 1972), p. 69.

[36]Ibid., p. 67.

[37]Antonio de Egaña, S.J. *Historia de la Iglesia en la América Española,* Hemisferio Sur (Madrid: Biblioteca de Autores Cristianos, 1966), p. 100.

[38]For a historical description of the role of the Church in colonial Brazil, see the first three chapters in Thomas C. Bruneau, *The Political Transformation of the Brazilian Church* (London: Cambridge University Press, 1974).

[39]Egaña, p. 154.

[40]Ibid., p. 362.

[41]This observation was based on a detailed study of the practice of the Catholic religion in Latin America conducted in 1965 by Francois Houtart and Emile Pin, *The Church and the Latin American Revolution,* trans. from the French by Gilbert Barth (New York: Sheed and Ward), p. 162. The authors add:

> "One does not look to the Church to define Catholicism, but to culture, tradition, and custom. The priest . . . is not a leader of the community who must be obeyed, but a servant of both national and religious culture." (p. 181)

[42]Paul Janet characterizes Suárez' view as follows:

> "He adopts in all its force the principle of popular sovereignty; he excludes the doctrine of divine law . . . and he causes not simply government but even society to rest upon unanimous consent. But these principles serve only to allow him immediately to effect the absolute and unconditional alienation of popular sovereignty into the hands of one person. He denies the need for consent of the people in the formulation of law; and as a guarantee against the unjust law he offers only a disobedience both seditious and disloyal. Finally, he shelters the prince under the power of the law and sees over him only the judgment of the Church." (Quoted by Richard M. Morse in *The Founding of New Societies,* edited by Louis Hartz, and reprinted in Liss and Liss, p. 76)

[43]Diderot in a private letter, in Will and Ariel Durant, *The Story of Civilization,* vol. 9: *The Age of Voltaire* (New York: Simon and Schuster, 1965), p. 656.

[44]Jean Meslier, a former priest who had lost his faith, and one of the harshest critics of the Christian faith during the Enlightenment, ibid., pp. 612-613.

[45]For the Church's views on the ideas of the Enlightenment see the following papal documents: Pius IX's *Quanta cura,* on the social and political apsects of Naturalism; *Syllabus,* on the errors of modern political philosophy; also, Leo XIII's *Inscrutabili Dei,* on the Church and civilization; *Immortale Dei,* on the Christian view of the State; and *Libertas praestantissimum,* on liberty and liberalism.

[46]Pius IX, *Quanta cura,* no. 3.

[47]Excerpt from Frederick B. Pike, *The Conflict Between Church and State in Latin America,* reprinted in Liss and Liss, p. 206.

[48]Pope Pius IX writes in mid-nineteenth century:

> "It is well known the great care and extreme pastoral concern with which our predecessors, the Roman Pontiffs, have complied with the ministry and obligations that were trusted to them by the same Jesus Christ in the person of St. Peter . . . of tending the lamb and the sheep. Never have the Pontiffs ceased to carefully feed the flock with words of faith and the doctrine of salvation, keeping it far from poisonous pastures. Because our predecessors, . . . anxious over the salvation of souls, have tried above all . . . (to assure) the

discovery and condemnation of all heresies and errors that, contrary to our divine faith, . . . morality and the eternal salvation of the souls, have provoked violent conflicts which have brought unfortunate ills both to the Church and the State." (*Quanta cura,* no. 1)

[49]Excerpt from Stanley J. Stein and Barbara H. Stein, *The Colonial Heritage of Latin America: Essays on Economic Dependence in Perspective,* reprinted in Liss and Liss, pp. 191-192.

[50]Pike, *The Conflict,* in Liss and Liss, pp. 208-210.

[51]Houtart and Pin, p. 39.

[52]Stein and Stein, in Liss and Liss, pp. 187-191.

[53]Quoted by Frederick B. Pike, "Catholicism in Latin America since 1848," cited in Frederick C. Turner, *Catholicism and Political Development in Latin America* (Chapel Hill, North Carolina: University of North Carolina Press, 1971), p. 96.

[54]Turner, p. 107.

2.
THE ROOTS OF LIBERATION THEOLOGY

The next three chapters will focus on the most significant elements that have contributed to the development of a liberation theology. A confluence of ideas will come into view, along with personalities, historical conditions, events, and attitudes that eventually coalesced into a movement that has sought to question an archaic cultural interpretation of faith and conventional Church postures.

The Rejection of European Theology and Spirituality

> Modern European theology, individualized and imperialistic, is reproduced in the colonies as progressive theology by those who operate as an oppressive colonial minority and take as the scheme of salvation a theology which for the periphery is meaningless and therefore uncritical. The status-quo is once again supported.[1]

In the elaboration of liberation theology, Latin American theologians have consciously rejected "imported" theology. This rejection is not absolute. Some aspects of traditional spirituality and fresh ideas from contemporary European authors have contributed to liberation theology, even though such contribution has gone largely uncredited.[2] The rejection and the development of theology have gone hand in hand. Discontent with what theologians call "European theology," to distinguish it from Latin American liberation theology, has led to a search for new approaches that are more in line with the region's problems and needs. If this is so, what lies at the basis of their complaints?

European theology, according to proponents of liberation theology, has a strong tendency to deal philosophically with social issues while leaving concrete conditions of human suffering largely intact. Conditioned by a highly technological and democratic culture, this theology presents a different view of human progress. Thus the biblical call to subdue nature is primarily understood in terms of scientific advancement. In underdeveloped nations, however, where conditions are characterized by poverty and oppression, progress is seen in terms of liberation from those conditions.[3]

Invariably, all liberation theologians cite as a major flaw in European theology its lack of attention to the social and political dimensions of the gospel and the faith, neutralizing their full impact. By reducing faith to a spiritual and personal level this theology has created a "private" religion, one that points mostly toward the self and the "visible other" (interpersonal relationships), while it practically overlooks the political nature of human problems. Even though new progressive European theologies have attempted to approach temporal questions, they have done so by trying primarily to understand reality outside of its historical context. Their methodology is deductive. It starts with revelation and then seeks to interpret reality. Liberation theology proceeds inductively by establishing the analysis of historical reality and its interpretation as the point of departure, and then seeking to change it. In addition, traditional spirituality advocated the "separation of planes," i.e., the sacred-profane dialectic, which in modern Latin America has unconsciously worked in favor of the status quo by keeping the Church away from the political realm. Too often this view has led the institution into collusion with governments, thereby silencing the Church's "prophetic" or critical role in society.[4]

There is yet another criticism of European theology. Christianity, say liberation theologians, cannot be reduced to any political system; it transcends them all, since it finds its ultimate realization with the coming of the kingdom at the end of history. Hence theology needs to serve as a reminder of the social and political conditioning to which faith and religion can be subjected throughout history. Conscious of temporal trappings, theology "accuses other theologies for not being sufficiently critical and politically vigilant," in this respect.[5]

These charges establish a liberation criterion to evaluate political systems and theology. They may, however, have a boomerang effect, in that they can be used to evaluate the liberation movement as well. While the rejection of the separation of planes contributes toward temporal liberation since it increases the religious significance of building the earthly city, erasing its distinctions completely presents serious problems. Some, caught up in the process, either have failed to see these problems or have ignored them. As Segundo Galilea has observed, the separation has to be rejected but some distinctions have to be kept, lest the gospel and the kingdom become completely temporalized.[6] In other words, liberation may run the risk of deviating from the path of the kingdom by secularizing its eschatological link with salvation and becoming identified with a political system. Already there are strong indications that, to a certain extent, some elements of the so-called "popular" church in Nicaragua are following this route.

Traditional spirituality also is found to be excessively abstract. This has significant social implications. Already it has been mentioned how cultural Christianity placed undue emphasis on internal freedom. It is not difficult to see why, from the standpoint of liberation, such spirituality can become very alienating in modern times. For example, in Stoicism the Stoic's satisfaction with his internal freedom leads him to be indifferent to the material conditions that surround him. Thus there is no longer a distinction between Master and Slave, for the Stoic has "dismissed the complex substance of reality from his consciousness."[7] In traditional Christianity, this translates into giving less importance to political conditions and to human rights, since external freedom is perceived as being secondary to the freedom that people find in God. Also, as Raúl Vidales, another liberation theologian, explains, when religion addresses only the spiritual realm and focuses exclusively on the salvation of the soul, the Gospel is presented to all in the same "neutral, indefinite, and antiseptic terms." Thus, it becomes difficult to distinguish between the exploiter and the exploited.[8]

Christianity's cultural version of a spiritualized religion had long equated faith with orthodoxy, largely as a result of the defensive posture of the Church toward the Reformation. An unbalanced form of sacramentalism developed. That is, reliance on the sacraments and on correct beliefs became the measure of the "true" Christian.[9] This has led to the strongest criticism ever leveled against European theology. It centers on the feature that most clearly distinguishes liberation theology from its counterpart, the praxis. For liberation theologians Christianity becomes the "opiate of the people" when ideas and beliefs are given more importance than practice and human action. Excessive concern with orthodoxy, at the expense of "orthopraxis," i.e., correct action, prevents liberation from being attained. It denies our ability to become an agent of our own destiny. Instead, it leaves us subjected to the laws of nature, which in an oppressive society implies the perpetuation of an undignified condition.

In traditional spirituality, the theologians point out, people are characterized by passiveness with regard to social issues. There is reliance on the cult, prayer, and the sacraments as a way of asking God to act on people and in historical events. This approach presents Christianity as a "magical" religion, in the words of Juan Luis Segundo, the Uruguayan theologian, for it looks "for divine efficacy in certain procedures without any relation to historical efficacy." Consequently, "any orthodoxy that does not essentially point toward orthopraxy is magical."[10]

A literal interpretation of the gospel, again, helps to understand what otherwise appears as an excessive dependency on God. In the New Testament, for example, the power of prayer "knows no boundaries," and faith "can move mountains." Traditional spirituality also dwells on the same theme from another angle by pointing out the efficacy of grace and our inefficacy. Hence we need Christ, for without Him the believer "cannot bear fruit." Moreover, the traditional religious mentality tends to accept suffering and poverty, which are in turn "offered" to God through prayer. From a liberation standpoint, this attitude is alienating, for we should not rely on God without first trying to solve our own problems. Neither prayer nor the sacraments alone will feed the hungry or liberate the oppressed. Liberation theology would add that we have a duty to attend our own responsibilities without expecting miraculous interventions from God.

These two views pose a serious dilemma. On the one hand Christians acknowledge their dependency on God. The question is, though, to what extent should they depend? The issue is similar to the philosophical argument concerning God's existence: there are no empirical proofs to either sustain His existence or to deny it. Christians admit the presence of grace and the need for prayer, but no one "knows" how the former manifests itself or how the latter functions. Thus liberation theology, without denying the above, has chosen to accentuate the praxis, the need to act, as being more reasonable and logical. In so doing, it adopts what traditional spirituality would consider a neo-promethean tendency, in that the cult, the sacraments, and prayer are de-emphasized, in some theologians and activists more than in others.

Much of the criticism of traditional spirituality and European theology would appear to be less pertinent nowadays, given the Church's new outlook stemming from Vatican II. But although a theological renewal began to take place after the Council, in

Latin America ecclesiastical structures and popular religion continue to be influenced by traditionalism and by the European mentality. The fundamental differences between the two theologies, points out Central American liberation theologian Jon Sobrino, centers around the faith. For European theology, faith in itself is the issue, insofar as it is confronted by secularism and atheism. For liberation theology what matters most are subhuman living conditions, in the region in which both the oppressor and the oppressed are believers. Hence it is faith that needs to be redefined within the context of Latin American reality.[11]

Liberation theologians have sought not just an intellectual but an operational redefinition of the faith, one that can be implemented through social and political action yet remain true to the biblical tradition. For the movement, faith and praxis are one and the same. Much of this emphasis on the praxis comes as a reaction to the lack of a substantive pastoral program in the Church. Despite arguments by critics pointing out that Christianity has elaborated the concept of the praxis since the seventh century, it is only now that the institution is beginning to stress it. The late French Cardinal Jean Danielou pinpointed the problem, writing during the years of the Council. He said that the reason Christians remained indifferent to the temporal city was, essentially, that their consciences had not been sufficiently educated.[12] In other words, the Church has not done its job well. There is, to be sure, a social doctrine within the teachings of the institution, but until recently there had been no "follow-through" — no urge and little desire to deal with the social question in Latin America, except through occasional reminders. Part of the problem lies in the fact that the social doctrine is written from the perspective of the First world and falls into the cultural conditions of consumer-oriented societies, in which the issues of poverty, oppression and repression are seen in a different — less of an emergency — light. As a Venezuelan theologian has stated: "Christian social doctrine has been characterized by a profound human sensitivity, vigorous denunciation and analytical capability, and total incapacity to propose solutions that go beyond the established order."[13] As a result, Catholics in that region had to first be "liberated" from that theology. Liberation theology, then, appears in the continent as an attempt to "rescue" religion from extreme spiritualism, traditionalism, and personalism.

Pierre Teilhard de Chardin

> Our faith imposes on us the right and the duty to throw ourselves into the things of the earth.[14]

Liberation theology does not exactly arise out of its rejection of a spiritualized view of reality, although the biting criticism by some of its advocates of theology's abstractness may indicate otherwise. But in many other writers there appears to be an authentic Christian love for the world and a positive inclination toward its affairs. It is precisely this love and inclination that distinguishes liberation spirituality from the traditional one. But as much as the Latin American theology wishes to establish its originality and distinctness from traditional and modern European theology, its development must be seen in light of a process that, within the Church, dates back to Pierre Teilhard de Chardin.

It has been said that the figure of this Jesuit, who died in 1955, was present throughout the Second Vatican Council, and that his ideas steered the course of the Church in its meeting with the modern world. Forbidden by his superiors to publish his writings because they were considered too controversial, Teilhard could not benefit from peer criticism. Most of his writings were published posthumously in the 1950s, a few years before the opening of the Council.

Although Teilherd is well known in scientific circles due to his interest, writings, and accomplishments in this area, it is his spirituality that is relevant to our topic. At a time when the world had changed and the Church was still relying on traditional theology, Teilhard came forth with *The Divine Milieu,* which in keeping with his spiritual bent was dedicated "To those who love the world." More than anything else, he expressed a religious view of reality that was more attuned to a secular age directing humanity more and more toward self and toward the world.

> By virtue of the Creation, and still more, of the Incarnation, *nothing* here below is *profane* for those who know how to see. On the contrary, everything is sacred to those capable of distinguishing that portion of chosen being which is subject to the attraction of Christ in the process of consummation. Try, with God's help, to perceive the connection — even physical and natural — which binds your labour with the building of the Kingdom of Heaven; . . . then, as you leave church for the noisy streets, you will remain with only one feeling, that of continuing to immerse yourself in God.[15]

Teilhard was actually paraphrasing an idea originally expressed by Jesuit founder Ignatius of Loyola, who in the sixteenth century suggested that an authentic Christian spirituality needed to have that "diaphaneity" or translucent attitude that would enable one to be "contemplative in action." In other words, a spirituality should combine belief, prayer, and action into a "Christian praxis," so that action becomes an effective form of prayer. The eschatological dimension, which saves praxis from being temporalized, is a necessary component to this approach. The difference, of course, is that while Ignatius' comments referred to the context of a "sacralized" and abstract spiritual milieu, Teilhard used his words to represent the opposite standpoint, a secularized society and a materially oriented spirituality. Ignatius' reasoning is in line with his epoch; with Teilhard, there is a radical departure.

Following his own idea of the "movement which answers the challenge of matter in order to save it, immersion and emergence, possession and renunciation," Teilhard speaks of the "spiritual power of matter," and of the "divinisation of human activity," and even suggests a close relationship between our temporal activity and the bringing forth of the kingdom.[16] All these found echo in the Church's orientation toward the world during the Second Vatican Council. They constitute the theological basis on which a theology of liberation is developed. Properly speaking, this theology is born when temporal liberation can be linked to eschatological salvation and the building of the kingdom on earth. This Teilhard saw happening through the material (or temporal) as well as the spiritual evolution of humanity toward God. His concept of history seems to be an answer to Marxian dialectics. History, for Teilhard, moves inexorably along a divine *milieu* toward its final realization in Christ. At times this process will be guided by the spiritual conscience, which reminds the world of its ultimate destination. At other times, the spirit, speaking through temporal events, "forces" changes that align the human conscience, including religious conscience, with the kingdom.

The Second Vatican Council

> Coming together in unity from every nation under the sun, we carry in our hearts the hardships, the bodily and mental distress, the sorrows, longings, and hopes of all the peoples entrusted to us. We urgently turn our thoughts to all the anxieties by which modern man is afflicted. Hence, let our concern swiftly focus first of all on those who are specially lowly, poor, and weak.
>
> As we undertake our work, therefore, we would emphasize whatever concerns the dignity of man, whatever contributes to a genuine community of peoples. 'Christ's love impels us.' . . .[17]

This quotation from the opening message reflects to a large extent the thrust of the Second Vatican Council. Events related in the last chapter may have given the impression that radical change had taken place within the Church almost overnight. This is not strictly so, for although a radical shift of focus did occur, it was not sudden. Pope Leo XIII, pressured to respond on the one hand to a hostile liberalism and the injustices of capitalism, and on the other to the Marxist alternative, began, around the close of the last century, a more systematic development of what is formally known today as the Social Doctrine of the Church.[18]

Cognizant of the impact of secularism and secularization, the new technology, emerging nations, war, poverty, and the conditions of the working class, successive popes became more involved in temporal matters, but without the clericalist orientation of the Middle Ages. Until the pontificate of Pius XII the Church had been undergoing the process of adjusting, with great reluctance, to not having the prominent role it had enjoyed in past centuries. It was under Pope Pius XII, and even more so under Pope John XXIII, that the Catholic Church came of age. The latter's two encyclicals, *Mater et Magistra* and *Pacem in Terris* (this last one published months after the Council opened), set the tone for the institution's plans to embrace the modern world.

The overall objective pursued by Pope John XXIII in convening an ecumenical council was *aggiornamento,* or a spiritual renewal of the Church. It implies a desire on the part of the Church not to be considered irrelevant or outdated by the world at large, and, from a positive standpoint, it reflects an urgent need to assert its moral and spiritual influence in a world torn by materialism, atheism, and injustice; the Church truly believes it has a message to communicate to all the world.[19]

The Council serves as the vehicle through which the Church officially approves, and signals to all peoples, its acceptance of the conditions of the modern world and concern over its affairs.[20] In doing so it is foregoing all political authority. By reaffirming "that no one is to be coerced into faith," the Church is rejecting clericalism as a means to transform the world into a Christian abode. The Church does reserve the right to intervene in issues that are social or political in nature as part of its religious mission.[21] In other words, the Church realizes that its spiritual function to spread the gospel, proclaim the kingdom, and serve as instrument of salvation has a material or temporal dimension through which it "witnesses," i.e. acts, like Christ.[22]

In addition to endorsing religious freedom, the Church now incorporates many of the views and attitudes to which it had been opposed in the past. No longer static, the Church has shown itself to be a dynamic society that changes through history. Its tone is pastoral, meaning that its message is addressed to all people. It projects the image of "feeling at home" in the world without having to react defensively or issue dogmatic condemnations as in the past. Open to self-criticism and to the opportunity of learning from the world, the Church displays a high degree of self-assurance.

In *Gaudium et spes* — the Pastoral Constitution of the Church in the Modern World — more than anywhere else, the Council responds to what the Church thinks of the world, how it sees it, and the Church's relationship to it. The significance it gives to temporal involvement and human activity in the world is unprecedented in modern history. Reacting, this time in a positive manner, to the Marxist charge that religion is the "opiate of the people," the institution dispels all myths to that effect. Given the importance of the issue, it is worth quoting the passage at length:

> This Council exhorts Christians, as citizens of two cities, to strive to discharge their earthly duties conscientiously and in response to the Gospel spirit. They are mistaken who, knowing that we have here no abiding city but seek one which is to come, think

> that they may therefore shirk their earthly responsibilities. For they are forgetting that by the faith itself they are more than ever obliged to measure up to these duties, . . .
>
> Nor, on the contrary, are they any less wide of the mark who think that religion consists in acts of worship alone and in the discharge of certain moral obligations, and who imagine they can plunge themselves into earthly affairs in such a way as to imply that these are altogether divorced from the religious life.[23]

Thus the Council not only gives a socio-political role to the faith, but accords a religious and spiritual connotation to one's temporal duties by tying these to salvation.[24] Along these lines it recognizes the autonomy and the proper values of the earthly city, and a person's initiative — independent of the Church — to improve one's life, thereby accepting the concept of people as agents of history. In another turnabout, the Council recognizes the legitimate autonomy of the sciences, and goes as far as recommending that they be used in the development of Christian doctrine.[26]

In dealing with the dignity of the human being, the Council Fathers deviate from the dualist view even more by reuniting body and soul, regarding a person as one and the body as "good and honorable," meaning that we are not allowed to despise it.[27] Also, they lay the foundation for the Church's doctrine on human rights by concerning themselves with, and attacking, anything that violates this dignity, such as genocide, torture, exploitation, oppression, slavery, abortion, economic manipulation, poverty, unemployment, murder, euthanasia, prostitution, sexual discrimination, war, and the arms race. In addition, they support political participation by citizens, and the modern concept of civil liberties.[28]

It would be difficult to imagine, much less to understand, liberation theology without Vatican II. The Council, indeed, paved the way for a spiritual renewal, one in which the antagonism between heaven and earth, spirit and matter, and the love of God and the love of the person diminished considerably. The Church and Christians have begun to orient themselves toward "the duty to build a better world based upon truth and justice," while acknowledging that temporal activity does not hinder one's spiritual growth in Christ.

Pope Paul VI

After the Council ended, Pope Paul VI issued his encyclical *Populorum Progressio* — On the Development of Peoples. The influence of this document on the liberation theology movement is quite perceptible. Coming fifteen months after Vatican II, the encyclical is inevitably seen in the light of *Gaudium et spes* as a development of the Church's Social Doctrine. The document reflects the Pontiff's personal concern for the situation in developing countries. It represents an indictment of the effects and of some of the principles of liberal capitalism, worded in a way that causes consternation among capitalist circles.

The encyclical reminds "that private ownership confers on no one a supreme and unconditional right," as well as that "if the earth has been created for the purpose of furnishing individuals either with the necessities of a livelihood or the means for progress, it follows that each person has the right to get from it what is necessary for life."[29] It warns of the danger of violence due to conditions that "cry out bitterly for God's punishment . . . to remove by force the injustice done to human dignity."[30] And in perhaps one of its most controversial passages, the document alludes to the conditions in which a morally justifiable violent revolution may take place.[31]

In giving the parable of the Good Samaritan a new twist, used years later by liberation theology, the encyclical elevates charity to the status of a moral duty to be observed at the international level, warning of the impending class struggle caused when the anger of the poor is aroused by the avarice of the rich.[32] It calls for the creation of a new society in which "freedom is not an empty word, and where Lazarus the poor man can sit at the same table as the rich man."[33]

Still, Pope Paul VI appeals for radical changes within the capitalist system, which puts him in line with reformists and those who favor the developmental approach. At the same time he cautions that the omen of a totalitarian Marxism will become a reality if rich societies choose not to heed unjust conditions.[34] Gustavo Gutiérrez himself observed that the encyclical follows the traditional pattern of ameliorating the conditions of the poor by seeking the conversion of the rich. That is, the document is addressed mainly to the developed nations, so that these can gain awareness and in turn change their behavior and their policies toward developing countries.[35] This is seen as reflecting the traditional emphasis on personal sin and individual salvation, although most likely it represents the Pontiff's attempt at avoiding a call for social revolution, which could have created a very unstable political situation in many parts of the world. Nonetheless, in the context of the Latin American situation, these words appear to have struck a different note. There, it was perceived as being supportive of liberation theology's target, capitalism, and thus it paved the direction which the movement would eventually take.

The Cuban Revolution

> Cuba remains the encouraging symbol and the hope for the Latin American people.[36]

The Cuban Revolution was highly praised by many within the movement for having opened a perspective of liberation among underdeveloped nations.[37] The liberation approach, however, was not a viable alternative within Latin American Catholicism until years after Castro came into power (in January 1959).

Until it was proclaimed Socialist during Castro's speech on April 16, 1961, the revolution had not been identified with Marxism. Even then, the socially conscious elements within the Church were not geared toward socialism. Instead, they entertained a variety of reformist models based on the developmentalist economic approach to growth. Marxism was not considered a viable alternative, mainly because of its opposition to religion and the Church's strong condemnation of its atheism and its orientation toward violence.

Thus when the Cuban Revolution took place, few within the clergy knew what meaning it foretold for Latin America. But frustration over the failures of reformist policies, with right-wing dictatorships operating under capitalist structures (which were perceived as breeding poverty and oppression while associated with the United States), exacerbated the attitudes of those who were committed to social change. These were men who during the 1950s had been urged by their Church to take Christianity to the people by working and living among them, and sharing their feelings and their conditions. They had been educated under a social doctrine which had been very critical of the conditions, structures, and values espoused by liberal capitalism. This doctrine of the Church advocated the subordination of the economic system and the profit motive to the needs of the people. It called for a more equitable sharing of goods with the poor, just wages, and a concept of private property that would safeguard the freedom of all. The Church's doctrine was developing within a capitalist framework and rejected Marxist socialism. At the same time, though, it showed a deep sensitivity for the poor, something that was not part of the capitalist agenda.

The pre-Vatican II mentality among the socially-minded priests was then primarily anti-capitalist, and by association, somewhat anti-American. It was the Council, and later *Populorum Progressio,* that gave their socio-religious framework more latitude by allowing the use of the social sciences and, indirectly, by "legitimizing" their anti-capitalist stance. The Council, following the wishes of Pope John XXIII, was offering an olive branch to the world. Thus condemnations of all sorts, including of Marxism, were avoided. Therefore, concern for the poor, the need to acquire an instrument to combat capitalism, and strong anti-American feelings, plus the search for new formulas of development, brings Cuba into the picture. The socialist revolution is seen as the awaited experiment, and later on regarded as the watershed in Latin American history by setting the example of liberation.[38]

Within the above context the images of Fidel Castro and Che Guevara evoke a sense of respect and admiration. The latter even has been referred to as a "christological mediation" by a noted liberation writer, meaning that Christ is made present today, if only through a distorted image, in the figure of the revolutionary.[39] Thus the Cuban Revolution filled an ideological vacuum among liberation theology's priests. Not all share this view, or are so uncritical of the revolutionary process. But many within the movement embrace Cuba's accomplishments: its ability and boldness to reject capitalism as a mode of development, and to engage in a political and military struggle against it.

The Medellín Episcopal Conference

> The Latin American Church, convening in this the Second General Episcopal Conference, focused its attention on man in this continent, for he is experiencing a decisive stage of his historical process. Proceeding in this manner she has not 'diverted,' but instead has 'turned around' toward man, fully aware that 'to know God it is necessary to know man.'[40]

A new frame of reference, according to the Jesuit psychologist John Powell, provides a "basic perception of reality through which we integrate, evaluate, and interpret new persons, events, and ideas."[41] Vatican II and *Populorum Progressio* gave the Church a much needed new frame of reference in terms of a new spirituality. Through it the Church penetrates the essence of the material world and tries to make sense of it by relating it to faith. Attitudes are formed, and actions follow, supposedly in accordance with the new spiritual scheme.

At Medellín, the Latin American Church was going to build on the Council's foundations, but these would have to be adapted to fit the continent's reality. The given objective of the Latin American bishops conference in Medellín, Colombia, in 1968 was to define the role the Church would play in the process of transformation that the continent was undergoing. Specifically, the Church, finding itself at a crossroad, needed to know how it would respond to existing socio-political pressures following the dissolution of the Alliance for Progress, the opposition to reform by conservative circles, and the specter of Marxism.

It appears that some members of the hierarchy wanted to implement Vatican II in an attempt to use the Church to promote necessary changes while co-opting Marxist efforts, thereby diffusing the potential for violent revolution. Some bishops thought that the Latin American Church might be able to accomplish a virtually impossible task, counting on the majority of the population's devotion for the institution and the prestige it enjoyed. Furthermore, the support which the conference had received from the Pope, who intentionally traveled to Medellín to raise its credibility, added strength to their convictions. Also, there was no question that *Gaudium et spes* and *Populorum Progression* would generate radical ideas. Rather than allowing these two documents to be interpreted at random, which could have led to a split within the ranks, the conference attempted at least to give them meaning, and to set guidelines for their interpretation.

From a theological standpoint, the new vision of reality provided by the documents found a most receptive audience at

Medellín. Relying on the same approach used by *Gaudium et spes* (reflecting on reality with the assistance of the social sciences), the framers analyzed social conditions, and elaborated a theology and a method that radically departed from the traditional one. Although in line with Vatican II, Medellín was far more precise and innovative. The Council had diminished the antogonism between spirit and matter, which could allow religion's involvement with temporal realities. Right at the outset the bishops at Medellín accepted liberation as a socio-political process taking place within a religious framework. To support this view they declared that Christian liberation seeks to free people, not only from sin but from its effects ("ignorance, hunger, misery, and oppression") as well.[42] At the same time, they redefined the concept of sin, returning it to biblical roots, so as to include its social dimension, thereby regarding unjust social structures as sinful.[43]

As a means of eradicating "structural sin," the document favors both personal conversion and structural changes. Although at one time it lists these changes ahead of conversion,[44] in a previous section the document argues that the latter should precede changes, at which time Christians themselves would bring about the necessary social transformations.[45] Nevertheless, nowhere does it state that conversion should be to God or to the Catholic faith. In this the document reflects a shift away from a traditional ritualistic emphasis accompanied by orthodoxy, to its actual objective: an internal change of "hearts and minds" toward the values with which the faith is identified — love, justice, freedom, and peace.[46] This point presented the hierarchy with a few problems. From its own standpoint, the Church considers integral liberation to include conversion of belief to faith in Jesus Christ and conversion of attitudes. Although the Church contends that the combination of the two exemplifies the true and authentic Christian, in its communications to the world it cannot make belief and faith in Christ a precondition of temporal liberation. Such a stance would be tantamount to saying that only those who have the faith have the right to be treated with human dignity and become liberated. Liberation, like salvation, is extended to all, but the Chuch cannot force all to partake in the faith, in accordance with the spirit of Vatican II. Hence the Church tries to find a common basis in terms of temporal activity by calling for a change of attitudes and behavior.

Those, on the other hand, who favor the primacy of the political struggle could regard political conversion to the struggle for liberation as analogous to the one sought by the Church — love of people through a spiritual conversion to Christ. Politics then could acquire primacy over religion, and partisan political movements could be presented as representative of the Church and the faith.

Furthermore, the document approves and gives impulse to "ecclesiastical base communities," (henceforth "Cebs") or small homogeneous groups where Christians become more intimately aware of their faith, and from which they were to promote social development.[47] As it will be seen in another chapter, the Cebs have played a major role in the liberation movement. Also, the conference calls on religious and priests to become involved in social problems "with greater boldness than in the past," although it cautions them not to abandon their eschatological or spiritual dimension.[48]

In the first two sections there is an implicit recognition of the social reality of class struggles between social classes, which is denounced as an obstruction to justice and peace. And, although the document makes a stand against both liberal capitalism and Marxism, as "attempts against the dignity of the human person,"[49] it is the former that is indirectly targeted. The bishops' strong denunciations of unjust and sinful structures refer to the systems that have caused them, which in Latin America are capitalist in their orientation. In addition, the United States is also indirectly related to unjust conditions in the continent. Through the socio-economic term "dependency," used to characterize Latin American reality, the document blames such conditions on "those forces that, inspired by an unbridled profit motive, are conducive to economic dictatorship and to the 'international imperialism of money,' already condemned by Pope Pius XI in *Quadragesimo anno* and by Pope Paul VI in *Populorum Progressio.*"[50]

To be able to understand the radical nature of the Medellín document, one must place the above-mentioned features, which constitute the basis of liberation theology, within the context of the conference's program of pastoral action voted by the bishops. Their primary approach is based on a rough model of "conscientization," or consciousness-raising, a concept developed by the Brazilian educational expert Paulo Freire. He sees behavior oriented toward social change as being initiated through an awakening of the mind of the oppressed individual who, after developing a critical consciousness of reality and of one's situation, becomes an active agent in the struggle for one's own liberation.[51]

Among the pastoral guidelines adopted at Medellín were the following:

- To awaken in man and in the people . . . an active just conscience, instilling a dynamic sense of responsibility and solidarity.

- To defend, in accordance with the Gospel, the rights of the poor and the oppressed. . . .

- To denounce energetically the abuses and unjust consequences of excessive inequalities between rich and poor, between the powerful and the weak. . . .

- To encourage and to support all efforts by the people to foster and institute their own grassroots organizations, aiming at . . . the search for a true justice.[52]

Thus the document commits the bishops to the struggle for justice. As a priest who identifies himself with the movement has remarked: "The Medellín Conference is really a revolutionary pastoral document. In fact, I cannot understand how the bishops could have signed it."[53] He and others claim that since it was prepared by experts the bishops could not possibly have had such an understanding of the situation as described in the document. Therefore, it is suggested that they committed themselves practically blinded to the conclusions. This observation appears to be only partially true. Quite a few bishops were adamantly opposed to the implementation of Vatican II. They were affected by traditionalism and saw this break with the past as excessively radical. Others simply remained aloof from social reality. Their spiritualism, and their lack of knowledge of the social sciences, and even of modern European theology, prevented them from understanding the new terminology in the Medellín document. Still, many of these bishops probably gave their support because the document was endorsed by the Pope, who they thought was aware of its implications and whom they trusted.

The majority of the bishops, however, were probably aware of the socio-political reality in the continent. They understood Medellín, but in terms of another "intellectual exercise," as part of the Social Doctrine which was taught, but not with sufficient zeal. They did not see its revolutionary potential, most likely, because of their educational and religious training. That is, to them Medellín was a theological, not a political, document.

The bishops who were shouldering the Conference, nonetheless, were aware of its implications, and they had little if any choice in the way they proceeded. The document needed to remain similar to Vatican II and *Populorum Progressio,* both of which offered drastic suggestions in important areas. Medellín was to represent, after all, the implementation of these documents. Moreover, a less radical approach would have been described as "whitewash" by leftist elements, and Marxism would have remained as the only serious alternative committed to social change. In retrospect, some observers and participants have remarked that Medellín deviated from its original goal later on, giving way to the liberation theology movement.[54] And as Phillip Berryman, writing on the impact of the conference, points out, years later there were efforts by part of the hierarchy to dilute the "revolutionary interpretations being given to Medellín."[55]

To say that liberation theology is a deviation, however, constitutes too narrow a judgment. What Medellín suggests, from a historical perspective, is not a deviation but the existence of two Medellín messages, or rather one message being interpreted differently by two different audiences. Liberation theology is "crystallized" at Medellín, not afterwards. What comes later is its development and refinement. The conference served as a catalyst of diverse ideas, which had not found common expression, until then, at such a significant level.

There is, on the one hand, a Medellín that expresses itself in a pastoral terminology, similar to Vatican II and to *Populorum Progressio*. It emphasizes the human dimension of salvation and uses technical secular language to anchor its theology, i.e., to mediate the faith and to communicate with the secular world (governments, social, economic, political, and cultural organizations). This approach lets the Bible speak in terms of present-day reality, and has a more or less defined praxis and program of action. It seeks to affect reality but is not totally committed for fear of secularizing itself. This group finds its audience — the majority of the bishops — in those who have their background in an idealist or God-centered theology. It was this audience which received a jolt when it found out that biblical terminology is not as explosive in a spiritual context as when the Church says that "Lazarus ought to find space at the same table with the rich man," in a continent where there are millions of hungry and deprived Lazaruses. The Latin American Church as well as the Vatican were totally unprepared for this type of impact.

The other audience — liberation theologians and activists —

perceived Medellín in a socio-political tone, focusing instead on the eschatological aspect of liberation. That is, while the previous group showed the human and material aspect of religion so that the world would see that Christianity is not the "opiate" (a European-imported concept), this group shows the religious dimension of political action and liberation in order to protect itself against charges of being only a Marxist secular humanism. Therefore, it relies on theology to communicate with the faithful (the hierarchy and the laity). It is reality that speaks here, suggesting to the believer what to do in the light of Revelation. It comes with nothing except faith, and elaborates the praxis as it develops. It prefers to focus on the temporal dimension for fear of being co-opted by an abstract and "passive" spiritualism. Finally, its audience consists of people that respond to an anthropologically-centered theology. Hence these people, too, have appropriated Medellín, and claim it as a milestone in the history of the Latin American Church.[56]

What we have, then, is a conflict between two theological approaches which are unable to come to terms with one another because of their different perspectives and their defensive postures. Thus, Medellín presents a pastoral rhetoric which reality transforms into a revolutionary platform. It places the religious ahead of politics, but social conditions as they are described upset the order. The rhetoric does not preach class struggle, but socio-economic conditions make the strife inevitable. The document condemns violence, but awakens the consciences of people and denounces their oppression. It rejects Marxist ideology, yet its criticism of economic injustices makes Marxism look very appealing. And it speaks more of conversion as the road to justice and peace, but the urgency of the task it describes suggests that a radical change of structures is first required.

The impact of Medellín may be gauged by the fact that in the 1960s and before, the Church was rarely persecuted. On the contrary, it was respected, received privileges, and was in harmony with governments. Around the time of Medellín, people began to focus their attention on the poor and toward their own liberation. This constituted a threat to governments, a view that came forth in the 1969 Rockefeller Commission hearings, which stated that the Catholic Church could pose a danger to regional stability if it decided to act in consonance with Medellín. Around this time, conservative Protestant sects began to arrive in Latin America, allegedly being financed by groups in the United States, so that with conservative Catholic elements in the region they would foment the growth of a "spiritualized" Christianity.[57]

Looking back, it is doubtful that Pope Paul VI had regrets about the impact of Medellín. As much as he abhorred violence, his deeper sense of justice and compassion for the poor and for the oppressed led him to extend his support for the document, with the realization that the alternatives would have been much worse.

[1]Enrique Dussel, "Domination — Liberation: A new Approach," *The Mystical and Political Dimension of the Christian Faith,* eds. Claude Geffré and Gustavo Gutiérrez, CONCILIUM Series No. 96 (New York: Herder and Herder, 1974), p. 54.

[2]Liberation Theology has built on ideas coming from Catholic and Protestant authors such as Karl Rahner, Johann Baptist Metz, P. Blanquart, Edward Schillebeeckx, Jean Cardonnel, Herve Chaigne, Jules Girardi, Rudolf Bultmann, Oscar Cullman, and Jurgen Moltman among others, in addition to relying on the methodology and ideas provided by the Second Vatican Council.

[3]Gutiérrez, *Teología de la Liberación,* p. 232.

[4]Boff, *Teología Desde el Cautiverio,* pp. 31-35.

[5]Ibid., p. 35.

[6]Personal interview with Segundo Galilea, New York, July 18, 1979.

[7]Louis Dupré, *The Philosophical Foundations of Marxism* (New York: Harcourt, Brace & World, Inc., 1966), p. 33.

[8]Raúl Vidales, "Methodological Issues in Liberation Theology," in Gibellini, ed., *Frontiers of Theology*, pp. 52-53.

[9]Johannes Hofinger, S.J., *Evangelization and Catechesis* (New York: Paulist Press, 1976), p. 68.

[10]Both quotes are taken from Alfred T. Hennelly, *Theologies in Conflict, The Challenge of Juan Luis Segundo* (Maryknoll, New York: Orbis Books, 1979), pp. 96-97.

[11]Jon Sobrino, "El Conocimiento Teológico en la Teología Europea y Latinoamericana," in Encuentro Latinoamericano de Teología, *Liberación y Cautiverio*, p. 184.

[12]Jean Danielou, *Oración y Política*, trans. O.L.M.S. (Barcelona, Spain: Editorial Pomaire, S.A., 1966), p. 127.

[13]Pedro Trigo, "¿Doctrina Social de la Iglesia?" *Nueva Sociedad* 36 (mayo-junio 1978): 36.

[14]Pierre Teilhard de Chardin, *The Divine Milieu*, Bernard Wall, gen. ed. of the English edition (New York: Harper and Brothers, Publishers, 1960), p. 39.

[15]Ibid., p. 35; italicizing is mine.

[16]Ibid., the quotation appears on p. 86; on the spiritual power of matter, see pp. 81-88; on the divinization of human activity, see pp. 17-44; on the link between temporal activity and the kingdom, see pp. 25-31.

[17]From the Opening Message, issued at the beginning of the Second Vatican Council by its Fathers, in Abbott, *Documents of Vatican II*, p. 5.

[18]*Rerum novarum*, Pope Leo XIII's most eloquent and precise document along these lines, was promulgated on May 15, 1891. Although it criticizes the unbridled capitalist economic order, the encyclical's main target is the "Socialist solution" that was being presented as an alternative to capitalism in Europe.

[19]As the editors of *The Documents of Vatican II* point out, "For the first time in the history of Ecumenical Councils, a Council addresses itself to all men (sic), not just members of the Catholic Church." (In Abbott, p. 3, n.)

[20]The preface to the Second Vatican Council's Pastoral Constitution on the Church in the Modern World, *Gaudium et spes*, states:

> "The joys and the hopes, the griefs and the anxieties of the men (sic) of this age, especially those who are poor or in any way afflicted, these too are the joys and hopes, the griefs and anxieties of the followers of Christ. Indeed, nothing genuinely human fails to raise an echo in their hearts. . . . That is why this community realizes that it is truly and intimately linked with mankind and its history."

[21] *Gaudium et spes,* nos. 42, 76.

[22]"Indeed, she (the Church) recognizes in the poor and the suffering the likeness of her poor and suffering Founder. She does all she can to relieve their need and in them she strives to serve Christ." *Lumen Gentium,* no. 8.

[23]*Gaudium et spes,* no. 43.

[24]"The Christian who neglects his temporal duties neglects his duties toward his neighbor and even God, and jeopardizes his eternal salvation." Ibid.

[25]Ibid., nos. 34-36.

[26]Ibid., no. 62.

[27]Ibid., no. 14.

[28]Ibid., nos. 27, 29, 31, 41, 63-75, 79-82.

[29]Pope Paul VI, *Populorum Progressio,* 26 March 1967, nos. 23, 22.

[30]Ibid., no. 30.

[31]Pope Paul VI's novelty lies not in developing a moral doctrine on revolution, which is quite traditional in the Church, but in suggesting it as a remote possibility within a context in which the Church appears challenging the legitimacy of a secular modern power, and in pointing to that alternative following his description of the injustices caused by liberal capitalism. Still, the Pontiff's views are not that radical. His statement is qualified by his remark that "insurrection and rebellion . . . beget new injustices, inflict new inequalities, and goad men on to new destruction." Ibid., n. 31. For a fine analysis of Pope Paul VI's views on revolution, see Gonzalo Higuera Udías, ¿"Evolución o Revolución"? in *Teología y Sociología del Desarrollo,* ed. Matías García, S.J. (Madrid: Editorial Razón y Fe, S.A., 1968), pp. 209-226.

[32]Paul VI, *Populorum,* no. 49.

[33]Ibid., no. 47.

[34]Ibid., no. 11.

[35]Gutiérrez, *Teología de la Liberación,* pp. 64-65. The author does not pretend through his critique to reject the encyclical. He acknowledges its valuable contribution to liberation, while at the same time he shows its limitations from the standpoint of the urgency of the problem.

[36]Roberto Oliveros, S.J., *Liberación y Teología* (Lima: Centro de Estudios y Publicaciones, 1977), p. 367.

[37]Eagleson, *Christians and Socialism,* p. 28.

[38]Gutiérrez, *Teología de la Liberación,* p. 127.

[39]Assman, *Theology for a Nomad Church,* p. 104.

[40]From the Introductory Statement of the document, Segunda Conferencia General del Episcopado Latinoamericano, *La Iglesia en la Actual Transformación de América Latina a la Luz del Concilio,* Vol II: Conclusiones, 5ta edicion (Bogotá, Colombia: Indo-American Press, 1970), no. 1 (Henceforth *Medellín*).

[41]John Powell, S.J., *Fully Human Fully Alive — A New Life Through a New Vision* (Niles, Illinois: Argus Communications, 1976), p. 10.

[42]*Medellín,* no. 1.3.

[43]Ibid., nos. 2.1; 2.14c.

[44]Ibid., no. 2.14b.

[45]Ibid., no. 1.3.

[46]Ibid. In the next paragraph the document indicates, nonetheless, that complete conversion is that which takes place in Christ, Ibid., no. 1.4.

[47]Ibid., no. 15.10.

[48]Ibid., no. 12.3.

[49]Ibid., no. 1.10.

[50]Ibid., no. 2.10e.

[51]See his article "Conscientizing as a Way of Liberating," in *Paulo Freire,* ed. LADOC, Keyhole Series N. 1 (Washington, D.C.: U.S. Catholic Conference, 1980), pp. 3-10, for a more detailed version.

[52]*Medellín,* nos. 2.21, 22, 23, 27.

[53]From a talk given by Jose A. Alemán, S.J., published in U.S. Catholic Conference LADOC series, No. 4, p. 15.

[54]Armando Bandera, *La Iglesia Ante el Proceso de Liberación Cristiana* (Madrid: Biblioteca de Autores Cristianos, 1975), p. 102. The author also cites Cardinal Pironio, who favors a less radical and more evangelical approach, as sharing this view. Also Cardinal Lopez Trujillo subscribes to this opinion in "Las Teologías de la Liberación," in *Diálogos.*

[55]Phillip Berryman, "What Happened at Puebla," in Daniel H. Levine, *Churches and Politics in Latin America,* Pref. by John P. Harrison (Beverly Hills: SAGE Publications, Inc., 1979), p. 59.

[56]Oliveros, p. 113.

[57]Jon Sobrino, "Persecución a la Iglesia en Centro América," *ECA* (julio 1981): pp. 645-664 passim. The point about the Rockefeller Commission is also taken from the above.

3.
MARXISM AND LIBERATION THEOLOGY

The Impact of Marxism in the Church

Nowadays it is easy to get the impression that Marxism has infected liberation theology to the point where the latter has become totally unacceptable to the Church. It can be ascertained that there is no liberation theology without Marxist input.[1] But then, the Church also has developed its present social doctrine with the assistance of liberalism and Marxism as well. Without the contributions of these two political ideologies Vatican II, which should rightfully be considered a watershed in Church history, could not have happened. Though the three may appear to be strange bedfellows, according to the Church, God works in mysterious ways, He writes in twisted lines, He makes it rain and shine on all alike, and the "Spirit blows on whomever it wants to."

The fact remains that Christianity has been constantly interpellated by ideologies. This was the case with dualist Stoicism and Platonism, Averroist Aristotelianism, anti-religious liberalism, atheistic phenomenology and existentialism, and Freudian psychoanalysis. Today, amid reaction and condemnation, reluctantly yet with firm conviction and humility, the Church appears to be in the process of separating "the wheat from the chaff" in both Marxism and liberation theology. The process has involved a profound self-examination but has renewed the institution's outlook on the temporal city by removing unnecessary cultural crust from its doctrine.

The antagonism that the Church has traditionally expressed toward Marxism is well known.[2] At times, however, the Church has linked Marxism, Socialism, and Communism indiscriminantly together, without distinguishing between their theoretical and the ideological aspects, and without wanting to differentiate between the ideology and the historical movement to which it gave rise. Too often the Church has reacted in terms of Marxism's historical realization, evaluating its doctrine from an organic viewpoint which analyzed society in terms of order and stability, without acknowledging the presence of conflictual reality.

The Church's criticism of Marxism has been directed against its philosophy, its ideology, and its historical manifestation. The most common charges have been: its atheistic and materialist orientation, its totalitarian aspect, its tendency toward violence and its exacerbation of the social conflict, its debasement of marriage, its attacks against the Christian concept of the family, against private property, and against legitimately constituted authority.

These denunciations have not ceased. The above notwithstanding, three trends may be observed in the Church's attitude toward Marxism. First, the institution has at times displayed a positive reaction to the Marxist critique, manifested by tacitly allowing itself to be questioned by it, by deriving knowledge of the world and of reality from its ideas, and even by using aspects of the theory. Second, the church has become progressively sophisticated in its understanding of Marxism and its historical origins, showing a more discriminating view of its complexity and its intentions. Finally, beginning with Pope John XXIII, the Church has tried to reach out to Marxists in an effort to establish an on-going dialogue that may allow a lessening of tensions between the two. No doubt the Church has shown more willingness to communicate than have Communist governments. The latters' continuous dogmatism, most likely a reflection of their own insecurity and weak doctrinal basis in modern times, impedes them from opening up to such dialogue.

The Church has consistently opposed Marxism; nonetheless the institution and culture have been influenced, both directly and indirectly, by Marxist ideas. It must be stressed that in this assessment Marxism is not considered in its dogmatic political aspect or as a strict scientific method, or even as a philosophy. Instead, Marxism is seen in its broadest sense as a cultural current, and as a heuristic approach in scientific analysis and praxis, capable of inducing or stirring up new ideas.

As was mentioned in chapter two, throughout the Middle Ages the Church, notwithstanding its strong spiritualistic and dualistic tendencies and its often individualistic orientation, had been concerned with the poor and with justice. Moreover, with the advent of capitalism in the fifteenth century, the Church kept pace by legislating moral principles dealing with the use of wealth. Part of the reason was that the first "capitalists" in Europe arose within ecclesiastical circles under strong clerical influence.[3] It was after the Reformation, especially after commercial capitalism appeared to have received religious approval by John Calvin in the sixteenth century, that the Church began to react negatively to some of its economic practices and values. In 1745, Pope Benedict XIV wrote the encyclical *Vix Pervenit* addressing the issue of usury, an activity that had become widely propagated at the time. Though the pope acknowledged the contributions of the nascent capitalism to commerce and industry and to the general progress of the common good, he denounced avarice, the profit motive, usury, and the ambition to which the capitalist activity gives way when wealth is considered as an end in itself.[4]

The social crisis in Europe became acute during the Industrial Revolution, following the emergence of urban workers congregating around newly established factories. While the socialists had assumed the defense of the workers and the systematic attack against capitalism in most of Western Europe, the Church continued to focus on the traditional approach: criticism and denunciation of individualistic morality. The intricacies and the problems of the temporal sphere were still secondary to the Church. Of primary interest was orthodoxy and doctrine, in part because throughout this period it found itself assailed by philosophical naturalism.

The revolution of 1848, which had both liberal and socialist tendencies, had a strong impact on the Church, which reacted negatively against them. However, at the local level these events made the Church attempt a closer relationship with urban and agrarian workers, partly out of an increasing awareness of their poor material conditions, and also because it needed the support of the masses to offset the influence of the two emerging political ideologies. Around this time liberal and social Catholicism began to appear.[5] At the same time, however, the Church in Rome was taking a conservative turn. The major encyclical of this period was Pope Pius IX's *Quanta cura* and its addendum *Syllabus,* published in December 1864. Although they contain a brief paragraph dealing with economic liberalism, both documents are strong condemnations of the philosophical aspects of naturalism, which pretended to organize society without a need of religion.[6] They represent by far the Church's strongest reaction against the social and political ideas of the modern world. In them there is hardly any assessment, much less understanding, of the social and economic conditions of the time.

By the end of the nineteenth century when Marxism began to gain popularity, the Church stood isolated with respect to the social question except for minor local movements. The liberation critique of the institution's self-alienating tendency throughout the ages is succinctly expressed by a Latin American priest:

> Christianity appears before the eyes of modern man (sic) dependent upon a series of values and institutions that are considered definitely outdated. For example, it appears linked to the Aristotelian cosmology at the time when Modern Science is born, defending the legitimacy of the structures of the Ancient Regime when the origins of the Liberal Revolution takes place, defending the social status-quo during the beginning of contemporary social struggles, insisting almost exclusively in a hereafter life amid a Humanity that is obsessed by the call of the Earth.[7]

Thus it is not until 1891 when Pope Leo XIII publishes his encyclical *Rerum novarum* that the Church begins to understand the critical situation of the workers, to denounce the excesses of capitalism, and to advocate "structural reforms." That the Church acts in the shadow of socialism, and prompted by the fear of Marxism, is evident. To begin with, the capitalist critique and the support for labor organizations are undertaken from within a framework which attacks the socialist alternative and the class struggle.[8] As Church historian Robert Aubert points out, "the Church allowed herself to be outdistanced by socialism," not out of insensitivity or ignorance of the workers' conditions, but because of "sheer incomprehension of the new problems posed by the industrial revolution."[9] And this, it may be added, has a lot to do with the orientaion of the Church's theology at the time and the way in which it arranged its priorities. The *Communist Manifesto* already had been published in 1848, and Marx had established the First International in 1864. The Church by then had lost the support of the working class. The latter were largely distrustful of the institution's paternalistic attitude and its vacillating responses concerning workers initiatives.[10]

The Church wasted no time in responding to the plight of the proletariat, and up to the present, lacking its own social theory and words, it has often echoed the Marxist criticism, its terminology, and a view of reality in line with its theory:

(On exploitation)

> Not only labor bargaining, but commercial relations of all sorts, are controlled by a few, to the extent that a substantially reduced number of opulent and rich people have imposed somewhat less than the yoke of slavery upon an infinite mass of proletarians. (Leo XIII, *Rerum novarum,* n.1).
>
> The first thing that needs to be done is to liberate the poor workers from the cruelty of the ambitious, who abuse people without moderation, as if they were objects of their own personal progress. (Ibid., n. 31)

(Denunciation of 'death wages')

> If the worker, forced either by necessity or fear of a greater evil, unwillingly accepts harsher conditions, imposed by the Master, this certainly signifies having to bear violence, which is denounced by justice. (Ibid., n. 32)

(Labor alienation and class struggle)

> Labor . . . is not a worthless merchandise . . . so that it cannot be sold or purchased. . . . Labor bargaining and the lease of workmanship, in what is called the market of labor, divides men into two groups or armies, that with their rivalry transform such market into a palisade in which these two armies attack each other harshly. (Pius XI *Quadragesimo anno,* n. 83)

(Need of a social ethic)

> It grows increasingly true that the obligations of justice and love are fulfilled only if each person, contributing to the common good, *according to his own abilities and the needs of others,* also promotes and

assists the public and private institutions dedicated to bettering the conditions of human life. (Vatican II, *Gaudium et spes,* n. 30. Italicizing is mine)

(On colonialism)

It must be admitted that colonizing countries at times sought nothing but their own advantage, aggrandizement, and glory, and when they relinquished their rule, left those countries in an ill-balanced economy, based on the production of one kind of crop, the market price of which is subject to very great and sudden changes. (Paul VI, *Populorum progressio,* n. 7).

(On imperialism)

Opinions have crept into human society according to which profit was considered the chief incentive to foster economic development, competition the supreme law of economics, private ownership of the means of production an absolute right which recognizes neither limits nor concomitant social duty. This type of unbridled liberalism paved the way for a type of tyranny rightly condemned . . . as the source of . . . international imperialism (Ibid., n. 26)

(On alienation)

All too soon, and often in an unforeseeable way, what this manifold activity of man (labor) yields is not only subjected to "alienation," in the sense that it is simply taken away from the person who produces it, but rather it turns against man himself. . . . (John Paul II, *Redemptor hominis,* n. 15).

(On degradation of labor)

Today's society, . . . often treats work as a special kind of merchandise. Man is often treated as a mere instrument of production, like a material tool that

> should cost as little as possible while producing the maximum. (John Paul II, "Address to Workers," Pusan, Korea, May 5, 1984)
>
> (On materialism)
>
> Free individuals, not inexorably subjected to the economic and political processes, though humbly we recognize that we are *conditioned* by these and we are compelled to make them more humane. (Latin American bishops, *Puebla*, n. 335. Italicizing is mine)
>
> Man is born and develops himself in the center of a *determined* society, *conditioned* and enriched by a particular culture. (Ibid., n. 392. Italicizing is mine)
>
> (On Structural reforms)
>
> The Church urges a swift and profound transformation of the structures, since these are called by its own nature, to contain the evil that stems from the heart of man. (Ibid., n. 438)

This new approach notwithstanding, the Church is still struggling for the credibility of its social doctrine and for its own identity. Marxism has effectively co-opted essential aspects of Christianity, such as social justice, concern for the oppressed, and liberation. This process of co-optation has been so successful nowadays that anyone who stands up for these issues risks being labled leftist, radical, or communist by many people in the Western world. Hence, largely because of a lack of education (or shall we say of evangelization), the cause of the poor, social justice, and liberation still only have a political connotation, with little or no religious implications. Thus while modern social liberals (socialists and Marxists) still regard the Church as reactionary, many within the Judeo-Christian tradition see the social question in terms of Marxism, and fear its implications.

Ironically, Marxism has, in the positive sense, materialized Christianity. This does not mean that the Christian religion has given up its spiritual dimension, but rather that faith and Christian praxis have taken material reality more into account. This signifies that concern for the human condition in the temporal city has become an important part of the Church's mission. The impact of Marxism has challenged the validity and identity of Christianity, to which it feels compelled to respond. In the process, the Church has developed a greater sensitivity for the material well-being of the human person, not just the soul, and within a social and political community, not only as individuals. Indirectly, Marxism has driven into Christianity the realization that spiritual individualism was a cultural reaction that could be shaped into a spirituality leading to salvation by placing the needs of others ahead of one's own.

The development of modern political theology, one that exercises its prophetic role through criticism and denunciation of social, economic and political values and structures, which signifies a return to the roots of Christianity, has been incorporated by the Church. For this it was necessary that faith acquire a social and political dimension; that faith be, in the term that liberation theologians have borrowed from European theologian Johann Metz, "deprivatized," or made social and public, in addition to being private. This prevents "the reduction of the praxis of faith to an alienating individualistic decision which has led to a separation of religion and society."[11]

The presence of a political theology in Church doctrine, as well as the incorporation of other "secular" views, does not mean that Marxism has subversively infiltrated ideas alien to Christianity. As Alfredo Fierro states, "a political theology is possible because there are grounds for it in biblical and Christian tradition."[12] Also, the popes, so watchful of the purity of the dogma and of orthodoxy, would not consent to the assimilation of an ideology that otherwise threatens its own existence. Indeed, the basis and the roots of Social Christianity are found in the Gospel. But, as Fierro adds, after two thousand years it is now that the Bible is being subjected to a political hermeneutics, and it is happening on the "humus of Marxism."[13]

It is important to recall that the Church has reconciled its doctrine with the major principles of the Enlightenment. Today, the institution not only accepts but defends political freedoms, freedom of religion, the autonomy of the State, the rights of people to self-determination, democracy, the autonomy of the sciences, and technological progress. These have been incorporated under the influence of liberalism, which for two hundred years had been its most formidable antagonist.

Marxism, as a cultural movement, has forced a recognition of new attitudes and practices, and through these it has indirectly provided capitalism a more ample scope of operation. Among these attitudes and practices are acceptance of labor organizations, government intervention in economic matters and regulation of the private sector, a new view of the role of private property, State assistance to the poor, the sick, and the weak. In society, Marxist theory has contributed to a psychological and a sociological understanding of alienation and of class divisions. And, though the development of science antecedes Marxism, the latter has given a stimulus to the human sciences and to the recognition of the social or material conditioning of culture and of human behavior. In this sense a heuristic and undogmatic understanding of historical materialism has led to a deeper awareness and a more rigorous approach to social reality, all without the need of accepting the Marxist ideology in its dogmatic form.

From the standpoint of the Church's social theology, as we have seen, Marxism has provided a wider perspective of the functioning of the capitalist system. Lacking its own methodology, the Church has relied on Marxist-popularized terms and concepts, such as exploitation, oppression, dependence, imperialism, class struggle, praxis, proletariat, alienation, surplus value, conscientization, fetishism of commodities, liberation, and others. Moreover, the Marxist concepts of people realizing themselves through work, and people as the architects of history and of their own destiny, both versions of widely held Renaissance beliefs, have brought out the essence of Christianity, whereas its previous cultural orientation stressed a "superstitious" and inordinate dependence on God.[14]

Today, the Church sees with new eyes God's call to humans to subdue the earth. Though it teaches and announces the kingdom, the Church is aware that no magical faith, no sacrament or indulgence alone, will lead to salvation. This requires our cooperation with grace. Only through actions is the truth in Christianity realized. This view lies at the core of evangelization today, though it still fails to reach the conscience of the masses of believers. However, this is not a new phenomenon. Such a Christian Promethean attitude finds its intellectual roots in sixteenth-century Ignatian spirituality, which taught the faithful to formulate their own praxis as if everything depended on each believer alone, leaving the outcome to God, on whom things ultimately depend.

In addition to its contribution to deprivatization, Marxist theory has brought new insights to the development of liberation theology, which have been accepted by the Church. Thus, again through historical materialism, the Church and liberation theology highlight the importance of economic structures, of dependency, and the need for structural transformations instead of focusing only on conversion. This has led to the study of ideologies and the subtle manner in which ideological values in society justify domination of one group by another. The development of a critical consciousness vis-á-vis the State lies at the base of Marxism. Through this approach liberation theology uncovers religious collusion with the State, and the latter's co-optation of Christianity in Latin America. Further, it questions those societies that uphold traditional values, God, honesty, fidelity, justice, and charity, while allowing misery, corruption, and injustice to take place.

Ideology here means that which mediates theory and praxis by making a call to solidarity and to the transformation of society in order to attain the aspirations, values, or interests that have guided the theory.[15] However, at this level it is difficult to distinguish between the theory, praxis, and ideology, for they all become one comprehensive aspect that views reality in a certain manner, interprets it, attempts to change it, and even motivates such change. From the standpoints of both the Church and liberation theology, this aspect of ideology does not have any pejorative connotation, thus it is not condemned.

The problem arises when the ideology, which the praxis needs to be effective, seeks to present itself as an ultimate answer and the only valid interpreter of reality. This in turn leads to absolutization of the social project by closing the ideology to criticism, by identifying its interests with those of the society, and by making a claim to the unconditionality of its exigencies. When an individual adheres to this vision, we may speak of the ideologization of the human conscience in which the individual's ideas and behavior are unconsciously conditioned by an ideology. This is the negative aspect which both the Church and liberation theology criticize.

Liberation as a Religious Issue

A selective use of Marxism also has led to significant changes in other aspects of theology. One concerns the issue of freedom. Liberalism sensitized the Church to the concept of individual freedom. It is Marxism, however, which in liberation theology completes the process by, indirectly, giving external freedom (e.g., freedom from material deprivation or political oppression and repression) a religious significance. We recall from our second chapter that the Christian view of freedom stressed the spiritual aspect by focusing on the individual's freedom from sin, and freedom to form an intimate relationship with God. External freedom not only was secondary but the effects of evil on others were regarded as temporal afflictions that people had to bear during their lifetime. Thus the Marxist critique of religion, largely inspired by Feurerbach:

> The social principles of Christianity place in heaven the compensation of all infamies, and in that manner justify the permanence of these infamies on earth. . . .
>
> The social principles of Christianity explain all infamies committed by oppressors against the oppressed, either as just punishment for original sin or other sins, or as trials that the Lord inflicts upon his redeemed ones in accordance with his infinite wisdom.[16]

Though the Church was in the process of altering its image as the "opiate of the people" when such criticism was aired, properly speaking it is not until *Rerum novarum* that one's suffering on earth as a result of human injustice is treated independently of personal attitudes and philosophical ideas. The previous tendency was to deal with social and political issues from a philosophical standpoint; such was the Thomist approach. In *Rerum novarum* the criticism of social conditions is examined in the context of concrete reality in a more positivistic manner. And it was not until Vatican II that the Church formally pronounced that the love of God and the dignity of the human person regard liberation from one's evil actions as an important teaching. The hierarchy opted to accept the "City of Man" and to work actively toward its material well-being. The temporal project became a high priority because of its increasingly apparent link with the eschatological kingdom. As a result, the theological understanding of God changed from that of an omnipotent and omniscient judge to that of a merciful father who forgives us and who is faithful to his promises.

In Latin America, it is not until just before liberation theology enters the socio-political arena that the hierarchy begins to react positively and concretely to injustice and to oppression. As will be seen in chapter four, by pressing the demand for socio-political liberation the new theology has taken the Church to task in going even further than it had gone in Vatican II. It must be taken into account that the 1950s and the 1960s were characterized by the numerous national liberation movements, including the Cuban Revoluion. It is within this context that liberation theology arises, resurrecting the term "liberation" both as a religious and as a socio-political concept.

The Mediation of Theology

A second aspect in which Marxism has been influential has to do with the political mediation of theology. The privatization of faith was the product of cultural Christianity. Deprivatization now allows Christianity to manifest itself politically through the action of belivers. Yet this rudimentary praxis does not reach a level of critical consciousness until a better appreciation and understanding of the demands of historical reality and God's kingdom are attained. This is one way of defining the role of theology. From another perspective, theology is seen as fulfilling the obligation of seeking from the Scriptures answers to new questions formulated under different conditions than in past epochs. When the issue at hand is the political sphere, theology is then presented with the need to mediate between the strictly religious and the political realms.

Liberation theology's use of Marxism pushes theology to materialize itself, that is, to become grounded in concrete human reality. Thus if the Church wishes to keep God in communication with people in today's society, the relevance of theology must be shown in less abstract terms. This is especially important today because by the time theology becomes religion, faith is soon culturalized and usually retains whatever characteristics and orientations were imparted at the theological level.

To materialize theology has nothing to do with theology becoming Marxist in the ideological sense, or with faith losing its eschatological dimension. Rather, it refers to two things: first, to a more operative conceptualization of religious concepts such as salvation, grace, kingdom, providence, sacrament, faith, love, sin, liberation, and others, so that religion may be a force in social relationships and in action, instead of being only a source of devotion and piety.[17] To some extent, de Chardin's writings were able to bridge the gap between the non-believer scientist and the believer through the use of concepts that better relate the two minds. And in Latin America, part of the reason liberation theology is so appealing is that people can associate their material reality with their faith in a way in which they become conscious of themselves as people who are able to act to change their conditions.

Second, materializing theology implies the incorporation of the human sciences in its development as the only means of studying reality. This is only a matter of practicality, since the former cannot reach where the latter can and vice versa. Thus theology loses relevance and credibility if it attempts to speak to human problems without having sufficient technical knowledge of the issues it examines. Indeed, it is ironic that the lack of a more scientific input in theology, which in Latin America has justified the use of Marxism as a tool of analysis, has given way both to an "evasive spiritualism" and to an uncritical acceptance of the Marxist ideology.[18]

Marxism and the Praxis in Liberation Theology

By far, the greatest impact of Marx in liberation theology has to do with two postulates that he developed before his theory was fully formulated. They have become sources of inspiration and intellectual guides of the theology:

> The question whether human thought can achieve objective truth is not a question of theory but a practical question. In practice (Praxis) man must prove the truth, i.e., the reality, power and this-sidedness of his thought. The dispute concerning the reality or unreality of thought — which is isolated from practice

> (Praxis) — is a purely scholastic question. (Thesis II on Feuerbach)
>
> Philosophers have only interpreted the world differently: the point is, however, to change it. (Thesis XI on Feuerbach)

The two theses serve as the basis of the praxis in liberation theology.[19] The Church itself has taken hold of their essence, and we may add, both ideas find similar roots in Jesus' message, given the objective that he pursued and the criteria he outlined for believers. With regard to the theses, Marx was not thinking in terms of setting a criteria to test the scientific truth of all philosophical, much less all theological, issues. Nor was it his intention to reject as scientifically false those that did not pass such test. The issue of proving the existence of God to Marx was "purely scholastic." That does not mean that his theses are irrelevant to Christianity and to faith.

His two postulates on Feuerbach must be seen within the context of a man who sought, above all, to change social conditions. That is why he transformed philosophy into praxis. In *The Holy Family* Marx makes the point, if passionately and with some exaggeration, that "ideas can accomplish absolutely nothing," thus, "to become real, ideas require men (sic) who apply a practical force."[20] In other words, Marx wanted to do away with abstract and passive thinking, because of the static nature of ideas. If ideas are not realized they can have no impact on social life. If, on the other hand, people pursue their own self-realization, they need to change themselves and change the environment; rather, they need to change their way of thinking so that they can act on the environment. Once the latter is accomplished one's human nature changes accordingly. This process requires not only thinking but also acting, i.e., praxis. True, through philosophy we may change our outlook in life, and may even discover our private truth. This process may make it easier to adapt to our new reality by understanding it. But Marx also rejects the concept of a passive being, one that is content with resigning oneself to human events, one who becomes the object rather than the subject of nature.

To change reality, ideas must first penetrate the minds of the masses, according to Marx. Afterward, the truth of these ideas, i.e. "the reality and power" in them, must be acted out through the praxis if one is really determined to change one's conditions.[21] Ironically, such is the basis of present Church evangelization. The praxis is the difference between a passive and an active spirituality, between an alienated and a committed religion. The divorce of praxis from orthodoxy was duly recognized by Vatican II "as among the more serious errors of our age."[22] However, although the Church finds the responsibility with Christians for this phenomenon, we must say that the institution itself was not as forceful on the issue (largely because it was not theologically prepared) as it would be a century later. As a result, the Christian religion appeared as an abstraction of reality leading to the estrangement of one's consciousness. As he did with respect to capitalism, Marx generalized from a static and cultural model of Christianity, which to him was no more than an illusion:

> Religion is indeed man's self-consciousness and self-awareness so long as he has not found himself or has lost himself again. . . .
>
> (Thus) the criticism of religion disillusions man so that he will think, act and fashion his reality as a man who has lost his illusions and regained his reason.[23]

Liberation theologians do not accept Marx's views on religion, but neither do they accept a contemplative religion alone. Ironically, through Marx, liberation theology destroys his own caricature of religion as "opium."[24] This is done by stressing a Christian revolutionary praxis. Through it the Church, and to a greater extent liberation theology, has rediscovered the practicality, the effectiveness and, as many within the movement will add, the subversive elements of the Gospel. Liberation theology is above all concerned with and about the poor, but that is not enough. Neither is it enough to analyze the causes of their conditions. The concern for the poor and awareness of their situation constitutes an alienated faith in Christians unless these are accompanied by an intentional praxis that is geared to transform social conditions.[25]

Sidney Hook, one of Marx's many interpreters, comments on his Thesis II:

> What a man wants to believe is relevant only to *what* he believes, but not to its truth. There is no will to believe in Marx but a will to action. . . . What takes place as a result of practice is not a relevant consequence of the theory unless the conditions involved in the meaning of the theory are met.[26]

In Christian theology we may reformulate the above statement in line with liberation theology. Christianity, like Marxism, has a conception of how society should operate. Not a specific one, but a sketch of conditions based on certain values. Segundo puts it as follows:

> Neither the Christian message nor the Church makes sense for an end other than to lead history toward a more human society, and toward more human conditions of life. God did not reveal things nor did He found a Church simply to call men toward Him, vertically, for example through a sacrament, but everything that He included in the Christian message, in the Scripture and in the Church had a function, that is, a historic end; it tended to realize God's plan in history, which is man's humanization and his divinization within humanization.[27]

This means that Christian praxis, at any one moment in history, has to be attuned with its conception and pursue, so as to meet, the conditions in it. Here we are not referring to a fixed *a priori* model of a social project that is deduced from Revelation, but to conditions that any political and social system should include. This approach is no different from Marxism, which also postulates its own set of conditions that include a classless society, nationalization of the means of production, and an economic system based on "from each according to his ability, to each according to his needs," or from capitalism, which calls for a market that responds to supply and demand and the initiative from private capital.

In a way Christ himself was a firm believer in truth being actualized through the praxis,[28] and he was a positivist in judging behavior. Innumerable times he gave examples carrying the same message: "Not everyone who calls me Lord, Lord, shall enter the kingdom of heaven, but only those who *do* God's will."[29] The praxis cannot be separated from conditions any more than the actions of Christians are relevant if they are not related to the theory: "For the tree can only be told by its fruits."[30] Obviously, many criteria can be used to evaluate the quality of the tree, but for Christ the most important one was the end result, just as for Marx it was the objective of realizing philosophy.

Historical Materialism and Social Change

The issue of social change, as expressed in liberation theology, has resulted in a conflict with the Church. The institution has approached social change in its traditional way: social structures cannot be changed apart from the person. Since hearts and minds fashion social structures, the Church insists that conversion must be preached. Liberation theology does not disagree with the Church on this issue. However, precisely because the Church's doctrine has insisted on conversion, taken in the sense of changing beliefs (orthodoxy), without much emphasis on the need for structural transformations, the theologians overstress the point that the person cannot be changed apart from his social conditioning. This is done for pedagogical reasons as well as to express the urgency of the task amid the seriousness of social conditions.

The Church is under the impression that the emphasis on social transformation is due to the influence of Marxist thought. This may be so, but it is due more to a reaction against traditional Church praxis. The method of analysis in liberation theology is related to the Marxist postulate that material life or social existence is not determined by consciousness, but that consciousness, being a "social product" from the beginning, is determined by material life.[31] Without falling into a mechanistic interpretation of that relationship, which is not what Marx had in mind, he adds:

> Therefore, in any interpretation of history one has first of all to observe this fundamental fact in all its due importance. . . .
> This conception of history depends on our ability to expound the real process of production, starting out from the material production of life itself, and to comprehend the form of intercourse connected with this and created by this mode of production as the basis of all history, . . . to explain all the different theoretical products and forms of consciousness, religion, philosophy, ethics, and trace their origins and growth from that basis. . . .[32]

Marx's dialectical materialism is first of all epistemological, not praxiological. In reacting to the Young Hegelians, he shifts his focus of analysis from the study of ideas to that of material reality, which later on leads him to switch from an idealistic praxis based on the criticism of ideas to a historical one based on the transformation of social reality. But to pursue that objective it is necessary to gather knowledge, not from ideas (which according to Marx are the product of social existence), but from social reality, especially material production and economic relationships, thereby being responsible for one's actions). Liberation theology adopts this approach of focusing on historical material reality in order to understand it and change it.

However, it would be misleading to assume that this view of Marxism has to be interpreted in a way that leads only to a praxis of structural changes while excluding, at one stage or another, a personal conversion of some sort. Change would then amount only to a different type of social conditioning. Even in Marx the revolutionary praxis is possible only when philosophy, i.e., ideas, takes hold of proletariat minds, that is, when people become aware and are "converted" to the revolutionary process. Only in that way can they participate actively in the creation of their new society.

It appears that there is a contradiction in Marx when he states that his epistemology leads "to the conclusion that all forms of products of consciousness cannot be dissolved by mental criticism, but only by the practical overthrow of the actual social relations which gave rise to the (idealistic view of history)," i.e., that ideas fashion social existence.[33] Here, he seems to be saying that conversion to certain ideas is not the correct approach to change reality — revolution is. On a closer look, this idea not only makes sense, but actually involves no contradiction. Marx's main criticism against the Young Hegelians is stated in his Thesis XI on Feuerbach, namely that they have made mental adjustments about the world, without these affecting material reality in any concrete manner. Thus, it does not make sense for someone to be converted to new ideas about reality if these do not lead that person to effect changes that correspond to the ideas. In such a case the social reality that is responsible for an alienated consciousness will continue exerting its influence on people. On the other hand, the transformation of structures presupposes a personal conversion to the ideas of socialism, otherwise we would be talking about programmed robots who proceed without any awareness of their motives and their objectives. Hence in Marx the praxis of social transformation and conversion are directly related. The former implies the latter, and the latter leads to the former.

The Church's praxis stresses the importance of conversion over structural transformation because of the fundamental value of internal freedom and because it sees that excluding conversion may lead to political revolutions and violence. The Church does not realize, however, that such conversion inevitably will lead to revolution and to violence unless it speaks of an idealistic conversion to the status quo, which is not the case in either the Church's latest pronouncements or in the Puebla document as it will be seen further ahead. Nonetheless, it is true that the fear is real that a call for structural changes without conversion to religious values may lead only to a radical political conversion identified with a Marxist strategy, which in turn may lead to a totalitarian system. In other words, conversion will only be useful to motivate the masses to join the revolutionary process, but once it attains power the group may become a ruthless dictatorship of the proletariat. For the most part, liberation theologians are concerned that conversion, which they do not reject, will give way to a criticism of ideas instead of reality, so that change will imply only making philosophical or idealistic adaptations in the mind, thereby detracting from a revolutionary praxis.[34]

Faith, Praxis, and Methodology in Liberation Theology

In contraposition to Marx, there is in liberation theology a will to believe. Liberation theology originates in a faith in Christ. It is precisely because those involved in liberation believe that they operationalize their faith through action or praxis. Raúl Vidales emphasizes this point by saying that liberation theology "can be none other than an interpretation of what is lived, of historic faith as praxis of liberation." Thus liberation seeks this consonance between theory and praxis.[35]

The striking characteristic of faith in liberation theology is the way in which it is oriented. Here are two noted liberation theologians expressing the same view. First, Juan Luis Segundo:

> The profound shift which makes me transcend the relative Christian testimonies that surround me, which propels me in an open, receptive way toward Jesus himself; that which grounds my faith in him and no longer in any other person, no matter how trustworthy or attractive, appears on the level of political commitment and of revolutionary political commitment on behalf of the oppressed.[36]

Then we have Leonardo Boff:

> A faith that is truly a faith in God and in Jesus Christ leads to a liberation process, denouncing concrete oppression that embodies sin as rejection of God and our brother, and to an effective commitment in the gestation and creation of a more just and egalitarian society.[37]

Hence, it is not that Marxist theory has subverted faith in the hands of liberation theologians, but rather it has helped them (in a heuristic manner) to discover a method through which they can bring out essential aspects of the Christian faith that because of its social conditioning had remained hidden: faith expressed in terms of an option for the poor and the oppressed, realized through a praxis in favor of their liberation. Here we see how the theology of liberation, the theory, follows Marx's Thesis XI on Feuerbach in that theology does not stop once it understands reality. Instead, it seeks to change reality, supposedly in the light of faith. In so doing theology recovers "the lost or threatened dimension of faith," which is that of its realization and the realization of the freedom of the children of God.[38]

It should be clear by now that liberation theology is oriented, through socio-political action, toward both external and internal freedom, influenced by a transcending Christianity.[39] Compared with traditional theology, liberation theology's use of Marxist ideas provides the theologians with a different religious perspective, which is, according to its authors, more attuned with present reality in Latin America and with an anthropological view of humanity that seems to prevail in today's culture. It is this perspective that leads to the issue of liberation of the poor from present social conditions, a value with which the Church has reconciled itself, to which it has given increasing importance in the last decades, and whose religious significance Marxism has helped to uncover.[40] However, this is not to say that serious methodological errors have not been made by some liberation theologians and activists by incorporating unrevised Marxist ideas, which have led them to omit reflection on the faith by focusing primarily on the praxis. This point will be further elaborated ahead in this chapter.

In the process of criticizing ideologies, liberation theology questions religion itself as a possible major cause of alienation. It focuses on the cultural conditioning of the faith and attempts to present a new interpretation of the Christian message through a "rereading" of the Bible from a totally different perspective: the reality of the poor. Rereading operates in a twofold manner. First, it uncovers the ideological functions that a traditional hermeneutics has played in religion and denounces them. Second, it serves as the basis on which reflection on the faith, the development of theology, takes place.[41] These roles become necessary for liberation theology. The conflict arises when the interpretation of the message is done within a framework that today may be considered alienating. For example, in many parts of Latin America a spiritualistic emphasis would be favored by conservative groups because it tends toward the status quo. Here it would be easy to see how some would prefer a literal interpretation of Christ's predilection for the "poor in spirit," which may be totally unrelated to those who are materially poor and may serve as a rationalization of one's accumulation of wealth while ignoring the needs of others, yet one would still be regarded as among God's chosen ones.

The suggestion by the Latin American bishops at Puebla that the political aspect be read from the standpoint of the Scripture, instead of the inverse as proposed by liberation theology,[42] is based on the concern that if rereading is done from an ideological perspective, the praxis may result in the reduction of the gospel to a socio-political dimension and the temporalization of religion. But in retrospect, the bishops' rule, which has been the practice of the Church, did not prevent the doctrine in the past from reducing the Scriptures to personalist and spiritualized dimensions, as well as to collusion with political systems. In this sense, Galilea is correct when he says that there can be interpretations of the Scripture which, as the product of cultural conditioning, betray the authenticity of the message of Christ. In these cases the teaching authority of the Church may not be of any help. This authority prevents heresy, he says, but does not necessarily preclude the ideologization of the biblical message.[43] And, as Galilea would admit, not even liberation theology can remain impervious to ideologization. Thus it has happened that, conditioned by the reality that surrounds them and by a lack of critical consciousness with respect to the Marxist instrument of analysis, some within the movement have adopted values and attitudes that seem to erode if not openly contradict their original critique.

Liberation theologians also like to assert that the praxis comes before the theory (the theology).[44] In a sense this is the proper course. Otherwise, they would commit the traditional error of elaborating a program of action based on a rigid model established *a priori,* which is the result of ideological and cultural conditioning that have little or no relevance to the reality that a Christian praxis seeks to change. Since the Gospel does not provide specific answers to concrete social problems, it does not make sense to prescribe solutions until after the commitment to liberation, i.e., a rudimentary praxis of becoming involved, is made.[45] Once in touch with reality, the person can assess the nature of the problem and its difficulties, thereby gaining a firsthand understanding of what is required to deal with it effectively. It is such reflection on the praxis and on reality that constitutes the theology. Once this is elaborated, the believer brings with him a better perspective to continue the praxis.[46]

Nevertheless, liberation theology's vague and ambiguous exposition of its approach has created confusion and conflict with Church authorities and critics who view the process as theology being guided by Marxist ideology.[47] The following appears among some liberation theologians:

> It is not what are called 'evangelical values' that give meaning to social praxis. Quite the opposite is the case. Social praxis gives meaning to the former. Christians should not redefine social praxis by starting with the Gospel message. They should do just the opposite. They should seek out the historical import of the Gospel by starting with social praxis.[48]

It would appear that the above contradicts liberation theology's own assertion that the praxis originates with faith. However, it is the other way around. In their desire to free themselves from an ideologized ecclesiastical praxis, liberation theologians forget to mention a previous step in the process, which is nonetheless present: prior to the praxis and to reflection on such praxis, there is a reflection on the faith. It is this, precisely, that distinguishes liberation praxis from the Marxist one. Gustavo Gutiérrez makes it clear that "from a perspective of faith, what prompts Christians to participate in the liberation of oppressed people and of the exploited social classes is the conviction of the radical incompatibility of the evangelical exigencies with an unjust and alienating society."[49] Leonardo Boff would confirm this by saying that liberation theology is the result of "an ethical indignation," in which "the situation of poverty of the masses produced a commotion of Christian love seeking a way of being efficacious."[50]

It is not surprising, then, for Gutiérrez to state that faith is the foundation of praxis.[51] More than that, one has to add that faith is the source of principles, of intentions, and of analysis in liberation. Faith becomes the bridging element between praxis and theory. Thus, love of Christ in the neighbor, compassion for the weak and the oppressed, the precept of putting the other before oneself, and the requirement to realize the faith through action — all distinctive Gospel values — are present in the consciousness of the believer before the initial praxis takes place. They color liberation's perception of reality and its action upon that reality.

This point is brought out by Segundo while arguing against Hugo Assman's contention that a personal understanding of the Gospel is not possible without a prior commitment to the revolutionary praxis.[52] Segundo shows that Assman's position is neither realistic or logical, for any type of revolutionary commitment has to be preceded by some kind of ideology, be it from "Marx, or Mao's saying, or the Gospel message."[53] Even in Assman's case this appears to be true, since he claims to be motivated by both Marxist and Christian values.[54]

The issue of *a priori* views rejected by liberation theology has to do with any series of acceptable and taboo behavior that may restrict the freedom of a pastoral or a political praxis when those are absolutized. If faith is ideologized, given its relationship with God, then it would hinder the praxis and the theology. Not only that but, from a theological standpoint, to politically ideologize the faith presupposes the relativism of God's plan, holding it to temporal limitations. Nonetheless, as Segundo sees it, the problem is that one's faith necessitates an ideology to help it to realize itself. Without an ideology rational action is impossible for it would lack direction. By ideology here he means "a system of goals and means that serves as the necessary backdrop for any human option or line of action;"[55] that is, any perspective that allows the believer to mediate between the general (and abstract) and the specific (and concrete).

Segundo sees the solution in suggesting that the believer must fashion for himself an ideology and use it in the relative sense, i.e. without holding it, dependent on the faith, in an absolute manner, and doing so in a critical way; that is, being mindful that it offers no guarantees for success and being open to the possibility of changing it if a better one comes along. In addition, his solution implies — and this is characteristic of all liberation theologians — that the historical context of the Gospel should be relativized too. In other words, the solutions to problems narrated in the Scripture are not always applicable to today's problems in the same way as they were at the time they were used. Nor can they suggest that Christ's own attitudes and the decisions he made are binding on all in the same manner. If the believer fails to relativize the attitudes and decisions in the gospel, his brand of Christianity becomes, for all practical purposes, static and bound to end in failure.[56] He applies the same principle to Marxism, saying that its failure to relativize its revolutionary ideology leads to absolutism.[57] Segundo sums up the relationship between faith and ideology, which as he indicates finds its theological basis in Vatican II, as follows:

> Faith has as its function the task of guiding the human mind towards more fully human solutions in history; the Church does not possess those solutions in advance but does possess elements that have been revealed by God; these revealed elements do not preserve the Church from ideologies; instead the Church must take advantage of those elements to go out in search of ideological solutions to the problem posed

by the historical process; and such solutions will always remain provisional.[58]

The Analysis of Social Reality

Once faith is deprivatized, reality has to be examined in order to relate faith to the temporal world. Again, deprivatization means that faith has a socio-political role (in addition to its traditional vertical or private dimension), that it has a message with political implications. And since faith assumes that present social conditions in Latin America are not in accordance with certain human and Christian values, "the analysis of reality becomes a condition for its transformation."[59] An abstract or idealistic theology cannot effectively undertake such a task because it lacks a proper understanding of that reality.

Such transformation of social conditions presupposes a valid religious basis, otherwise theology becomes sociology. Liberation theology finds this basis in the concept of the Kingdom of God already present on earth and progressing toward its ultimate consummation at the end of history. Since this kingdom is rooted in the world, it is affected by many of the human/natural processes that influence other institutions. Moreover, the kingdom is intimately related to the world:

> The Kingdom of God, in effect, has to do in the first place with historical reality, with a structural reality that to a large extent shapes personal destinies; it has to do with a historical praxis that, without abandoning the personal dimension, has incidence over strictly social dimensions; it has to do, . . . at least as a purpose, with the whole of humanity; and finally, it has to do with evil and structural sins which, to the extent they are historical, need sociological factors for their interpretation.[60]

Not only do we find that the Kingdom of God is a historical, thus a social, reality, but also that even the major witness of the Christian faith, as Boff calls the Scripture, does not come to us directly from its source. Instead, what we have is God's word mediated by and presented to us through the human word, thus subjected to human limitations.[61] This does not mean that the word of God loses its transcendence or its freedom, but that when we speak of faith "we have to discern what constitutes the exigent call of God (its never-changing message), and what are properly theological, social, and even ideological articulations that are linked to a historical past and say little or nothing to our time."[62]

It has been established how faith already has helped liberation theology to identify the perspective from which the theology will be elaborated: the dimension of the poor. As Ellacuría maintains, this choice of context supposes a certain evangelical preference, although not an exclusive one, which will consciously determine the way in which the word of God will be interpreted, the tools of analysis and the theories chosen to examine reality, and the type of praxis undertaken.[63] From this perspective and through a more discriminating analysis of reality, liberation theology views poverty not as something accidental, the result of fate or the will of God, but as an evil that is largely the product of sin. The poor are largely victims of unjust and oppressive relations among people, and of social structures that perpetuate those relations. Relying on Vatican II, on *Populorum progressio,* and on Marxist ideas, the theological objective surpasses (though it does not negate) the traditional goal of ameliorating poverty through personal and social charity, and focuses instead on ways to eradicate the cause of the poor's conditions which prevents their development, violates their dignity, and subjects them, as Vatican II has stated, "to conditions unworthy of human beings."[64] These conditions already point to the liberation of the poor as the justifying factor in liberation theology.

A liberation praxis and the theology on which it is dependent are intimately related to the analysis of reality. If the latter is misleading, because of its inaccurate or biased perception, both the praxis and the theology will be negatively affected. From the standpoints of both the Church's social doctrine and liberation theology, the relationship between theology and science is characterized by a relative interdependence: that between the abstract and the concrete, and the normative and the empirical. An effective choice of a course of action requires as much concrete information as possible. But the application of scientific results to society and the choice of praxis always entail value judgments. The results by themselves never indicate a definite praxis independent of normative considerations. This is true even of Marxism.

The selection of any method of analysis is not only preceded by certain values, but these values will also guide the research, including the concepts that are used and those aspects of reality on which the scientist wishes to focus. In addition, when the method is incorporated in a theory of social change or of action, those same values will condition the general ends towards which the theory is headed. These ends in turn will judge and justify the means that are chosen. The determining role of values in this process is simply unavoidable. At this stage, a social theory of action is related to its praxis through ideology, here meaning a body of ideas and values that must accompany the praxis and that seeks to explain and legitimate changes. At this point, it may be added, ideology tends to be absolutized.

When choosing its categories for the analysis, or a particular praxis, theology confronts three basic limitations. The first one is that faith lacks its own methodology for analyzing social reality. It needs the assistance of secular human science, for faith speaks largely in a metaphysical language, which is inadequate to deal with concrete reality. The second point is that faith, as we have said, does not provide a specific type of social system — this needs to be improvised. However, the Christian message contains a heuristic dimension. It possesses certain distinctive values, and points to certain distinctive conditions of social life.[65] These basic values and conditions constitute the *evangelical criteria,* and make Christianity what it is. So, for example, Christianity tends to favor the weak rather than the strong, freedom rather than oppression, cooperation over crude competition, the other more than oneself and thus it is altruistic not selfish; it preaches peace and harmony more than violence and discord, love and forgiveness instead of hatred, justice and equity instead of their opposite; it is inclusive or universal rather than exclusive, and it upholds the dignity of the person which links one to certain individual and social rights. Granted, these preferences do not constitute a social system. What they do is to set parameters and boundaries, establish criteria for the critique of society, and influence the choices for specific conditions and for decision-making.[66]

Segundo is correct when he points out that "Christian morality is precisely a morality of ends, that the specific task of the Christian message is to lead people to ends that are the most communitarian and generous-hearted ends imaginable."[67] There are some norms of behavior, however, that are an essential part of the message which no end may justifiably contradict, and which will condition both the praxis and the concrete ends in a society. These norms may be subsumed in the concept of love as *modus operandi* that does not allow selfishness, contempt, or hatred, or their concomitant result of excluding others.

From a theological standpoint, the third limitation to a Christian praxis, i.e., one that originates with faith, is that it cannot alter the dogmatic truths about God, Jesus Christ, the human person, and the Church, even if doing so hinders the effectiveness of a political praxis. Otherwise it would affect the essence of the source of the values that we have enunciated, and most likely will distort them.

These aspects have been, in one way or another, overlooked by some (not all) in liberation theology. As liberation theology maintains, Revelation cannot simply be accepted the way it is.

Its essence has to be extracted, and with that in hand the reflection on the praxis in the light of faith takes place. However, concerned as they are with avoiding culturally conditioned elements *a priori,* some liberation theologians and activists argue that a supposedly "rational praxis" dictates ethics, means, ends, and the message itself. For example, Christians for Socialism have stated that:

> The specific nature of the Christian contribution should not be viewed as something prior to revolutionary praxis, as something ready made that the Christian brings with him to the revolutionary struggle. Rather, in the course of his real-life experience in that struggle, faith reveals its capacity to provide creative contributions which neither the Christian nor anyone else could have foreseen outside the revolutionary process.[68]

For a group so rooted in historical materialism and concrete reality, one would assume that such abstract mysticism would have no place in their analysis. Nonetheless, in line with the above, Christians must rid themselves of what Pablo Richard calls their "antecedent identity," their *a priori* configuration of faith, before they join the revolutionary struggle. It is after they are committed to liberation that their true "consequent identity" will be revealed.[69] Richard does not distinguish between the ideological and the permanent in the Christian message. It is one thing to reject what is historically an *a priori* method of analysis and a praxis that does not consider the historical context, and it is quite another to disregard what are the distinctive values which influence the Christians' initial commitment, the interpretation of reality, and the praxis, Even someone as radical in his commitment and in the praxis he outlines as Jules Girardi, acknowledges that love has such capacity to root itself in concrete reality and demand its transformation, that it can lead to a new social project.[70]

In Christians for Socialism and in Richard, we have the personification of history and of revolution. Richard, for example, speaks of the rationality of historical transformation which "justifies itself and by itself without need of any foreign argument or motives."[71] It would seem naive, following that statement, to ask what values give legitimacy and ascribe rationality to that particular type of historical transformation. It appears to be a self-evident truth. And so it is with revolutionary praxis which is "either assumed for its own intrinsic rationality or else it is simply not assumed at all, . . . for it already carries the legitimacy of its existence and can only be assumed from its own reason for being."[72] Does that mean that any revolution justifies itself? Are there any ethics that guide the internal process? Is it the liberation of the poor that justifies the revolution? If so, why do we have to assume that particular project? Richard may have answers for these questions, but are we expected to know them *a priori,* as was the case with Natural Law?

The problem here is that we are not dealing with a Christian praxis, but with a Leninist praxis that is assumed by Christians. In Leninism as in Maoism, revolutionary ends and means are rather well defined. The specific steps to be taken are not given, since those will be dictated by the praxis, but without any criteria other than the success of the revolution. But it is that lack of ethical criteria that historically has led to the indiscriminate use of power during and after a revolution. That is not the case with a praxis if it is to be called "Christian," as such would be normatively conditioned before, during, and after the revolution by the evangelical criteria. Without this balance, what we have is simply praxis dictating a course, although nonetheless a distinctive type of normative praxis making choices.

The Marxist Theory

The above discussion paves the way for the use of the Marxist theory in liberation theology.[73] The argument explains in somewhat greater detail Pope Paul VI's reasons for warning about the danger of resorting to the Marxist theory, or for that matter to any other. Paul VI distinguishes among several versions of Marxism: an active practice of class struggle, a system of political and economic collectives, an ideology based on historical materialism and "the denial of everything transcendent," and a "scientific activity, as a rigorous method of examining social and political reality, and as the rational link, tested by history, between the theoretical knowledge and the practice of revolutionary transformation."[74] In other words, he is saying that each aspect may be viewed independent of the other, and adds that they all pose questions that could be useful "for the reflection and activity of Christians." But then he states, "it would be illusory and dangerous to reach a point of forgetting the intimate link which radically binds them (the aspects) together, to accept the elements of Marxist analysis without recognizing their relationship with ideology, and to enter into the practice of class struggle and its Marxist interpretations, while failing to note the kind of totalitarian and violent society to which this process leads.[75]

The link between the analysis and the realization of Marxism-Leninism, however, is not axiomatically but historically determined.[76] This indicates the extent to which the values that guide the analysis are congruent with those that establish the conceptions of a Marxist-socialist system, which in turn justify the means to attain them. Some would point out that Marxism, independent of those who implement it, remains a valid theory with valid and just social principles. Sidney Hook, for example, contends that:

> What Marx understood by Communism was profoundly different from the system of political despotism and terror . . . which prevails in the Soviet Union. Marx was a democratic socialist, a secular humanist, and a fighter for human freedom. . . . His differences with (other socialists) were over the means and conditions necessary to establish a ration-

> ally planned economy in which there would be no opportunity for human beings to exploit other human beings.[77]

Be that as it may, there is a thin and passable line between the strong use of power to prevent injustice and its despotic use. And it is precisely this sincere effort to prevent people from exploiting others that (along with frustrations, anguish, and contempt for capitalist practices in Latin America) has resulted in the absence in liberation theology of a critique of totalitarian Marxism-Leninism and of the possible ways of avoiding it. A major reason for this is the failure to take into consideration the evangelical criteria as a means to temper the harshness of the Marxist historical realization.

Given the intimate relationship in Marxism between the analysis and the values in the theory, and its tendency to present a global explanation of social life and absolutize its "scientific" observations, its uncritical incorporation into a Christian theology or its acceptance as a theory independent of the theology, will distort any Christian praxis. On the one hand, value-laden concepts that do not necessarily conform with Christian values and the results of the analysis, will present a Marxist view of social reality, just the same as capitalist values will result in the opposite view. On the other, a theology that does not have the last word will result in a course of action determined by the values in the theory. That is, in a Christian praxis it is not science or reality but theology that ultimately must pass judgment on action.

There is no reason why a Christian theology may not use the Marxist analysis. However, as Pierre Bigó contends, it cannot do so without having to revise all Marxist categories because of their ambivalence and their roots in a different social ethic.[78] This is not mere arbitrariness or dogmatism, but a matter of two opposing comprehensive outlooks of reality. Thus logically, as Bigó points out, "the person who possesses a Christian revelation of authentic human relations will not make the same diagnosis as one who does not have it and who explicitly denies it."[79] Hence, for example, historical materialism cannot be interpreted as meaning that the human consciousness is so determined by historical processes, particularly economic relations, that religion is regarded simply as false consciousness, or that individual consciousness lacks the freedom to liberate itself from social conditioning. The point that religion makes today is that the person has within one's power the ability to search for truth and to develop as a human person, precisely by constantly freeing oneself from both external and internal limitations. The only thing that faith acknowledges is God's role in the process. However, neither faith nor theology is certain of the manner or the extent of God's role, except that theology affirms that providence and grace do not eliminate one's freedom of choice and action. That is no reason to eliminate the useful sociological insight provided by historical materialism, which if properly understood makes science, religion and the person aware of the conditioning influence of social structures in life. This knowledge allows us to be critical and vigilant of ideologies in both political and religious spheres.

A theological methodology requires that the scientific analysis not be divorced from faith and the values that such faith presupposes. To do otherwise leads to a dualist view of reality which ends with faith being interpreted not by reality but by different values altogether. It is a myth that science or praxis interprets reality. The person interprets reality, and in doing so injects his own values in the process. Also, it is a mistake to assume that either a Marxist or a capitalist analysis is necessarily in conformity with the Christian view of reality. Antoncich expresses the relationship between faith and science rather succinctly:

> With regard to acquiring knowledge of society and its problems, it is necessary to start not from a naive un-

> derstanding, which is frequently imbued with the dominant ideology, but from a critical and analytical understanding capable of explaining social causality, its dynamisms and forces. Now, such socio-analytical mediation, sufficient for the social scientist, is not enough for the theologian or the social doctrine, since their socio-analytical view is linked with the view of the faith, which is not dependent on science or human knowledge, but on revelation.[80]

It is within this context that, mindful of the role of values in the human sciences, some have spoken about the need for a "theo-sociology," one in which "the interpretation of the analysis of reality already incorporates a theologically scientific structure."[81] At the beginning of liberation theology, the Church's social doctrine lacked its own methodology, and it still does. Hence, the circumstances in Latin America gave way to the use of what was available at the time. The Marxist approach was, from the standpoint of concrete social reality, the only one to oppose capitalism. Since the struggle against capitalism became the religious and political objective, given the methodological vacuum, the urgency of the situation led many to use Marxism in a somewhat uncritical fashion. Marxism had become for many the missing and necessary link between theology and reality.

Despite all the problems that have arisen as a result, the process has led to a dialectical incorporation of liberation theology into the Latin American Church. This does not reduce the potential value of a "theo-sociology." It only points out the risk of it becoming a self-contained discipline that may end up isolating itself once it sees that it has no need of secular human sciences. In other words, there is a significant value in continuing to analyze reality and to question faith from a strict secular approach.

The need remains to be able to explain social reality in Latin

America, and to determine as well as possible the economic, social, and political causes of poverty and oppression. The use of Marxist theory in a liberation theology presents some problems, not unsurmountable, though they require a disciplined critical attitude. Marxism is said to have a scientific component. That is not denied. The issue is that for Marx, in line with the social intellectuals of his time, science was a rational approach with strong positivistic orientations. As a full-fledged theory of social relationships, however, it has lacked rigorous interdisciplinary empiricism. Most of its attention has been devoted to the economics of capitalism, but we yet have to see serious studies incorporating the sociological and political aspects and their interrelation with the economic.

Liberation theologians have relied on studies analyzing the situation in the continent from a general Marxist perspective. However, despite their important theoretical contributions, those studies still present serious pitfalls.[82] Other than this, liberation theology is based mostly on Marxist-colored perceptions in which it is difficult to separate what is ideological from what is truly scientific. This has led to global affirmations, extrapolations, and the faulty use and interpretation of some of its categories. Reality is not so much analyzed in the strict sense of the term, as it is portrayed, thereby resulting in a blurry picture which is later adapted by the theologian to formulate his interpretation and the praxis. It is in this respect that the Church has objected to the methodology in liberation theology. In its 1984 statement on the issue the Vatican does not reject entirely the use of the Marxist analysis.[83] Nor is its complaint that Marxist categories have been misused in the scientific analysis. The objection is rather that Marxist categories and values have been adopted in an insufficiently critical way at the moment they are adapted to the theology. In other words, it is Marxism and not theology that in some cases is having the last word. Hence, the Vatican has reiterated its position that "the use of philosophical positions or of human sciences by the theologian has a value which might be called instrumental, but yet must undergo a critical study from a theological perspective."[84] Thus a proper methodological procedure requires that Marxism undergo two revisions, one at the scientific level, to deal with reality, and the other at the theological level, to deal with the pastoral task from the standpoint of faith.

Any liberation theology needs to be aware of the limitations of the Marxist theory at the stage of operationalizing its concepts and categories, because these sometimes do not provide adequate scientific explanations. In addition, if the ideological content, i.e., the Marxist view of reality (which could interrogate religion and faith in a positive manner), is not critically examined in the light of the evangelical criteria, it alone usually ends up guiding the analysis and interpreting the results. A link would be made between the Marxist theory and theology at the theoretical level without their fusion ever taking place. At the praxiological level, however, the fusion would take place but in a manner in which theology is subordinated to the theory. Hence we search in vain for the Christian contribution to the liberation praxis in some of the writers only to find out that there is none. Or, to put it differently, the non-Christian contribution is the Christian contribution. The role of faith is to motivate the Christian to join the revolution. Although that would be quite advantageous for the political praxis, and even though that does not constitute a problem in and by itself, from the standpoint of religion it does, for faith would cease its role there. That is, one simply dives into the Marxist approach and allows it to do both the thinking and the acting. It is within this context that an often-cited phrase by Che Guevara is understood and accepted:

> Christians should opt definitely for the revolution — particularly on this continent where the Christian faith is so important among the masses of the people. But in the revolutionary struggle Christians cannot presume to impose their own dogmas or to proselytize for their churches. They should come without any in-

> tention of evangelizing Marxists and without cowardly concealing their faith to assimilate themselves to the latter. . . . When Christians dare to give full-fledged revolutionary witness, then the Latin American revolution will be invincible; because up to now Christians have allowed their doctrine to be used as a tool by the reactionaries.[85]

The last part of the statement has been historically true, and in part because of it we presume that many have reacted with a sense of guilt to a Marxist-called revolution, when instead they could have opted for a Christian-called one. These Christians have failed to notice that they are not asked to give a Christian testimony but a "full-fledged revolutionary witness," which in practice translates into observing a Marxist revolutionary ethic and praxis. This point is obscured and overlooked by some in liberation theology because of their failure to distinguish, once again, between what is historically or idealistically *a priori* and what is distinctively and permanently so, in the Christian message. Hence Segundo, through a single historical example, the failure of the Chilean Christian Democratic Party to follow through with their political program, pretends to confirm Hugo Assman's hypothesis that " 'evangelical' conditions imposed on the revolutionary process on *a priori* terms eventually turn into a third alternative, and that they also turn into counter-revolutionary forces when and if the revolution becomes feasible."[86]

The major flaw in the argument is the sweeping generalization of something that indeed may take place, as in the case of the Chilean Christian Democrats. However, even Segundo seems to acknowledge a certain validity in the third option proclaimed by the Christian Democrats between the Conservative parties and the dictatorship of the proletariat posed by Marxist Socialism. But he does not distinguish a third way out between the improbability of "converting the hearts of the people who would be affected by the changes" (on which he based the success of the Christian Democrats program) and a Marxist conception of the dictatorship of the proletariat. Identifying the former as an *a priori* "evangelical ideal" with the Christian Democrats' failure leads, in Segundo's view, to a reaffirmation of Assman's hypothesis. Assuming that Assman's postulate stands, in the Chilean case the alternative would have been to accede to a dictatorship of the proletariat, interpreted not by any evangelical criteria but by a Marxist ideology. It is this outcome that concerns the Church most.

It cannot be ascertained whether Segundo would accept this conclusion. He simply limits himself to stating the axiom in liberation methodology that a Christian theology is only possible following a political commitment. The problem remains that in the absence of any *a priori* Christian conditions, it is no longer a Christian liberation praxis, but essentially a Marxist one. The pretension appears to be that a revolution is morally neutral or amoral, when in fact the praxis does not speak; a person interprets reality and makes choices for action based on historical projects that are impregnated with values. If what Segundo is saying is that it is only through the commitment to liberation that the essence of the Christian message emerges and that it will somehow condition the praxis, that would be something quite different and even possible. Still, even in the case of a more human socialism (as in the case of any system including capitalism), as many in liberation theology propose, the presence of *a priori* conceptions is inevitable. And these conceptions are determined by values. The question is, which values?[87]

In conclusion, from the standpoint of a political or a theological methodology, the insufficiency of the Marxist theory does not preclude its use. However, it points out the need to broaden the methodological scope and to integrate other approaches in a critical manner. The Church would place no objections then, for a Christian praxis would be able to operate more effectively when based on a more accurate picture of reality.

NOTES

[1]Juan Luis Segundo states:

> "Whether or not everything Marx said is accepted, and no matter how his 'essential' thought is explained, it will always remain certain that there is no contemporary social thought that is not to some degree 'Marxist,' that is, profoundly indebted to Marx. In that sense, liberation theology in Latin America is certainly 'Marxist.' " (*The Liberation of Theology,* p. 10).

[2]For an excellent detailed and critical exposition of the Church's doctrine on Marxism, see Christine E. Gudorf, *Catholic Social Teaching on Liberation Themes* (Lanham, Md.: University Press of America, Inc., 1980).

[3]Jacques Coeur, the Medicis, the Albertis, the Peruzzis, the Bardis, and the Fuggers were all intimately associated with popes, serving as financial counselors and bankers for the Church. For a concise historical background see A. Dauphin Meunier, *La Iglesia Ante el Capitalismo,* trans. Francisco Sabate (Valencia, España: Ediciones Fomento de Cultura, 1956), pp. 11-51.

[4]Pope Benedict XIV, *Vix pervenit,* Nov. 1, 1745.

[5]Bishops Ketteler, in Germany; Mermillod, in France; Manning, in England; Gibbons, in the United States. Also laity and clergy such as La Tour du Pin, Lorin, Vogelsang, Le Play, Decurtins, Pothier, Hitze, Toniolo and others. Note taken from Federico Rodriquez, ed., *Doctrina Pontificia — Documentos Sociales* (Madrid: Biblioteca de Autores Cristianos, 1959), p. 307. Also, see Meunier for brief explanation, pp. 147-154. For more detail, see Hubert Jedin and John Dolan, gen. eds., *History of the Church,* 10 vols. (New York: The Crossroads Publishing Co., 1965-1981), vol. 8: *The Church in the Age of Liberalism,* by Roger Aubert et al., trans. Peter Becker, particularly, pp. 283-303.

[6]Dauphin Meunier, a French Catholic writing about this period argues that the documents constitute the Church's reaction against liberal capitalism. A thorough reading shows that this statement is not accurate. Ibid., p. 161.

[7]Victor Gil, "Ateismo y Marxismo Occidentales de Hoy," in *Vida Pastoral* 101 (órgano oficial de la Conferencia Episcopal Uruguaya), (enero-febrero 1984): 47.

[8]Pope Leo XIII, *Rerum novarum,* May 15, 1891, nos. 2-11, 15, 39.

[9]Louis J. Rogier, gen. ed. *The Christian Centuries — A New History of the Catholic Church,* 5 vols. (New York: Paulist Press, 1963-1978), vol. 5: *The Church in a Secularized Society,* by Roger Aubert (1978), p. 144.

[10]Ibid., p. 146.

[11]Johannes Baptist Metz, S.J., "Teología Política," trans. Javier Medina-Dávila, in *Selecciones de Teología* 38 (abril-junio 1971): 98.

[12]Alfredo Fierro, *The Militant Gospel: A Critical Introduction to Political Theologies,* trans. John Drury (Maryknoll, New York: Orbis Books, 1977), p. 77.

[13]Ibid., pp. 78-80.

[14]A European theologian writes one year after the end of Vatican II, while referring to Feuerbach and Marx:

> "Maybe they are right in reminding man (sic) that he has to work, that he can and ought to solve his immediate problems by himself, without recurring to extraordinary interventions by God . . . Perhaps . . . the atheist philosophy has reminded us that man should do a great deal more on his part and cooperate to attain his goals." (J. Gomez Cafferena, S.J., *Hacia el Verdadero Cristianismo* (Madrid: Razón y Fe, 1966), p. 351).

[15]Here we follow the explanation of ideologies provided by Ricardo Antoncich, S.J. based on the Puebla document. *Los Cristianos Ante la Injusticia* (Bogotá: Ediciones Grupo Social, Indo-American Press Service, 1980), pp. 183-192.

[16]Der Kommunismus der "Rheinischen Beobachters," Werke, v. 4, p. 200, quoted in Gregorio Rodriquez de Yurre, *El Marxismo,* 2 vols. (Madrid: Biblioteca de Autores Cristianos, 1976), vol. 2, p. 78.

[17]We are not saying that piety should be reduced or eliminated. On the contrary, piety is extremely important in a praxis-oriented faith. It arouses the person's feelings, motivates his action, and sustains him. Without it, religious praxis soon becomes sterile. Also, we do not use the term "social action" with a political connotation alone, but in the sense that religion supposes social and not isolated beings who are continuously interrelating with each other.

[18]Tercera Conferencia General del Episcopado Latinoamericano, *La Evangelización en el Presente y en el Futuro de América Latina,* 2da edicion. (Bogotá: Editora L. Canal y Asociados, 1979), n. 826. (Henceforth *Puebla*).

> [19]"In Latin America, our challenge is precisely to realize the historical truth of the Message of freedom. . . . In liberation theology the praxis appears as the criterion of historical and evangelical truth. The biblical notion of truth lies not so much in 'knowing' or in 'saying' as in 'making' (to verify). Biblically, truth and fidelity are closely linked; the 'promise' and its 'fulfillment' are manifested as two essential components of the truth in the Gospel." (Raúl Vidales, "Acotaciones a la Problemática Sobre el Método en la Teología de la Liberación," in *Liberación y Cautiverio,* pp. 256-257.)

[20]Karl Marx, Frederick Engels, *The Holy Family,* cited in David McLellan, *The Thought of Karl Marx —An Introduction* (New York: Harper & Row, 1971), p. 32.

[21]Sidney Hook, *From Hegel to Marx,* with New Introduction (Ann Arbor: The University of Michigan Press, 1971), p. 284.

[22]*Gaudium et spes,* no. 43.

[23]Karl Marx, "Contribution to the Critique of Hegel's Philosophy of Right," in T.B. Bottomore, *Karl Marx —Early writings,* Foreword by Erich Fromm (New York: McGraw-Hill, 1963), pp. 43-44. We must point out that Marx's criticism, in our opinion, is conditioned by Protestant Christianity in Prussia. However, he did not make significant distinctions when it came to his criticism of Christianity.

[24]In Gustavo Gutiérrez' words, "the proclamation of a God who loves all men (sic) equally must be given substance in history and must become history." In "Liberation, Theology and Proclamation," in Claude Geffré and Gustavo Gutiérrez, eds., *The Mystical and Political Dimension of the Christian Faith* (New York: Herder and Herder, 1974), p. 73.

[25]"Solidarity with the poor implies. . . a liberating social praxis: that is, a transforming activity directed towards the creation of a just, free society." Ibid., p. 60.

[26]Hook, p. 285.

[27]Juan Luis Segundo, "Condicionamientos Actuales de la Reflexión Teológica en Latinoamerica," in *Liberación y Cautiverio,* p.94.

[28]Juan Hernández Pico, a Jesuit who is presently involved in the Nicaraguan revolution, points out:

> "Jesus never remained passive, contemplative, exalted in the extasis of the irruption of the Kingdom: on the contrary, through word and action he carried out a 'questioning' praxis, one that delegitimized absolute oppression in his time: law, religion, the State, all sorts of discriminating stratification. Also, he actively faced hunger, pain, sickness and death, triumphing over them through attitudes that anticipated the Kingdom." (In "Método Teológico Latinoamericano y Normatividad del Jesús Histórico para la Praxis Política Mediada por el Análisis de la Realidad," in *Liberación y Cutiverio,* p. 602)

[29]Mt. 14:21.

[30]Mt. 12:33.

[31]Karl Marx and Frederick Engels. *The German Ideology,* trans. and ed. by S. Ryazanskaya (Moscow: Progress Publishers, 1968), pp. 38-42.

[32]Ibid., pp. 39, 50.

[33]Ibid., p. 50.

[34]Ignacio Ellacuría, "Hacia Una Fundamentación Filosófica del Método Teológico Latinoamericano," in *Liberación y Cautiverio,* p. 619.

[35]Raúl Vidales, in "Acotaciones," in Ibid., p. 256.

[36]Juan Luis Segundo, *Masas y Minorías en la Dialéctica Divina de la Liberación* (Buenos Aires: La Aurora, 1973), in Henelly, pp. 158-159.

[37]Leonardo Boff, ¿"Qué es Hacer Teología Desde América Latina"? in *Liberación y Cautiverio,* pp. 150-151.

[38]Jon Sobrino, "El Conocimiento Teológico," in Ibid., p. 185. He adds, "European theology tends to reconcile human misery within theological thinking," while liberation theology tends to free reality of such conditions. Ibid., p. 188.

[39]For a treatment of this concept of freedom in liberation theology see Joseph Comblin, "Freedom and Liberation as Theological Concepts," in Geffré, pp. 92-104. Also, see Ellacuría, *Freedom Made Flesh,* pp. 159-162.

[40]Ignacio Ellacuría, "El Auténtico Lugar Social de la Iglesia," in *Diakonia* 25 (enero-marzo 1983): 30-31. Also, today the Church has come to accept as valid the term "liberation theology," and gives liberation theologians credit for placing the poor and their liberation in a Biblical context. Vatican Congregation for the Doctrine of the Faith, Cardinal Joseph Ratzinger, *Instruction on Certain Aspects of the "Theology of Liberation,"* trans. the Vatican, Aug. 6, 1984, no. 9.9 (Henceforth *Instruction I*).

[41]For examples of rereading see Leonardo Boff "Christ's Liberation via Oppression," in Gibellini, pp. 100-131. Also, for a more radical interpretation of the Bible, see José P. Miranda, *Marx and the Bible* (Maryknoll, New York: Orbis Books, 1974).

[42]*Puebla,* no. 559.

[43]Galilea, personal interview.

[44]Raúl Vidales, Methodological Issues, in Gibellini, p. 43. Also, Boff, *Teología Desde El Cautiverio,* p. 15.

[45]Segundo, *Liberation of Theology,* p. 81. Sobrino, "El Conocimiento Teológico," in *Liberación y Cautiverio,* p. 190.

[46]We should note that this process is no different from the conventional systemic approach borrowed from Cybernetics and used for years in Political Science. See, for example, the pioneering work by Karl Deutsch, *The Nerves of Government* (New York: The Free Press, 1966), and David Easton, *A Framework for Political Analysis* (Englewood Cliffs, New Jersey: Prentice-Hall Inc., 1965).

[47]*Instruction I,* Introduction.

[48]J.P. Richard, cited without a reference by Adolfo Ham, "Introduction to the Theology of Liberation," in *Communio viatorum* (Prague), Summer 1973, quoted in Segundo, *The Liberation of Theology,* pp. 84-85.

[49]Gutiérrez, *Teología de la Liberación,* p. 189.

[50]Boff, *Teología Desde el Cautiverio,* p. 15.

[51]Gutiérrez, *Teología de la Liberación,* p. 27.

[52]The Issue is discussed by Assman in *Theology for a Nomad Church,* pp. 141-142.

[53]Segundo, *Liberation of Theology,* p. 101.

[54]Assman says, "operatively I am a Marxist; intentionally speaking I feel that I am a Christian." The statement is taken from a writing by Assman in *Discussion sur "la theologie de la Revolution"* (Paris, 1972), quoted in Bandera, p. 276, n.

[55]Segundo, *Liberation of Theology,* p. 102.

[56]See Chapter 4, "Ideologies and Faith," in Ibid., pp. 97-124, for a discussion of the issue.

[57]Ibid., pp. 101-102.

[58]Ibid., p. 126.

[59]Gustavo Gutiérrez, "Comunidades Cristianas de Base: Perspectivas Eclesiológicas," in *Diakonia* 19, agosto-octubre, 1981, p. 27.

[60]Ellacuría, "El Lugar Auténtico," p. 28.

[61]Boff, ¿"Qué es Hacer Teología"? p. 135.

[62]Ibid. (parentheses mine).

[63]Ellacuría, "El Lugar Auténtico," pp. 24-26.

[64]*Gaudium et spes,* no. 63.

[65]For example, Gutiérrez acknowledges as much when he says that "the demands of the Gospel are incompatible with the social situation which is being lived in Latin America, with the ways in which relations between men (sic) operate, with the structures in which these relations are found." In Geffré, p. 73.

[66]The Vatican, in its *Instruction on Christian Freedom,* chooses the Beatitudes as the embodiment of the authentic Christian spirit that can influence the praxis. Congregation for the Doctrine of the Faith, Cardinal Joseph Ratzinger, *Instruction on Christian Freedom and Liberation,* (Henceforth, *Instruction II*), Vatican City, March 22, 1986, no. 62.

[67]Segundo, *Liberation of Theology,* pp. 171-172.

[68]Christians for Socialism, "Final Document," in Eagleson, Part Two, n. 3.2.

[69]Richard, *La Iglesia Latinoamericana,* pp. 71-74. Ironically, Richard claims that liberation theology has an *a priori* idenity: anti-imperialism. Ibid., p. 16.

[70]Jules Girardi, *Amor Cristiano y Lucha de Clases* (Salamanca: Ediciones Sígueme, 1975), p. 49.

[71]Richard, *La Iglesia Latinoamericana,* p. 24.

[72]Ibid., p. 73.

[73]Not all in liberation theology rely on the Marxist theory as instrument of analysis. We think, for example, of Galilea, Marins, and Juan Carlos Scannone, among others.

[74]Pope Paul VI, *Octogesima adveniens,* 14 May 1971, no. 33.

[75]Ibid., no. 34.

[76]The 1984 statement by the Vatican misses the point when it ascribes "atheism and the denial of the human person, his liberty, and his rights" to the core of Marxist theory. Atheism is largely a historical product in Marxism with little philosophical basis. It is certainly not an essential aspect of the theory. As to the other aspects, it would have been more accurate to say that they are historical realizations, not theoretical formulations. *Instruction I,* no. 7.9.

[77]Hook, p. 2. Also, Michael Harrington sustains the same view in *Socialism* (New York: Bantam Books/Saturday Review Press, 1973), pp. 41-42.

[78]P. Pierre Bigó, S.J., "El 'Instrumental Científico' Marxista," in CELAM, *Diálogos,* p. 251.

[79]Ibid., p. 249.

[80]Antoncich, *Los Cristianos,* p. 96.

[81]Alberto Methol Ferré, in CELAM, *Diálogos,* p. 256.

[82]See Helio Jaguaribe, et al., *La Dependencia Política-Económica de América Latina* (Mexico, D.F.: Editores Siglo 21, 1969); Fernando H. Cardoso y Enzo Faletto, *Dependencia y Desarrollo en América Latina: Ensayo de Interpretación,* 6ta edición (Buenos Aires: Editores Siglo 21, 1973); André Gunder Frank, *Capitalism and Underdevelopment in Latin America* (New York: Monthly Review Press, 1969); Celso Furtado, *La Economía Latinoamericana Desde la Conquista Ibérica Hasta la Revolución Cubana,* trans. Angelica Gimpel Smith, 3ra edición (Santiago: Editorial Universitaria, 1973); Theotonio dos Santos, *Dependencia Económica y Cambio Revolucionario en América Latina* (Caracas: Editorial Nueva Izquierda. 1970); Osvaldo Sunkel, *El Subdesarrollo Latinoamericano y la Teoría del Desarrollo* (Mexico, D.F.: Editores Siglo 21, 1970).

[83]*Instruction I,* Introduction.

[84]Ibid., no. 7.10.

[85]Quoted in the Conclusion of the Final Document of Christians for Socialism, in Eagleson, pp. 174-175.

[86]Segundo, *Liberation of Theology,* p. 94.

[87]Galilea, for example, speaks of "attitudes and values that are rooted in the Gospel message that are capable of being fleshed out in history through the commitment . . . for the oppressed." In Gibellini, p. 177.

4. THE POLITICS OF SOCIAL CHANGE IN LIBERATION THEOLOGY

The objective of liberation theology is not only to interpret reality but to change it. For this, ideas need to be realized, so it is imperative that they be practical. Liberation theology encounters two dimensions of social reality. One is its analysis, and the other is the praxis. Eventually, liberation theology needs to make the transition from that which is desirable to that which is possible. This chapter will begin by examining the analysis of social reality on which liberation theology is based. It will take a close look at the critique of capitalism and its major objections over the issue of dependence. It will deal with the social conditions that liberation seeks and its means for attaining them. Finally, the chapter will analyze the movement's potential to foster social change.

The Liberation Critique of Capitalism

The fundamental socio-political characteristic encompassing liberation thought is anti-capitalism. Pablo Richard echoes the least radical and the non-Marxist within the movement when he says that liberation theology "is a theology indissolubly linked to the historical destiny of the Latin American continent and to the emancipation from imperialist and capitalist oppression."[1] In this sense, liberation theology is more opposed to an individualistic capitalism and more inclined toward some forms of socialism or social capitalism than it is toward Marxist communism *per se.* As seen in the previous chapter, Marxism has played a decisive role in the formulation of the theology. In its politics, however, a totalitarian Marxist-Leninist system does not necessarily constitute the theologians' political map.

Liberation theology's anti-capitalism is not so much Marxist as it is conditioned by Christian values. This is why, as will be seen in the next chapter, the theology's critique of capitalism is quite similar to that made by the Church. The Marxist influence is present in both, but it is transcended by the Christian orientation. Also, the critique of capitalism is not limited only to its economic aspects.

Capitalism represents the totality of a culture in which social, political, legal, and even religious values and practices are interrelated with the economic, and these in turn are tied to its international dimension. Ignacio Ellacuría describes the general features of the type of system prevailing in Latin America from a liberation theology standpoint:

> It positively and actively makes it impossible for people to lead a Christian life. . . .
> The sin is to be found in an overall way of life . . . that is grounded on the twin notions of profit and private property. . . . These are necessary to some extent, given the imperfect state of the world and human beings right now. But the very fact that our way of life is grounded and conditioned by the quest for profit and for more and more private property, represents a serious form of idolatry. It produces a whole series of pernicious consequences that give shape to consumer society.[2]

Among these consequences is the tendency to imitate the values and cultures of developed nations — materialism, individualism and selfishness, consumerism, escapism into drugs and sexuality, the idolatry of the future in the search for personal status and material well-being.[3] Others point to "the permanent recourse to the law of the stronger as a social norm," the control of workers by the private firm, and opposition to social reforms.[4]

Characteristic criticism among activists include denouncing their system for not taking into consideration the interests of the majority and for creating a privileged minority, persecuting members of the Church, and allowing concentration of wealth in the hands of the few, thus creating insensitive inequalities, and for deliberately setting up an economic model "that places the product before the producer. . . . wealth before work, and nationalism above life itself."[5] Seen from a liberation standpoint, the issue of capitalism versus Christianity is presented in terms of a conflict of values. As Segundo states it, the gospel "presents a human orientation that rejects profits and wealth as the center of one's activity and one's interpersonal relations."[6]

In real life, human behavior tends to be guided by values, interests, and priorities. Hence, two competing sets of values cannot operate simultaneously at the personal level. One must eventually give in to the other, and that other will then condition the ways in which the former expresses itself. Thus, either wealth and profits, power, status, and individual material satisfaction become the primary incentives in a socio-political and economic system that subordinates man and woman to these wants, or else the basic human needs and the values of solidarity, cooperation, and concern for one's neighbor are given precedence over the others. Such an "either-or" situation does not signify exclusion or rejection. Cooperation, for example, does not necessarily have to exclude private property or competition but would guide and condition the ways in which the latter two are used.

The issue that liberation theology raises is crucial to Christians who have not bothered to question the way in which the system has conditioned their faith. As Enrique Dussel points out, the real problem is not atheism but idolatry or fetishism:

> Many people who claim to be Christian will readily fall in with the idea of accepting the fetish (e.g. money) as a profane value which is not invested with any sacred character; and they will spend all their time preoccupied with that object. But if the same whole hearted preoccupation with money is evident in people who refuse to worship a creator God, Christians will be inclined to say that they have erased all thought of the divine from their lives. What is really happening here is that the person who is an "atheist" with respect to the Christian God is in practice worshipping the fetish; and so are Christians who spend all their time trying to make money. The latter cannot possibly offer any real criticism of fetishistic practice. Instead they secularize the fetish in theory while actually worshipping it in practice as the professed non-Christian does.[7]

A strict socialist critique in liberation, one following Marx's analysis, does not depart in great measure from a less Marxist approach. Thus, according to the socialist analysis, the colonialist and neocolonialist capitalism prevailing in Latin America has given way to a class-based society rooted in exploitation, profit, and competition. The ruling bourgeoisie operates within each country in complicity with imperialist agents that include multinational corporations and the CIA. Some of these governments end up creating fascist systems that, using the specter of communism, rely on repression, torture, and persecution.[8]

Many activists and theologians cannot reconcile themselves with a reformed capitalism in line with Christian values because they regard such a formulation as a contradiction. What happens is that they view socialism from a theoretical or philosophical standpoint, examining the goals and values it represents, while they evaluate capitalism on the basis of the way it has realized itself historically in Latin America. For them, capitalism is not simply the practical association of two factors of production, capital and labor, each supplying the other what it does not have or cannot provide itself. In theory, this model has two possible ethical configurations, one social and one somewhat more individual. Accordingly, since each factor complements the other and one cannot operate without the other, both should enjoy the fruits of production on an equitable basis. The criterion here would be that each person gives according to his ability in equal parts: the one provides his capital, his managerial experience, and his work day, while the other provides his labor, his skills, and also his work day. Since the product is the result of both working together, their share of the profits should be more or less the same for both. Going even further, if the social criterion is one of need, profits would be divided accordingly. Thus, a family of four, regardless of whether it is the entrepreneur's or the worker's family, should earn more than a family of two, all other things being equal.

The more individual ethic, on the other hand, places its emphasis on individual incentives such as previous effort to learn a profession, on thrift, and on risk. Since the entrepreneur stands to lose more if a venture fails, he also should be rewarded more for his daring effort, as well as for his willingness to invest his income in starting a business. Such diligence and ingenuity results in the entrepreneur getting a higher return than the workers. This ethnic does not necessarily contravene Christian values. To be sure, there are individual and social values in Christianity which, far from being in conflict with one another, reflect the nature of humans as social beings and yet individuals. Thus the individual entrepreneur, guided by his social responsibility, may seek to expand his business in order to provide more employment opportunities for the jobless and to allow workers a chance at higher wages. Workers in turn may want to become entrepreneurs investing their earnings in their workplaces, thereby assuming a more personal responsibility for the venture with the possibility of receiving more income. In this system, private property and the profit motive, far from being abusive and exploitative, guarantee a measure of personal freedom, initiative, and social responsibility without necessarily detracting from other social values.

To operate effectively, however, both the social and the individual capitalist models require that the entrepreneur's actions be guided by the social values which are in line with the social conditions that are desired. The degree of government intervention in this socio-economic process is inversely proportional to the degree in which the entrepreneurial class accepts these values, provided that the government and the workers share them too. Hence, the extreme case occurs when a revolutionary government takes power either through the electoral process or through force, in order to represent not only the interests of the workers but also the ideal conditions in which the system should operate.

In practice, the historical realization of these forms of capitalism has failed, not because of private property or the profit motive but because of sin. That is, from a religious standpoint, social values are replaced by individualistic and selfish priorities that distort the use of property and make profits the means for individualistic ends. In this situation accumulated wealth gives way to an unequal interdependence between the entrepreneur and the worker. With little or no savings, and because of his need to survive, the worker is placed in a disadvantageous position vis-á-vis the capitalist, who now can use his wealth as an instrument of control and domination. Even in a benign sense, he can impose conditions that maximize and realize that which he seeks: profits. The problem becomes more acute in a system in which competition is no longer guided by social considerations, but instead the capitalist's own need to survive is top priority. Thus, a selfish desire for profits and a need to survive force the capitalist to abandon the social ends of private property. Instead he relies on it only as a survival instrument or as personal pleasure.

When a full-fledged system evolves in the direction just described, such a *fait accompli* leads in time to a cultural legitimization of the system. What once would have considered idolatrous and materialistic is accepted as a way of life, side by side with the values that used to question such a system. Structures are set up that reinforce the operating values of the system, which bind the capitalist and his associates by claiming their allegiance. Once co-opted, it becomes very difficult for an individual to question the system from within. It is not likely that he will have any incentive to do so, and if he does his action will probably be ineffective. It is important to remember that we are not talking about forming an alternative system that would operate side-by-side with the existing one, but of reforming the existing system. This entails the simultaneous conversion of many in the upper echelons. In Latin America, where many private enterprises are family owned, the task may appear to be somewhat easier than in systems like those in the United States, in which objections would be freely voiced. However, precisely because these businesses are family-controlled, it becomes difficult to promote reforms. Individuals have a strong investment in and attachment to their own belongings, whereas in the case of impersonal ownership or management, as in the American corporation, individuals are more detached.

The reality of Latin American capitalism is viewed from the idealistic principles of socialism. Hence, the critique:

> When the productive force of labor becomes mere merchandise that is rented by capital, the system inverts the relationship man-instruments of labor. In consequence it generates, through the so-called work contract, a permanent unequal relation between the owners of capital and the wage earners. This type of relation is maintained by a series of institutional,

> ideological, and coercive mechanisms throughout the whole international capitalist system. Its effects are the concentration of wealth and power in the hands of the few. . . .[9]

The Marxist critique, far from invalidating the analysis of reality, shows the extent to which in this particular case it dovetails with the religious critique. The difference between the social and individual ethical models of capitalism and its concrete realization lies in the set of values that guides the relations between the owners of capital and the workers in the latter. The "sin," which consists in the distortion of an economic ethic, is attributed to the capitalist theory and its philosophical values. Most likely, what liberation theology has in mind here is the theory of economic liberalism and utilitarianism that finds its roots in the works of men such as John Stuart Mill, Adam Smith, and Jeremy Bentham, whose concept of a social ethic takes place through extreme individualism, and the political liberalism of the French Revolution, which asserted people's intellectual, social, political, and economic freedoms. This was influenced in part by the general orientation of the Reformation, whose net result, religious individualism, would give additional impetus to the Renaissance concept of one's adult status. Needless to say, liberation theology does not criticize the positive aspects that resulted from both the French Revolution and the Reformation, namely freedom and the concept of individual rights.

If somehow an individualistic ethic would not lead to excessive inequalities and to domination, but instead would foster solidarity, equal opportunities for personal growth for all, and a concern for the disadvantaged, there would not be a social conflict. By evaluating the concrete results of capitalist values in Latin American society, the liberation critique questions their morality. In effect, liberation theology incorporates the socialist view and the religious concept of sin to denounce the negative impact of the capitalist ethic. Thus, God has created the earth's resources for the benefit of the entire human family. Through the concept of Christian brotherhood it is understood that a fair and equitable use of these resources will be made by those who are stewards of God's property. The issue that liberation theology brings out is that people misuse their freedom in society, and distort the Christian view in a way that leads them to a sinful use of the resources by focusing on their own needs and desires while forgetting those of others. To simplify with an analogy, those obsessed with capital gain are like thieves who steal whenever possible simply because the opportunity is there and no one is present to deter them. Here we are dealing with children of God who are conditioned into acting as social thieves by a system that legitimizes such behavior.

The liberation response lies in the eventual need to replace an individualistic ethic through the personal internalization of social principles. This is in line with the Church's call for conversion to human values which would make possible the realization of an economic model based on a social ethic. It is clear that the object is to prevent capital from becoming a factor of domination and oppression. Thus, what is required is an altruistic ethic that permeates not only the individual but the entire culture, and places the needs of the entire social family (including the individual's) ahead of one's own. In other words, the person will think and act socially (the Christian concept of brotherhood) instead of thinking and acting selfishly. Moreover, this ethic assumes a non-materialist attitude in which a person is not interested in accumulating riches in this world beyond what one needs to maintain a moderate life style, taking into consideration the fact that others do not have enough to meet their basic needs. The social example would be the Judeo-Christian concept of the family, in which each member is aware of the needs of the others and is virtually incapable of being selfish.

Also, liberation's approach to socialism advocates an attitutde that would regard property as having a social function, which would prevent the misappropriation of the fruits of labor:

> A new man and a new society will become possible only when labor is considered the only human source of wealth; when the social interest becomes man's fundamental incentive in economic activity; when capital is subordinated to labor, and hence when the means of production become social property.[10]

One may ask, however, why the call is made for the nationalization of the means of production when the changed attitude can be attained without it through personal conversion. Lacking further qualifications, the statement seems to assert that nationalization is required to create a new attitude within the individual. This would correspond to a dogmatic (uncritical) interpretation of Marxist materialism, since one may not necessarily follow the other.

Thus, by identifying the ethical values and objectives of an ideal socialism with those that are distinctively Christian, many within the liberation movement base their criticism of capitalism and the choice of a socialist alternative on religious grounds, believing that the historical realization of socialism will result in accordance with the ideal scheme:

> Building this new society is an attempt at creating disinterested relations, propitiate solidary structures, and authentic human values, all of which translate historically the exigencies of our fidelity to the Gospel. Christ reveals himself . . . where men realize themselves as brothers and as children of the Father. Hence, all that contributes toward an effective true fraternity is a sign of the progress of the kingdom of God in history. . . .[11]

Dependence and Capitalism

The liberation critique is not limited to economics. This is not to say that problems in Latin America do not have strong economic roots, but only that the complete picture is far more complex, encompassing social, political, and religious dimensions, with ties to international politics. Nearly all within the liberation movement perceive the Latin American question in terms of dependence. Following the failure of developmentalist and integrationist attempts during the 1950s and the early 1960s in which capitalist approaches were utilized, some Latin American social scientists began to deal with the problem of underdevelopment from a dependence angle.[12] Essentially, they were seeking more concrete explanations, based on the analysis of Latin American conditions, that past theories were not able to provide. These theories had failed largely because they stemmed from a different historical perspective — that of the developed nations — while conditions that favored economic growth and political stability had become impossible to duplicate in Latin America given the existing economic relationships, and because they were based on abstract models that did not take historical conditions and reality into account.[13]

As the dependence perspective gained acceptance, the social scientists began to incorporate some aspects of the Marxist analysis into their studies. But, as Gonzalo Arroyo points out, one cannot speak of the "theory of dependence" in terms of a coherent Marxist theory, but as a paradigmatic view of Latin American relations with regard to the United States and the international capitalist system.[14] Its notable feature is the interdisciplinary approach to development. It views underdevelopment within a historical context, as a socio-economic, political, and religious issue having global dimensions, thus bringing into play external variables that were absent in previous studies.

It would be relatively easy to view this approach as an ideological effort to shift the blame and the causes of Latin American problems to "American imperialism" and international capitalism.[15] But even when we grant a high degree of bias, there is a certain logic inherent in the theory that corresponds with reality to some extent. For one thing, the approach does not say that the United States is able to pull all strings within a Latin American country strictly from the outside. It does say, however, that there is a coincidence between the center (the developed nations) and the periphery (the less developed nations) that makes possible conditions of dependence through domestic social and political groups, who rule the nations on the periphery and who respond to the interests of the center with whom the periphery interests are identified.[16] Hence, dependence refers to a confluence of interests and values taking place in a relationship of otherwise asymmetrical interdependence that produces compartmentalized and conditioned growth.

The functioning of the system has an adverse impact on the dependent societies. Among these are:

- regressive appropriation of income among workers and the upper strata who control the means of production.
- creation of a consumerist class that prevents capital accumulation from being used more productively in depressed sectors of the economy, or to build the infrastructure.
- the export of income through the multinatio

The functioning of the system has an adverse impact on the dependent societies. Among these are:

- regressive appropriation of income among workers and the upper strata who control the means of production.
- creation of a consumerist class that prevents capi-

tal accumulation from being used more productively in depressed sectors of the economy, or to build the infrastructure.

- the export of income through the multinationals, from the periphery to the center.

- hindering the development of the agricultural sector, so vital in many of these countries, due to low demand for products (often due to protectionist policies by the center), which in turn prevents its diversification.[17]

The term dependence carries an ideological connotation of imperialism and neocolonialism which suggests exploitation of one nation by another. Nevertheless, as Klaus Knorr has pointed out, to use the latter terms empirically one must show intent, "an effective use of power for deliberately establishing and maintaining an exploitative relationship."[18] Intent in relationships between powerful and weak nations cannot be ruled out. The means are present today as they were in the past to seek unilateral advantages from a weaker nation, though today it is difficult to achieve them without some costs to the imperialist power.[19] Nonetheless, given the difficulty of proving intent, the term dependence denotes an attitude that is more congruent with the real conditions of poverty and injustice that prevail in Latin America: indifference. This does not refer to an attitude of callousness on the part of the developed capitalist nations. Although this attitude exists among some of the ruling classes of the less developed nations, here it refers to a general insensitivity due to lack of awareness of the many ways in which the everyday policies of the developed nations negatively affect the overall situation within many of the Latin American countries, and the extent to which the former ignore the potential resources they have at their command to help change the plight of the less developed countries.

Indifference is largely the result of the rules and the values that prevail in the international system, which are a reflection of the same rules and values that have been accepted and legitimized domestically among the capitalist developed nations. Political actors abide by these rules without profoundly questioning their overall impact.[20] In a way this attitude resembles that which is commonly found within less developed and traditional societies in which obsolete methods of production and instruments and religious rituals approximating magic are so deeply ingrained that they actually hinder development because they are difficult to change. Thus, an ideological self-centeredness and a strong sense of individualistic materialism prevent the more powerful nations from formulating and implementing policies that are truly sensitive to the needs of the Third World. The reality of dependence addresses a situation which according to one of its exponents is the following:

> In a certain group of countries their economy is conditioned by the development and expansion of another economy to which the dependent one is subjected. Relations of interdependence between two or more economies, and between these and world commerce, assume the form of dependency when the dominant nations can expand and propel themselves, while the dependent nations can (only) do so as a reflection of that expansion, which can have a positive or negative impact over its immediate development.[21]

Today, the theory of dependence still provides the scientific framework on which liberation theology bases much of its analysis, in spite of limitations recognized by some in the liberation movement, given the complexity of the analysis and the fluidity of politics in the region.[22] Yet an essential feature of the theory is its insistence on showing that dependence is not simply an external variable that contributes to slow and uneven growth, but that it is internalized in the culture of the dependent nation. In this manner it reinforces the structures and practices that cause social and political injustice, and erodes traditional cultural values:

> It is not possible to think of the influence of the United States as an external variable, that acts over the national economic structure by determining it through external commerce and financing. Our dependency is actually much more complex and profound, affecting the bases of the entire social and economic structure, constituting a network, . . . from which the less developed nations will have to extricate themselves if they pretend to realize all of their potential. It is necessary to think about imperialism as a structural element, inserted and acting within the center of our national structures, conforming to the roots of an economic, technological, political, and cultural dependence.[23]

Setting aside the ideological reference to American imperialism, which is less precise given the need to show the intent to subjugate, this line of thinking is in the minds of not only the theologians but of the Church itself. It alludes to the progressive co-opting of the Latin American culture by the values of a liberal individualistic capitalism. It is this aspect, more than anything else, that creates an anti-American rhetoric and leads many to seek socialism. In effect, the issue of dependence has become more of a political than an analytical tool in liberation theology. This is not to say that dependence is a myth, but that for many people reality can be felt and seen easier than it can be scientifically explained. The disease is there, its effects can be observed, even though its causes cannot be fully understood.

Dependence as a social paradigm still offers useful insight concerning some of the problems in the region. Renato Poblete, one of the theory's critics, acknowledges that the conflictual framework on which dependence is based is more in line with Latin American reality, thus it leads the scientist to focus on the causes of the conflict. By identifying and isolating the parties involved, the theory also allows for a more effective social and political mobilization of the masses, while it suggests the path to follow in the analysis.[24] At the same time, however, he points out that its ideological use could result in partial blindness to reality. By overstressing the class conflict issue, the theory may fail to acknowledge that social groups are also motivated by national interests and expectations of development. Moreover, given a plurality of interests among the masses, in order to effect political mobilization there is a need to promote alliances that often include collaboration among classes.[25]

Even though dependence as a theory attempts to approach the issue of underdevelopment from global and historical perspectives, and despite its incorporation of the various cultural and political aspects, its common denominator and its explanatory variable continues to be economic. This is not necessarily because of any exaggerated Marxist influence, as much as that development has been traditionally considered an economic issue. Still, to increase the explanatory potential of the theory, an effective incorporation of other disciplines will be required. This calls for dynamic systemic models capable of focusing on the three levels which seem to affect development: the international, the national or state, and the personal.

From a liberation standpoint the personal level is particularly important since it is often overlooked. Any time that a structural analysis is undertaken, even with a dialectical perspective in mind, the solutions invariably will be along the line of structural changes. This is where the scientist tends to find injustice, inefficiency, and corruption. A dialectical analysis of structures, however, usually precludes attention to the evangelization of the culture, which is the role that the theologian and the Church have to play. In effect, the tendency here is to forget that, as theologians are aware, the objective of social transformation, which includes structures, must be able to cause a change in cultural values that may eventually reach the individual. Such internalization of values is not based on religious pietism, but on the psychological and social reality of the individual, whose motivations, priorities, and social praxis are ultimately guided by personal values and conditioned by culture. Thus, for a new society to function as liberation theologians envision, their values must reach the people as well as the social institutions.

Dependence and Socialism

From a capitalist perspective, there is in Latin America a consensus among governments that a move by the periphery toward a more balanced interdependence vis-á-vis the center is necessary. This view favors a reformist approach that is based on politics of national and regional assertiveness that may translate into greater political and economic autonomy. The theory of dependence suggests in part that the conditions affecting Latin America are caused by the center. This is true to the extent that developed nations fail to do what is in their power to foster and seek to change those conditions, to the extent that they continue to exert their power to maintain asymmetrical relations, and to the extent to which a Latin American government in collusion with domestic groups agrees with and abides by the center's rules because it serves their particular interests.

With regard to the first point, the most that Latin America can realistically hope to accomplish is to plead its case and seek to persuade or convert the center to a greater sensitivity to its needs. It cannot expect to change the center by force, nor undermine it economically. As to the second point, a sort of nationalistic capitalism that focuses more on the nation as a whole or regional pacts that strive toward autonomy vis-á-vis the center may indeed force more equitable terms in relations. The nation would also seek to diversify its economy by increasing its relations and trade with other countries. Finally, a strong nationalist and populist government may, with some degree of success, eliminate domestic disparities caused by internal collusion.

If the problems in Latin America were caused only by the center, then the strategy just outlined could be effective. What is it, however, that makes the type of capitalist culture prevailing in the region so unjust, as liberation theology says, and which impedes the social, political, and economic transformations that are necessary? The following characteristics are typical:

- lack of natural resources in some countries.

- lack of human resources, exist untapped, due to lack of skills, technical and professional education, and human incentives among the native population.

- political repression that discourages social and governmental reforms.

- the presence of cultural values that reinforce and accept a distorted sense of individualism, ambition, and the profit motive that gives way to a market system that does not take into account social values.

- ethos and mores that tend to accept, or remain indifferent to, civic dishonesty and corruption, i.e., tax evasions and weak implementation of laws, bribery, etc.

- collusion of political officials with dominant groups that results in policies that favor their interests.

- unequal distribution of land.

- expectations and aspirations created by a consumerist system that go unfulfilled, thereby fostering social unrest and repression.

- militaristic policies that result in high expenditures on arms.

- asymmetrical relations of interdependence that tend to favor the center and create disparities in the periphery.

- indifference by the center with regard to the plight of the periphery that prevents the former from being more sensitive to the latter's needs.

These features are basically responsible for structures that lead to unequal and regressive policies in the distribution of resources. They hinder the establishment and functioning of stable social and legal institutions that could reinforce the concept of a government of laws. Also, they prevent the market system from attending social ills, create conflict among groups, and in general, allow marginalization of masses of poor people. Most of the conditions outlined above, however, have strong domestic roots that are not caused by the center. True, the center, if motivated, has some political, economic, and military resources to foster necessary changes. But the major responsibility for the transformation of structures and the solution of its domestic problems remain with the periphery. Hence, an altruistic center with sensitive multinationals and the infusion of billions of dollars and technology into the area will not ameliorate conditions significantly, unless there exist, at the periphery level, a domestic system and a culture capable of making an effective use of the center's resources.

The theory of dependence does not state that by achieving more autonomy alone vis-á-vis the center, development is guaranteed. Nor does liberation theology maintain that socialism is the *sine qua non* of such development, since a socialist economic system by itself will not necessarily reduce the reality of external dependence. Moreover, neither the theory of dependence nor liberation theology advocate an absolute break with the capitalist center in favor of, say, joining the Soviet bloc, though their rhetoric may accidentally result in that. Liberation theology does not view the center as the only cause of Latin America's social ills, nor does it regard external dependence as the only root of the problems — if it were, external independence would be the solution. Instead, liberation theology regards external dependence as an impediment, though not the only one, to development. It is a constant reality that reflects on the domestic system of the periphery, and one of the contributing elements to injustice in the region.

If Latin American nations were able to break from a condition of external capitalist dependence but remain within a capitalist framework internally, the problems would by no means be solved in the eyes of liberation theologians. The issue of internal dependence remains, and all the other aspects that lead to injustice and to religious alienation. In other words, a model based on the American society is not necessarily the ideal in liberation theology. Thus, with regard to external dependence, the real purpose of socialism is not to liberate Latin America from the center, but to mitigate the negative impact that the region suffers internally. It is by eradicating capitalism at home that Latin American nations liberate themselves from internal oppression. And many believe that only through some form of socialism will that be possible. In addition, the socialist alternative is the link between the external and the internal variables, for it can break the confluence of interests and the collusion existing between dominant groups in the periphery and those in the center.

At this point it is worth stressing that liberation theology does not rely either on the theory of dependence or socialism to the extent that without the latter two the former would not exist as a theology or as a movement.[26] In other words, liberation is not a rationalization of the two. An inaccurate analysis of reality may result in the wrong praxis, but in no way does it invalidate the theological method, its bases, or the significance of the praxis itself. Insofar as the socialist alternative is concerned, it appears to be dictated not by Revelation or faith but by the temporal response to a personal commitment to one's faith.

Socialism and Liberation

Liberation seeks the realization of freedom from all servitude, including its external as well as its internal dimensions, and implies liberation from personal sin and from the effects of others' sins. Thus, there is a personal and a spiritual, as well as a socio-political and material, liberation. While the theology stresses the significance of the latter, it neither denies or rejects the former.[27] There is no doubt, however, that liberation theology assigns top priority to socio-political liberation, just as Church theology and praxis has traditionally stressed the private and the mystical aspects of liberation by seeing it in terms of an ahistorical salvation.[28] Liberation theology's emphasis on the socio-political level occurs in response to the needs of people who live under conditions of injustice.[29] It is this "sinful" reality that dictates their praxis, just as the reality of secularism in developed societies poses atheism as "among the most serious problems of this age," which the Church must confront.[30] The issue then is not necessarily one of orthodoxy, but of viewing the Christian faith from different perspectives of reality.

Since liberation theology provides socio-political liberation with a theological basis and a religious significance, the question is raised whether because of the strong support that exists for socialism, a socio-political and economic system is in effect being given a religious status. And if so, whether that constitutes a reduction of Christian salvation and faith to a temporal project, or, viewed from a different angle, whether liberation theology presents socialism as a path to salvation. Hence, from both theological and political standpoints, we have to ask why socialism is chosen over other models, for what purposes, and what type of socialism it is. Only then its viability in Latin America can be assessed.

Viewed as it is by liberation theology as a utopian project (utopia here referring to a creative imagination that deals with idealistic models that are capable of being realized), socialism is, indeed, given religious and eschatological significance, insofar as it constitutes a socio-political mediation of distinctive human values that have an eschatological transcendence. But this is not limited to socialism. The same occurs with any other system that is sought with the same ends. During the Middle Ages, in a theocratic system the king was regarded as an agent of the Church, since his role was in part to assist the institution in creating conditions that were conducive to personal salvation. Thus, it is quite possible to assign a theoretical political mediation to capitalism too.

To do so does not necessarily constitute an absolute temporalization of Christianity or God's Kingdom, unless the political system is predicated on a philosophical basis and concrete structures that, acting in the name of Christianity, deny all eschatological transcendence. Aside from that, it must be taken into account that all political systems are by nature temporal projects, and they all have a temporal orientation. To that extent, insofar as it attempts to realize conditions of life that are in tune with values that are distinctively religious, a political system will inevitably temporalize, though not necessarily in an absolute manner, God's Kingdom. Hence, there is nothing unorthodox about relative temporalization. On the contrary, it becomes a necessity. By the same token, there is nothing unorthodox, although it may lead to confusion among believers, about a political system that truly presents itself as a path to salvation, as long as it does not say "I am the Way, the Truth and the Life."[31] That is, as long as it does not pretend to be the only way and the only truth.

The close relationship between liberation and socialism is the result of identifying the aspirations of an idealized philosphical socialism with the needs and aspirations of the poor in Latin America, and further relating the values of socialism with human values that are distinctively Christian. At the philosophical level then, it is quite possible for Fidel Castro to assert that "There are no contradictions among the purposes of religion and those of socialism," and for a non-Marxist Chilean Cardinal, to have stated that "there are more evangelical values in socialism than there are in capitalism."[32] Thus, the ideal conditions and values in Christian liberation (such as justice, fraternity, solidarity, the new person, freedom, equality, and the common good), and their specific indicators (development, human rights, a more equitable distribution of resources, a more symmetrical interdependence, cultural self-determination, union laws, participatory democracy, the social function of property, the overcoming of alienation, and others) coincide in the eyes of many within liberation theology with a socialist project.[33]

If identifying socialism with evangelical and human values in Christianity provides many in the liberation movement with an orthodox seal, the socialist project also benefits from the harsh reality for which Latin American capitalism is responsible and from the support which the latter finds in the United States. In liberation theology, anti-capitalism, through resentment and frustration, becomes a propelling force toward socialism. The Chilean Catholic Workers Movement, for example, in giving its support to the Allende government, made known its social responsibility within the new system: "to actively collaborate to make a more just society that allows the integral liberation of those who are oppressed by such an inhuman and anti-Christian system as capitalism."[34]

While not all within the liberation movement subscribe to

socialism via the anti-capitalist reaction, this tendency appears to be common and natural for many. Their frustration in dealing with the pernicious effects of the present system leads them to support an ideal system whose concrete effects they have never questioned largely because they have never experienced them. This is similar to those who, having been affected by communism, come to resent it to the extent of being indifferent to and adamant in not recognizing the negative aspects of capitalism in other parts of the world. Hence, an ideological posture develops which is critical of the system they resent, yet somewhat uncritical toward the one they favor. Within this context one may understand why many are so eager to enter into questionable alliances with Marxists, to point to Cuba as an example of a true Christian revolution, to elevate the figure of Che Guevara to quasi-religious status, and to regard socialism "as a fundamental step toward the arrival of God's Kingdom."[35] The question may be raised if at the ideological level there is any difference in the approach between a Marxist Christian ideology and a capitalist one. Arguments will abound that qualitatively speaking each one is more just and humane than the other. But such comparisons are meaningless when the concrete realization of one system is evaluated from the ideal standpoint of the other. Without an objective analysis and historical awareness, what we have is an ideological conflict carried to almost absolute levels, showing the tensions between heaven and earth or spirit and matter, this time reflected through the personal-universal dialectic. In politics, there is the inherent tendency to dichotomize the Christian reality "individual-social being." The American political process, for example, has conditioned Judeo-Christian values to the extent that they are almost neatly divided along the lines of political parties, with one stressing the more personal and private values while the other stresses the social issues.

The ideological element adds another dimension to the issue of why many people favor socialism in Latin America. Here we are referring to the subdued influence of Marxism among Christians due to its attraction as a supposedly scientific and coherent means of explaining reality. Theology is able to transpose some of its categories to the social level. Thus sin is the explanation of conditions of injustice from a religious standpoint, faith is related to a political praxis, and socio-political liberation is linked to eschatology. Still, it is theology's lack of explanatory capability at the social level that calls for the use of science. Given the existing vacuum, Marxism became the link between science and theology. Nonetheless, what is meant by the ideological element are those aspects of Marxism that are incorporated largely without being critically questioned.

The primary objectives of socialism as espoused by liberation theology are: 1) eradicating the sinful injustices produced by a system that distorts the essential human values concerning the use of property and political power, disregards personal dignity, and creates selfish and highly insensitive structures that condition human behavior (this is done by replacing old structures and policies with socialist ones); 2) preventing such values and attitudes, insofar as they remain within the individual, from acting in detriment to the common well-being of the society, by enforcing those conditions that are in line with the social ethic model. As a group of priests in Chile posed the issue:

> Inasmuch as it is true that socialism does not free itself of the injustices that stem from personal attitudes, . . . it offers through a change in the relations of production, a fundamental equality of opportunities, it dignifies labor, . . . and offers the conjuctive development of the nation that benefits all, especially those who have been left behind, and a valorization of moral and fraternal motivations over individual self-interest.[36]

The reason underlying these socialist objectives is a basic distrust of anyone who, while unconverted to the social ethic or refusing to undergo conversion, will misuse the means of production in detriment to society as a whole if allowed to operate freely in a competitive market system. Although the motive that inspires the socialist option is the individual's social irresponsibility, the target is the private means of production. The objective is to take away from a person that which is used as a weapon of domination. The implication is that if the individual does not abuse property and the freedom one has been given to use it with a sense of responsibility, there would not be a need to change the production relations in a private enterprise system. Such is the basic premise in the type of socialism espoused by liberation theology. Neither the theologians nor the activists advocate this option based on the technical economic advantages that may be derived from nationalization, central planning of production and distribution, and the possibility of ensuring rapid growth. These considerations, while important, are secondary to the ethical orientation they pursue. The counterpart of this motivation is to lay the groundwork that may lead to the creation of a new society and a new person:

> We do not believe that man (sic) will automatically become less selfish in socialism, but we say that, having established a more egalitarian socio-economic foundation, it is possible to work more effectively for human solidarity, than in a society that is torn by inequalities.[37]

This relates to the long-term goals of socialism, the basis of which is conversion. The term "goal" refers to ideal conditions that are attainable in a complete sense. It differs from an "objective," which refers to a specific and concrete end that can be realized. Hence socialism entails the creation of new structures in line with liberation objectives, but at the same time it is supposed to generate a system of human values that reflects a social ethic and which is distinctively Judeo-Christian.

Insofar as socialism is realized through the electoral process and is constantly dependent on it, the creation of the new society becomes possible only in the degree to which these values are internalized by the people. This is similar to the socialization process that takes place in all societies. In ours, for example, we can point to the civilizing process in the western United States, or the enforcement of desegregation laws in the South. Overt governmental action was necessary until people began to accept or at least abide by the notion of a society based on law, order, and justice, instead of shootouts and discrimination. To the extent that old attitudes do not change, coercion becomes necessary to deter illegal overt behavior. Likewise, if socialism comes to a society via a revolution based on force, its coercive effects toward a sector of the population will be harshly felt, and may become destructive of the social fabric if the government is unable to get institutional support at the grassroots level, and if people ultimately fail to be persuaded of the necessity to accept the new norms.

In Latin America the institutional Church has based its program of action primarily on conversion, not only because it is proper to its religious function, but also because of the sociological insight that there can be no free new society without conversion. Instead, a totalitarian system will result. Traditionally, however, the Church has de-emphasized and even omitted at times the need for structural transformation, or it has only advocated social change as the by-product of individual conversion. The underlying reasons have been to prevent violent upheavals and because until lately it has not been receptive to the fact that social structures have a conditioning effect on human behavior. Because of the above, but also due to the ideological influence of Marxism and to the urgent need to put an end to social injustice, many within the liberation movement have placed a strong emphasis on structural transformation relative to the need for conversion. It is not that liberation theology should deal less with structural changes, but that conversion at the personal level seems to be taken for granted.

On the one hand, the dilemma is inescapable, and it is a matter of social strategy. While involved in conscientization and popular mobilization, the energy devoted by the Church to personal conversion would detract from the process of social change and further cause a shift of attention that may confuse the people and lead to a paralysis in the socio-political liberation praxis. This is because the approaches are different. Structural change is socially and externally oriented, while conversion is personal and inwardly guided. The one has an immediate objective, the end of social injustice, the other implies a never-ending process. Nonetheless the problem remains, in that social change will be repressive and coercive insofar as some type of conversion fails to take place. Again, we must emphasize that such conversion refers to the internalization of certain human values, although the Church has to preach a conversion to Christ. While a specific faith is not a requirement to partake in the fruits of socio-political liberation, a conversion to human values does become necessary.

As to the influence of Marxism in liberation theology's option for socialism and the small amount of attention given to conversion, the issue is twofold. First, it is due not so much to the value content of Marxism as to the approach itself. We return to our critique of the theory of dependence in this chapter. The Marxist analysis of social reality is basically structurally oriented. It focuses on individual behavior only insofar as the latter is conditioned by structure. Hence, the results of the analysis cannot possibly emphasize social and personal conversion until the structures are changed. The only conversion that is required is political, in order to mobilize the revolutionary forces.

Second, and more value-oriented, is the issue of how socialism deals with evil in a capitalist society. The question is not whether conversion is necessary or not, but how will it come about. Marx assumes the perfectibility of human nature, and rejects any notion of our sinful condition. Moreover, he does not see evil inherent in human nature. Since evil is external, through praxis we can redeem ourselves from bondage. There is nothing that we need to change within ourselves, except to become conscious of the surroundings that alienate us from our work, from nature, from others, and from ourselves. The socialization process that we have undergone in capitalist society is the result of structures that have conditioned us ideologically. The creation of a new person becomes possible when the individual is placed in a proper environment, one that is conducive to "social beingness":

> If man draws all his knowledge, sensations, etc. from the world of the senses and the experiences gained in it, the empirical world must be arranged so that in it man experiences and gets used to what is really human, and so that he becomes aware of himself as man. If interest correctly understood is the principle of all morality, man's private interest must be made to coincide with the interest of humanity. If man . . . is free through the positive power to assert his true individuality, crime must not be punished in the individual, but the anti-social source of crime must be destroyed. . . . If man is shaped by his surroundings, his surroundings must be made human.[38]

In liberation theology injustice is caused by the capitalist system. But even though there is awareness and acknowledgement of our responsibility for our sin against one another, when some of the theologians and many of the activists speak of the new society, they do so without referring to personal conversion or indicating how the new values will be internalized. Most of the emphasis is placed on the socialization of the means of production. Hence, it is not clear whether we will be converted or conditioned, or both. Social conditioning, even in personal conversion, is important because no matter what, it is unavoidable. But the question remains as to whether social conditioning is considered as a substitute for conversion.

Marxist materialism identifies evil in the structures. The

term "sinful structures," which has a valid sociological basis and has been used by the Church, refers to unjust or evil standard operating procedures that become part of a social organization and in time begin to operate independently of the individual's will.[39] This is not to say that the structures are the original cause of evil. Structures are the result of people's actions, but once these become culturally accepted and legitimized, many people conform to them without questioning them. Their morality and their values are basically co-opted by the structures. By simply being part of society, the individual adopts its rules and its values. The structures, through its members, give rise to evil no doubt, but the members cannot be blamed insofar as they are neither conscious of the wrong they do and hence not responsible, nor able to change the system on which they depend for a living.

In circumstances such as these one may rightfully allege that injustice and sin are not founded on the will of the oppressor, since they are the result of the way society is organized. Here we are referring to people who are convinced that even their selfish attitudes are not wrong, that their freedom allows them to do what they want. Anyone who threatens their freedom is regarded as an enemy who needs to be fought. In effect, we might even be dealing with insensitive individuals who are convinced of the morality of their actions. They do not think of questioning the system's impact on others, but simply accept it as part of life. The real sinner, on the other hand, is the one who is conscious of the sinfulness of selfishness and aware that these actions hurt others, but does not care.

When the structures become causative agents of evil, freedom is considerably diminished to the extent that personal responsibility is questionable. Hence there is no need for a personal conversion in which the individual becomes fully aware of the evil behavior of which one is part, accepts one's responsibility, and freely decides to change one's values and habits. The new structures will help one to accomplish that through the socialization process. As Paulo Freire has said, transforming the concrete circumstances in which one lives will transform the person too, "not automatically, of course, but quite certainly."[40]

One example is that of abortion in the United States. Many who favor abortion do not see anything wrong in it. Those holding the opposite view see abortion as a sin and as a social crime that is being legitimized by sinful structures. The person who commits an abortion, however, may not necessarily sin if one is not aware of its sinfulness and does not believe that such action is morally wrong, since society seems to condone it. In this situation, passing a law against abortion will have for its objective that of preventing a social crime, and creating an environment similar to that which was established when anti-slavery laws were passed. In time those laws ceased being the binding force because slavery as a socially acceptable norm had lost its value in society. Instead, it was looked upon as evil, both from a religious and a social perspective. Social conversion had taken place through conditioning. Hence, when the Vatican asserts that "structures, whether they are good or bad, are the result of man's actions and so are consequences more than causes,"[41] it is not taking fully into consideration that the statement is correct only in terms of the structures' origins, but not in terms of their continuous presence. If the statement "the root of evil lies in free and responsible persons who have to be converted . . . in order to live and act as new creatures"[42] is true as the Vatican's first document on liberation theology maintains, a fact we do not deny in some cases, then why is the Church so insistent in combating abortion through external reforms?

Marxist materialism assumes that a person can be conditioned into a social being in the same fashion as one was conditioned into being selfish, through the production relations. Liberation theologians and activists, however, are not reductionists. They do not believe that the new society is based only on economics. A change in the production relations represents the restructuring of society, including its laws and institutions, its ways of doing business, its advertising, and the production and distribution process.[43] Hence their assertion is that a socialist system based on human values that are transcending and distinctively Judeo-Christian will be able to generate those same values, which once embodied in culture will lead to social conversion of individuals. Here they are not following a mechanist view. Nor do they imply that there will not be a need for personal conversion and for evangelization. On the contrary, social change lays the groundwork for a more effective evangelization. Moreover, they can mutually reinforce each other. In the words of Gutiérrez:

> "Hearts" can also be transformed by altering sociocultural structures. Both aspects are interdependent and complementary because they are grounded on a common unity. The view that a structural transformation will automatically produce different human beings is no more and no less "mechanist" than the view that a "personal change of heart" will automatically lead to a transformation of society. Any such mechanist views are naive and unrealistic.[44]

Those who refuse to abide by the system, as in all societies, will be deterred from illicit behavior and coerced into obeying the laws.

The problem that people have with the term "social conditioning," however, relates to its negative connotation. Based on Marxist materialism, it lends itself to interpretations of a mechanist or deterministic process and to a denial of the spirit. However, this view does not take into account the difference between two types of conditioning. One is that in which the individual is aware of the influence of society's values, e.g. their explicit vocalization through social institutions, government, the school, the church, and the family. In this process of socialization, society not only condones, but actively supports, the propagation of those ethos, norms, and values that are deemed positive. The other involves passive or concealed conditioning, e.g. society's acceptance of certain behavioral norms that are spin-offs of cultural changes that are transmitted through the media. These norms and values on consumerism, sexual mores, corporate attitudes, crime, drug dependence, and others are not extolled and legitimized through the socialization process. Instead they are imitated and incorporated unconsciously by the individual. Eventually, they dictate behavior. The first type confronts and educates the individual, the other undermines or bypasses critical reflection.

In liberation theology social conversion focuses on active conditioning. Thus for example, an overt educational program may be instituted to deal with the problem of alcoholism and teenage pregnancies in society, or reeducation may be oriented toward social responsibility and *machismo*. The approach would have the same effects as they would have on a student whose parents change their child from one school to another because of the presence of significant values in one which are absent in the other. The idea is to provide the person with a suitable environment in which human values are nurtured. The basic issue is whether to make constructive and positive use of social conditioning, or to let its passive effects have an unintended impact in society.

The Church's greatest concern in this respect is that an uncritical Marxist materialism may lead to an atheist culture, thereby depriving individuals of spiritual transcendence and the foundation of ethics based on freedom and responsibility.[45] This fear is also reflected in the Vatican's recent *Instruction on Christian Freedom and Liberation,* which points out that giving priority to structures over conversion "is contrary to the construction of a just social order," supposedly because it stems from a "materialistic anthropology."[46] However, aside from the questionable premise that relates such anthropology to the moral outcome of a social order, the document fails to consider that in Western societies the individual is passively conditioned and one's freedom and responsibility may, too, diminish considerably. In this situation the Church has to face sinful conditions created by "non-sinners," people who are not aware of the evil they do or who do not accept that what they do is evil.

Another concern is that given the close relationship of many in the liberation movement with non-Christian Marxists, socialism may give way to repression and totalitarianism. This view is held by other liberation theologians and activists such as Enrique Dussel, Juan Carlos Scannone, Ronaldo Muñoz, José Marins, Segundo Galilea, and Helder Cámara, among others. Scannone, for example, believes that insofar as liberation is presented within the context of the master-slave or oppressor-oppressed dialectics, society cannot be authentically liberated. The new system arises as a reaction to the one it seeks to replace. It liberates the universal from the oppression by the particular, but ends in the oppression of the particular and the universal in the name of the totality. Thus, what is ontologically a dialectic of totality becomes in practice political totalitarianism.[47]

The issue reverts to the question of *a priori* values that determine social attitudes ideologically. If socialism is advocated as a reaction, it cannot evade the dialectical process, and by insisting on the social question that disregards the particular, the risk of totalitarianism increases. The new society has to remain itself closed to what its rulers consider alien ideologies and values, and to external as well as to internal self-criticism. Such has been the historical experience of socialist models that follow a strict Marxist materialism. The system cannot avoid absolutizing itself because freedom for the expression of critical reflection cannot be condoned until a new person is created in society. This would require political rehabilitation programs that use the entire political apparatus to produce a change of attitudes by way of imposing conformity to new external behavior patterns.

In this case, abuses of power are easily committed by the rulers who now seek to take the necessary measures to prevent the new society from being affected by capitalist values. The control of religious and intellectual freedom and the lack of development of a critical consciousness in a Marxist non-democratic socialism, are not so much the results of Marxist ideas as the logical pragmatic action that the goals themselves suggest. This is why this system's worst enemy is not necessarily a foreign power against whom military action can be taken, but the flourishing of an independent critical mind that can question the government's legitimacy and the wisdom of its policies. The other side of the issue is that by focusing only on structures the interpersonal dimension is overlooked. If serious injustice takes place in the structures, it is no less true that similar relations are also found at the personal level. As Enrique Dussel has stated, "if it is bad to be a mine worker in Bolivia, in many instances it is even worse to the mine worker's wife."[48]

For socialism to become a liberating force it requires not only economic but concrete moral indicators. Hervé Chaigne, a Franciscan monk, points out that if socialism fails to subject production relations to human rights, and does not allow room for people to develop and deepen their inner selves, it would amount to a substitution of one materialism for another, that is, a new version of state capitalism.[49] Here socialism runs the risk of contradicting the goals of liberation theology.

The socialist model may be created either through the democratic process or through a violent revolution. The democratic approach, however, does not insure the establishment of socialism, and once in power a democratic socialist government cannot necessarily produce the structural changes that are needed to create a new society. The democratic process within a capitalist framework only allows for the competition of political forces. Hence, the liberation movement has to rely on the Christian base communities to attain social and religious conscientization and political mobilization. These communities have become positive means for personal conversion, which may then have a strong impact on the cultural and political levels. Their effectiveness is well recognized by those involved in them:

> The political process is the great instrument that we have to build a just society like the one God wishes. . . . In our base communities we look for the strength that will motivate us in the struggle that takes place in the neighborhoods or in the villages, in the working place, or in a political party.[50]

The impact of the base communities is seen in the relationship between conversion and social change. Although they may lend themselves to political manipulation for narrow political purposes, these groups foster a deep, personal, and religious conversion that is also oriented toward structural changes. Another liberation theologian, Luis del Valle, points out that liberation at this level seeks in part to develop in its members the courage to question the system, to oppose power, and to overcome the fear of persecution and death to the extent that such fear will cease to paralyze their actions. This is done through study and reflection on the Bible and by analyzing reality, carefully weighing the cost and advantages of facing power in specific circumstances.[51] If the democratic process is possible, such human potential for change can be channeled peacefully.[52] On the other hand, in countries with dictatorships, or in others where political expression finds no outlet, personal conversion will most likely lead to violent confrontation.

If personal conversion fails to take place, the democratic process will not be able to create a new society. The old values of possession, oppression, consumerism, and power will resurface thereby hindering social change. For this reason Paulo Freire urges the development of a critical consciousness as the link between social and personal conversion. He sees the oppressed person as a slave of his inner being (oppressed mentality), as well as a slave of the objective reality that oppresses him. Conscientization implies a reflection of the causes and conditions that are responsible for his oppression, and the recognition that he is being oppressed. Next comes the realization that both his internal and external conditions can be overcome, the one through education that leads to the development of critical consciousness, and the other through the praxis of liberation. Throughout the process the oppressed focuses alternately on his subjective conditions and subjective reality in order to determine how a person should proceed.[53]

Hence, conscientization is not only consciousness-raising. It is above all a critical attitude with regard to reality (which the individual tries to unveil in order to see its contradictions) tied to a commitment to change that reality. Critical education is important because it prevents the values of the old society from continuing to influence the new society. Without this, changes in the infrastructure will not have the intended effect in the newly created structures.[54]

Liberation theology's anti-capitalist attitude, its approach in contrasting capitalism and socialism, its identification of the latter with Christian ideals and values, and the influence of Marxism have played a determining role in many of the theologians and activists. These aspects neither invalidate nor validate their socialist option. As Pope Paul VI had said, "It is up to the Christian communities to analyze with objectivity the situation which is proper to their own country, . . . and to discern the options and commitments which are called for in order to bring about . . . changes seen in many cases to be urgently needed."[55] Nonetheless, the weakest point in liberation theology is the lack of a critical attitude with regard to socialism.

The socialist option, in whatever form, is regarded as a temporal panacea without a sense of realism and objectivity. There is nothing so substantially unethical or impractical in a theoretical socialist model, that is not found in other aspects of capitalism that may rule out the former from offering a viable alternative under certain circumstances. By the same token, there is nothing that guarantees that an uncritical version of socialism may not end up being as contemptuous and insensitive to society and humans as the type of capitalism that is being rejected by liberation theology in Latin America.

For Juan Luis Segundo, one of the most prolific theologians in the liberation movement, socialism does not mean "a long-term project," but simply the removal of the means of production from the hands of private individuals and their control by higher institutions which are concerned with the common good.[56] Segundo is well aware that socialism has much deeper implications than the one mentioned. As someone who seeks to exercise an influential role among the masses, Segundo should be fully prepared to discuss that which he is asking others to do. He relies, however, on a biblical rationale to evade the issue altogether:

> The European advocates of political theology demand that we Latin Americans present them with a proposal for a socialist society that is guaranteed in advance to avoid the defects evident in existing brands of socialism. Why do they not demand the same thing of Jesus? Why do they not demand that Jesus, before telling someone that his faith has saved him and cured him, provide some guarantee that the cure will definitely not be followed by worse illnesses?[57]

Indeed, Europeans may often proceed with a caution that paralyzes their praxis. Their conditions are not the same as those in Latin America, hence they reflect some degree of insensitivity in asking for guaranteed success. Socialism, however, is not a theological issue in the strict use of the term. It is a political, social, and economic mediation. It is at these levels that the socialist option must be discussed. What is missing in liberation theology is not a full description of the model, which is unrealistic, but a sense of historical awareness and a description of the possible pitfalls that should be avoided. If reality dictates the praxis, then such reality cannot be ignored. Joseph Comblin brings the issue out into the open:

> The disillusionment of the socialist experiments have shown that there is no level of technical development which necessarily brings with it human relations of freedom. . . . The socialist experiment has shown that there is no such thing as innocent power. . . . There is no social change without the intervention of political power, but a socialism built by the power of the State is always a system of domination.[58]

Likewise, others who have argued in favor of socialism have done so but not without objections. Nicaraguan bishops, for example, supported a socialist project in their country, as long as it meant "the preeminence of the interests of the Nicaraguan majority and a model of a nationally planned economy, in solidarity and with progressive popular participation."[59] Furthermore, the bishops regard as compatible with Christian values a type of socialism that leads to a decrease of injustice and inequality, narrowing the gap between the intellectual and manual remuneration for work, the overcoming of economic alienation, and the transfer of power to the people. They object to a system, however, that seizes the people's role in history, that subjects them to political manipulation and abuses of power, and prevents them from manifesting publicly their religious convictions or denies parents the right to educate their own children.[60]

In Marxist terminology, it may be said that many advocates of socialism within the liberation movement have ignored the objective conditions for revolution. We may ask, how will they deal with the flight of capital and skilled personnel that ensues with a socialist government? How will they address the issue of incentives for production that seems to baffle socialist economies? Also, a socialist government will have to deal with international financial institutions whose capitalist approaches may prevent the fulfillment of immediate socialist expectations.

In addition, strong overt demonstrations of anti-Americanism may predispose stronger reactions from the United States. Such conflict may lead the new government to make considerable expenditures on arms to defend the revolution, thereby detracting from economic development and social services. Moreover, the government will close the doors to American capital and technology.

From this perspective, ironically, the theory of dependence brings forth a sense of realism. Liberation theology's objective is not only to free Latin American nations from the center, but to be able to develop the economies within the periphery. Is this something that can be done without the center? Prebisch himself acknowledges that the responsibility to transform the system lies with Latin Americans themselves. But he concedes that as difficult as it may be, the task would be worse without the cooperation from the center.[61] This suggests that liberation and structural changes will not be enough. Since the revolution cannot reach the center, as traditional as it may sound, the periphery will have to work diligently to persuade the center to adopt an altruistic attitude toward the region. Only a sense of social responsibility by the center will insure the development of the periphery.

Class Struggle or Social Conflict?

In Latin America there is a consensus among theologians and activists that neither reform nor the transformation of the system will take place without serious conflict. Not even the democratic and electoral process can guarantee that violence will be avoided. The process can be peaceful only insofar as the major groups that represent the status quo are willing to abide by democratic rules, which has not always been the case, or if they perceive that the opposition brings only moderate programs that will not alter the system significantly. But the acceptance of violence as a means to solve conflict is so deeply rooted in the Latin American experience that ideological struggles and serious conflicts of interest often lead to repression and to open confrontation. Thus resistance by the Right to changes by the Left, and vice versa, accounts for a high incidence of turmoil.

Liberation theology incorporates into its social analysis the reality of conflict. It may be argued that this is due to the influence of Marxism. To be sure, Marxism operates within a conflictual framework. It claims that class conflict is an observable fact in history. However, charges that liberation theology either creates or accepts the class struggle *a priori*[62] simplifies the problem. As we shall see ahead and in the next chapter, a non-Marxist Church that adopts the Puebla document may create conflict too.

For a Marxist class struggle to be successful, certain conditions must be present. In first place, we may speculate that the social conflict is avoidable if the workers are not abused by the owner or manager of capital, if they fail to become aware of their situation, if they do not mind their conditions, or if apathy leads workers to resign themselves to injustice. The last two conditions do not erase the reality of injustice, but they preclude a confrontation. Hence the existence of conflict in most instances implies that one group has been made aware of its condition and has decided to overcome them. This situation is not limited to Marxism. Without conscientization no liberation praxis is possible. Thus, a Church committed to the cause of the poor engaged in such activity will be perceived by the oppressor as operating under the shadow of Marxism, which most likely will lead to conflict.

The issue of class struggle in liberation theology is perhaps the most confusing and problematic of all. The term itself, because it is borrowed from Marxism and is so superficially and ambiguously treated in liberation theology, tends to be misinterpreted and misused. For example, the Vatican's major objection to the liberation praxis is its engagement in the class struggle because there it sees the means of linking Marxist ideology with a totalitarian atheist society.

The Church has traditionally viewed the Marxist class struggle in terms of its historical realization. Pope Pius XI saw it as a crusade based on hatred and destruction in which "all resisting forces, . . . should be without any distinction, annihilated as enemies of mankind."[63] And in the first Vatican publication on liberation theology the class struggle is seen as dividing society into two opposing classes, in which conflict is inevitable. Acceptance of the struggle, it affirms, leads to violence by pitting one class against another.[64] In general terms, the Church denounces a class struggle that favors one group against another, leads to hatred and violence instead of reconciliation, fosters a classist theology that in turn divides the Church itself, and paves the way to a reductionist and confusing interpretation of the Bible.[65] Moreover, the document implies that acceptance of the term by some of the theologies of liberation has led to the notion that people redeem themselves in history through the class struggle, thereby eliminating the eschatological dimension of liberation in Jesus Christ.[66]

The European Jules Girardi, however, has been among the most influential writers on the theologians in regard to this theme. The now Cardinal Alfonso López Trujillo blames Girardi for having a pernicious impact on men like Gutiérrez, Assman, Comblin, and others by relating the class struggle to a Christian praxis based on love.[67] Yet, a close reading of Girardi's much-quoted book, *Amor Cristiano y Lucha de Clases,* finds the author quite critical of the violence instituted by the socialist revolutions, objecting to an identification between redemption of the proletariat and human redemption, choosing non-violence as preferable over violence, praising the Czech people for their non-violent resistance against the Soviet invasion — all this while accepting the necessity of the class struggle and the use of violence as a last recourse in line with Pope Paul VI's *Populorum progressio.*[68] If we are to go beyond the confusion, how are we to understand the words of Pope John Paul II, who is so opposed to class struggle and yet indicts the "rich North," telling these nations that the "poor South" will judge them for depriving others of food, freedom, and other human rights by making use of "an imperialist monopoly of their economic and political power"?[69]

The root of the problem lies in the ambiguity of the term "class." At one time or another Marx identified several social groups as being organized into classes: the proletariat, the bourgeoisie, landowners, the petty bourgeoisie, peasants, professionals and intellectuals, farm laborers, and the lumpen-proletariat. Nonetheless, in *The Communist Manifesto* Marx claimed that capitalism simplifies class antagonism by dividing society into two major groups, the bougeoisie and the proletariat, each assigned a normative label by Marx. The former is the oppressor and the latter is the oppressed.[70] The distinction is based on each class's relation to the means of production: the oppressor owns these means, while the oppressed, having none, have to sell their labor to survive. From the standpoint of a revolutionary praxis this typology is not very helpful. It tells us that those who do not own the means of production constitute a class and will be the backbone of the revolution. However, as Marx reminds us, in order for the proletariat to be mobilized, members must identify with and see themselves as being proletarian. While the struggle aims at providing them with a class consciousness, many will not develop it in time, either because of competition among themselves or because they are effectively co-opted by the oppressor. In the end they will have to be liberated as a part of the dominant class. The Marxist scientific analysis, then, is ultimately based on the observation of group conflict throughout history. The two classes are divided according to consciousness alignment: those who think and feel like the proletariat belong to the "good" class that must seek its own liberation from those who sympathize or identify with the bourgeoisie, which is the "evil" class.

In liberation theology the ambiguity concerning the use of the term "class" is also present. No theologian or activist group divides society according to strict Marxist standards, nor do they use any specific scientific category to identify the participants in the class struggle. Their two main groups are the oppressed and the oppressor, under which are subsumed the opposites poor-rich, working class-ruling class, exploited-exploiter.[71] Moreover, in liberation theology the oppressed are above all those people that Marx saw as not having a great revolutionary potential, the lumpenproletariat, and the destitute who remain on the fringe of society. The term "class," despite its sociological connotation, has more of a religious significance in the writings of the theologians and refers primarily to the poor. Not only the "poor in spirit" whom Christ blessed as an ideal, but also the other category of poor — the naked, the hungry, the sick, those who are abused, who do not earn enough to support their families, whose needs are not taken into account either by their governments or their employers. In general, they are those whom the Church has identified in the Puebla document as embodying the aspirations to which all human beings as children of God are called.[72]

As an analytical term, the class struggle in liberation theology indicates a situation of conflict between two groups, the poor who try to overcome their condition and the other, whether it is called the rich, the oppressor, the dominant, or ruling classes, who either remain indifferent or prevent the inclusion and the development of the former in society. In practice, however, there is little or no difference between the term "class struggle" as it is used in liberation theology and the terms suggested by Cardinal López Trujillo, such as "conflict," "class struggle in general," and "struggle for justice,"[73] or that employed by the Vatican, "the disinherited classes."[74] Even the term chosen by the Church at Puebla, "option for the poor," can lead to a similar praxis as a class struggle. For example, López Trujillo attempts to differentiate the class struggle from the other terms by its tendency to divide society into two groups or classes in which antagonistic tensions lead to violence, the dictatorship of the proletariat, and a new dominant class.[75] However, the tactics that López Trujillo suggests may take place in a legitimate struggle for justice, such as popular manifestations, strikes, and public denunciations, already point to the existence of antagonistic opposition, and in Latin America these actions often may lead to repression and to violence.

Reading the Vatican's first *Instruction,* one cannot fail to notice a situation of conflict between two groups and the potential for violence given the realism and the tone with which conditions are denounced:

> Mankind will no longer passively submit to crushing poverty with its effects of death, disease and decline. He resents this misery as an intolerable violation of his native dignity.
> The powerful aspiration that people have for liberation . . . is above all among those people who bear the burdens of misery, and in the heart of the disinherited classes. . . . The scandal of the shocking inequality between the rich and the poor . . . is no longer tolerated.[76]

A major difference between liberation theology's concept of class struggle and the Church's is the latter's assertion that liberation theology identifies with systematic violence and a totalitarian dictatorship of the proletariat. A rather careful examination of liberation writings, however, does not reveal the above. On the contrary, throughout much of the debate surrounding the theology, a significant issue lies in the way that terms such as socialism, class struggle, revolution, dictatorship of the proletariat, materialism, and violence are used. Those who oppose this terminology are reacting more against the historical experience of communism. On the other hand, those in the liberation movement using these terms fail to conceptualize them rigorously. Their writings denote a lack of historical awareness of the ways in which they have been realized. Hence, the question is not whether to use those terms or not, but how they are to be used and what their objectives are: which concrete conditions are sought in socialism, and which should be avoided; which attitudes and values are to be found in a class struggle, and which should be shunned; what does the dictatorship of the proletariat entail for them; what do they understand by historical materialism; is there an ethic that should guide a revolution and the use of violence? López Trujillo himself is quite vague while approving the Church's tactics insofar as they do not transcend "certain limits," without mentioning what these limits are.[77] We think that as long as the theologians fail to focus on values, attitudes, and concrete guidelines the debate will generate more confusion, and will unnecessarily alienate those theologians and activists from the Church by creating reasonable fears of totalitarianism and atheism, thereby pushing the institution into a defensive posture with regard to social change.

There is, indeed, a concern on the part of the Church about the class struggle when viewed in a historical perspective. It refers mostly to the passive conditioning effect that it may have on its participants, which may obstruct the creation of the new person. Historically, the efficacy of the class struggle as a communist revolutionary strategy has resulted from making strong appeals to human emotions by fomenting discord, resentment, and hatred against the opposite class. This tactic fuels vengeful desires among the oppressed and urges them to drive the dominant group from power. In addition, it creates a revolutionary fervor within the people that serves as a cohesive political force. The use of labels against anyone who disagrees with the revolution is common: "bourgeoisie" and "reactionary" in the Soviet Union, "social scum" and "worms" in Cuba. In this type of revolutionary process there exists, conscious or not, a determined disposition to mobilize the masses with anger and hatred.

Another tactic commonly accepted among revolutionary regimes that come to power, whether of the Right or the Left, is that of "revolutionary justice" or the systematic and arbitrary annihilation of the opposition and its sympathizers. Its purpose is not only to eliminate internal opposition but to placate the anger of the masses and to win their support. The difficulty of diffusing these attitudes raises the question as to whether people who have been taught to hate can restrain their own dispositions at a later time. The psychological and sociological implications are such that even if a government attempts a tactical policy of reconciliation within society or vis-á-vis other nations once it feels secure in power, the masses may see such actions as a softening of the revolutionary posture and prevent them altogether.

Another conflictive issue is that of the alliance between Christians and Marxists, openly suggested by many within the liberation movement. Even though one cannot judge all Marxists alike, just as no one can say that all Christians think and act in the same manner, the point here is the extent to which Christian identity will be allowed to coexist in the event that Christians do not have military power in a revolution. Will this identity be allowed to exercise its critical role even when it does not act in a reactionary manner? Will a Marxist government tolerate a second, differing social conscience?

So far there remains a basic distrust on the part of Marxists toward Christians as a group, even when they are accepted as individual revolutionaries. Pedro Trigo, an observer of the religious situation in Cuba, for example, points out that in recent years there has been a slight positive change of policy by the government toward Christians in order to avoid unnecessary political friction at a time when it is not convenient, even though the overall objective is still to prevent the revitalization of Christianity.[78] In the last *Resolution* on politics in relation to religion in 1980, the Cuban government appears to signal a less doctrinaire approach than the one evidenced in a similar resolution in 1975. But, as Trigo adds, even though the government welcomes the new liberation phenomenon in Latin America, Christians as a group are seen as a potential source of internal criticism, and thus of civil disobedience.[79]

In Nicaragua, the process that seems to be taking place is different and much more complex, given the active role that many Christians and the local Church played in the revolution. There the government is not seeking to suppress the Christian religion. Instead, in conjunction with militant Christians it has tried to identify religion with the revolution itself by co-opting aspects of Christianity, and by making selective use of enunciations in the Puebla document and from the Nicaraguan bishops who appear to support their policies and objectives. Their aim appears to be that of neutralizing an independent Church by dividing it, while trying to discredit those who favor the revolutionary process but do not support some of their policies, and who may create a dissenting nucleus of opposition.[80] Since there are numerous aspects of the revolution with which Christians can sympathize, these militants are playing a major role in conscientizing the population along the lines of the revolution. However, they are also trying to instill a critical consciousness in the people, something which could backfire against the government, or against themselves, should the former adopt a more dogmatic form of Marxism.

The Church is also concerned that by adopting the term "class struggle," liberation theology may create a class conflict that does not yet exist. Or as the *Instruction* says, the "expression remains pregnant with the interpretation that Marx gave it, so it cannot be taken as the equivalent of 'severe social conflict,' in an empirical sense."[81] The use of the term by some theologians and activists is ill-chosen, not only due to its empirical ambiguity but because of the tendency to identify the movement with the historical Marxist process, and as such detracts from an objective dialogue with the Church. Still, the choice of terms should not avoid the point that Marx was trying to make: the real existence of a social conflict.

While it is up to the social scientist to find out where, when, and how the term may be appropriately used, in liberation theology its treatment is different. It is not so much whether it corresponds to the good-evil, love-selfishness struggle in Christian theology, regardless of its Marxist connotations. This means that even without the use of the term an analysis of a conflictive situation in Latin America will result in the unavoidable reality of two groups opposing each other. From a moral standpoint the struggle is not, as it may appear in a scientific analysis, between two groups or classes in conflict over similar interests. Rather, an ethical judgment is made that one group is treating the other unfairly by failing to abide by God's rules, thereby depriving the other from enjoying the same opportunities, rights, and rewards to which it is entitled. The Church indeed notices such antagonism between two groups, and not only makes an ethical evaluation of the conflict, but takes sides as well. The Church's support of the poor implies that it favors one group more than the other. And as a result, it will devote most of its efforts in defending the rights of the poor and denouncing the injustices committed against them. Engaged in that praxis, the institution inevitably has to go against the interests of the opposing group. In other words, something concrete is oppressing the poor, according to the Church, and when it denounces injustice that entity becomes visible.

Nonetheless, the Church is also concerned that liberation theology's use of the term "class struggle" may evoke a social phenomenon that will be exclusionary, based on hatred, and violent. In this respect, the analysis of the class struggle or social conflict differs from its praxis, and their Marxist version from that of the Church. As some in the liberation movement point out, the Marxist analysis should not lead to personal hatred at the class level since they find no fault in oppression. Since evil is rooted in the structures that condition people's unjust behavior, the analysis is not personal but structural. Its objective is to get the oppressed to see that what is needed is a reorganization of society, not revenge.[82] Such objective scientific analysis ought to lead to a praxis of conscientization that excludes hatred. Reconciliation between classes should not then be a major problem, at least from the perspective of the oppressed, who understand the truth in the conflict.

The Church's view of the social conflict tends to be more explosive. It finds sin not primarily in structures but in those who head them. As the *Instruction* points out, "the root of evil lies in free and responsible persons."[83] Conscientization of the poor along these lines inevitably leads to hatred, at least as an initial reaction on the part of the oppressed and also by the oppressor who is cast as the villain in the conflict. This situation creates the potential for violent class struggle. Now the historical Marxist realization of the class struggle has not followed its idealistic prognosis. Marx's own attitudes prevented him from making an aseptic and value-free judgment. But then he could not possibly do that, for oppression, even by human moral values, is theft. Explicitly, he appears to have assigned a moral responsibility to the bourgeoisie, whether realistically or not. This does not contradict his materialism, however, for the bourgeoisie acts evilly because it is conditioned to behave that way. But in the end, Marx's contempt for capitalist society is transferred from his structural analysis to the bourgeoisie; it is made personal, implicitly attributing to this class a moral freedom that it supposedly does not have.

Furthermore, given the natural tendency to defend its interests, but also because it does not see itself as an oppressive class, the bourgeoisie engages in an active resistance that provokes hatred among the oppressed. Violence by the oppressed, when unorganized, is a symptom of such hatred. When organized, however, it reflects a calculated option in view of a strong and well-coordinated opposition. Hatred continues to be present, but it gives way to a rational revolutionary praxis. In other words, in the end the Marxist finds that one does not struggle against structures but against people.

The Marxist idealism in the class struggle fails for the same reasons that the Church's own prediction should not. The institution is very much aware of the human aspects that are involved in a violence-prone conflict. Theoretically, its analytical approach should lead to violence, humanly speaking, and often it does. Nonetheless, in order to avoid this, it pursues a praxis that is different from the Marxist. In its option for the poor the Church places itself in a difficult position. It denounces oppression and identifies the oppressor:

> the seizure of the vast majority of the wealth by an oligarchy of owners bereft of social consciousness, the practical absence or the shortcomings of a rule of law, military dictators making a mockery of elementary human rights, the corruption of certain powerful officials, the savage practices of some foreign capital interests. . . .[84]

The Church, however, sees itself as a consciously biased mediator between two groups, attempting to avoid the division of society into two classes. It is interesting to observe that in none of the Church's recent documents do we see the poor being told to love their enemy, something that would make the dominant groups the Church's enemies.

In its role as "mother" the institution seeks to convert her two groups of children, the oppressed and the oppressor. It tells the disinherited classes that hatred, revenge, and violence should not guide their actions, while it appeals to the "moral potential" of the ruling classes and to their "constant need for interior conversion."[85] The reality of a class conflict is already present in the above situation.

The Church criticizes a supposedly "radical wing" in liberation theology because it sees this group as not following an orthodox praxis and instead assuming *a priori* the need for struggle and violence against the ruling classes. But this view cannot be sustained from a social standpoint. The dilemma in the Church's own praxis is that it contributes to a class struggle from the moment it identifies two contending groups and sides with one while it denounces the other. It then goes on to mediate between them by making moral appeals. The Marxist approach bypasses such appeals as inefficient. It considers it unrealistic to hope that the bourgeoisie will be converted, either because of its greed or because it rationalizes its own moral position. Liberation theologians do not reject the appeal to conversion, and believe that it is necessary that conversion takes place. Their attitude, however, is that it is unjust to wait until the oppressor has converted before social change can take place.

From the liberation theology standpoint, the struggle becomes violent when the poor are conscientized and put pressure on the ruling classes to convert, i.e., to become sensitive to their plight, but are unsuccessful. There is an implicit recognition that if the disinherited classes were not abused these groups would not in fact exist to oppose the dominant groups. In other words, a class struggle exists because there is a class or group conflict in which one side oppresses the other and refuses to alter the status quo. For the oppressed, peace and stability cannot be sought based on their own acceptance of unjust conditions. This view is not a Marxist invention, although in modern times Marxism has popularized it. The Church's acceptance of the struggle does not mean that Marxist ideas have penetrated the institution, but that the existence of a serious social conflict involves a moral dimension which cannot be overlooked. Hence, the Church's own praxis is as conducive to a form of class struggle as is liberation theology. Hatred and violence, when they occur, are secondary to the liberation praxis, just as the Church's intention is not to foster social conflict *per se*.

Altogether, the institution's dilemma with the class struggle is, as Lucien Pelissier points out, that it focuses on its brutal effects and takes these for its causes, preventing it from seriously concentrating on the latter.[86] However, once it analyzes social conditions, it realizes that its duty will involve and cannot avoid conflict. Once it accepts this reality, the Church cannot remain neutral, since a moral situation requires a moral judgment and ethical guidelines. But, the Church's role in the social conflict that results from its option for the poor, its denunciation of the oppressor has to be mitigated by its constant appeal for love and reconciliation and for the conversion of the dominant groups. In effect, such is the Church's version of the class struggle. As we have seen, the type of class struggle that is chosen can make a difference in the outcome. It is not the same when conscientization takes place with explicit hatred and desires for revenge, unwarranted violence, and the good-evil labeling according to dogmatic political views, as when such awareness takes place in terms of the need for an ultimate reconciliation, respect for opposing ideas and human dignity, justice based on human rights, truth, and freedom. The new society will be shaped according to the attitudes involved in the struggle.

The Church does not seek a class struggle any more than liberation theology does. As Gutiérrez says, in the first instance the struggle is neither an ideological strategy nor an option, it is a concrete reality, whether Marxist or not. Since it involves human beings who are subjected to injustice, the issue for the Christian is to find one's place in the struggle. And, according to the theologians and the Church, Christ's own commandment places the committed Christian on the side of the poor.[87]

In liberation theology the class struggle is above all a political process. The struggle is not based on dogmatic economic doctrines, however. Neither the Marxist theory of surplus value, nor the fetishism of commodities, nor the theory of alienation constitute the rallying points in the class struggle. These are merely explanations of observable conditions of poverty, injustice, and oppression. As we said, in liberation theology the term "class struggle" is not well defined sociologically or even politically. The theologians are interested in those who do not have any class consciousness but who have different relations to the means of production, and those who are even excluded from them. Socio-political liberation today is grounded more on religious doctrine than the struggle within the Church on behalf of individual human rights a century ago. In effect, it constitutes a liberation from the sin of those who do not wish to be converted.

In a personalist theology liberation from sin has a primary spiritual and abstract dimension that takes place within the person and vis-á-vis God. The result is not only spiritual but material, a change of attitudes in one's relations with other people. Liberation theology, on the other hand, includes and even begins with the same personal liberation from sin. Since a change of attitude is involved, one's behavior is not only characterized by abstaining from perpetrating injustice upon others, since not doing evil is only the negative result of conversion. A more positive aspect is the crux of the Gospel, namely to love, to assist those in need, to struggle for justice. What liberation theology says is that in order to be faithful to the Christian commandment, given the existence of a social conflict between two classes, one cannot remain on the sidelines as a spectator but must take a socio-political position because the conflict occurs at the political level. The struggle may acquire a more strictly religious dimension as it did during the time of Christ, who conscientized the situation in terms of two groups and did it through word and deed: "He who is not with me is against me."[88] In effect, the religious conflict assumed political and class conflict characteristics in the theocratic state: those who sided with Jesus and those who followed the Scribes and the Pharisees.

Personal liberation from sin needs to be manifested concretely, and so, too, does socio-political liberation. In this manner the struggle moves into the political arena. Here, the liberation praxis shows similarities with the electoral process in a democratic society. Both involve similar steps: identification of potential voters; political campaigns, neighborhood canvassing, and discussion groups aimed at conscientizing the people in favor of one party and against the other; party organization to solicit funds, to mail propaganda, set up political rallies, and coordinate decision-making; party mobilization to get people to attend rallies, to support the party, and ultimately to get them to vote for the party's leaders. Once the party is in power the process does not end. The organization continues to conscientize and mobilize political support for key issues as they are debated throughout an administration's term in office.

The differences in the struggle are due to the type of political culture existing within a country and the socio-economic conditions of the people. In countries that are ruled by dictatorial regimes, or in those where the political process prevents the input from the grassroots and living conditions are below acceptable human standards, the incidence of frustration, vociferous and strident rhetoric, antagonism, and possibly violence tends to be much higher than in countries where open democratic systems prevail and where the socio-economic gap between classes is not as wide. In other words, an anti-capitalist ideology finds wider acceptance in the former than, say, in the United States.

Hence in most parts of Latin America the socio-political conflict assumes the characteristics of a class struggle. The only aspect that is particularly Marxist is the anti-capitalist critique, and even here it finds a high degree of correspondence with the Church's social doctrine. In all other parts, the class struggle will conform to the nature of a social conflict. There, for example, even though hatred is not used tactically, a certain degree is unavoidable. Girardi is aware of this when he says:

> At the psychological and the sociological levels there occurs a certain logic of the struggle which gravitates toward hatred, or at least toward internal hostility; it unchains antipathy, resentment, personal or group rivalries, instinctive aggressive behavior, that favors the creation of a sectarian morality. . . .[89]

The only possible ways in which this social phenomenon fails to occur is either in the absence of a conflict or through one's decision to avoid involvement. It is interesting to observe that Girardi's description of the internal and external aspects of a conflict are similar to the attitudes and behavior that Jesus Christ manifested during his encounters with the Pharisees and with the merchants at the Temple.[90] In his case there actually was no religious conflict within the Jewish community; it was Jesus who created it.

The Class Struggle and Violence

Violence is among the most distasteful aspects of class struggle. Not only is it a threat to human life, but it is regarded as contrary to the spirit of the Gospel. Those who denounce liberation theology point to the theologians' and the activists' systematic preaching of violence, or to favoring or creating an attitude that leads to the use of violence. In this regard, once again liberation theology's close identification with Marxism and its advocacy of political revolution has negatively affected the movement's reputation. In liberation writings we notice that the issue of violence has to do with a gathered impression of violence whose correspondence with reality is somewhat complex. For example, there is no carte blanche approach to violence. There is, however, a condoning attitude by some, a reflective attitude on the use of violence as a limited alternative by others, an option for non-violence by some well-known theologians and activists, and a commitment to guerrilla warfare as a response to faith by still others.

The mainstream of liberation theologians and activists operate within an ethical context that considers violence an evil, though a lesser one in some circumstances and hence permissible within the Church's established social doctrine. For them violence occurs when dominant groups respond violently to nonviolent actions protesting social and political conditions. In other words, the oppressed do not initiate it. Moreover, they do not consider violence as the only means of liberation, though some acknowledge that historically, oppressive violence has not been overcome without recourse to violence. In addition, violence is always considered a means within the context of love, which may require its use at times when justifiable moral reasons can be presented, while striving toward its reduction.

Theologians point out that if resistance to change is present along with an unwillingness by the ruling groups to consider the demands and the aspirations of the poor, the only way to avoid violence is for the oppressed to accept their condition. In such circumstances a moral call for non-violence can be easily co-opted by the dominant classes to perpetuate the status quo. From a liberation perspective, violence by the oppressed appears as an act of struggle against sin. It is the external material manifestation of its counterpart, the internal spiritual struggle that takes place within the soul when the believer combats sin and eradicates it from the inside. In this respect violence is the means available to redeem, i.e., rescue, people from the sin of oppressive violence.

Theologians and activists find a biblical basis in the recourse to violence as manifestations of God's wrath, and in retribution against the oppressor. Hence there is a distinction between a violence that is evil and condemnable, and one that is just and a means of self-defense. The negative image that the oppressed project through violence is that it appears immoral and illegal because it goes against established authority and order.[91] The predominant view of those who accept violence in liberation theology is characterized by its limited and defensive use, guided by evangelical consideration and based on ethical reflection. Obviously, this is not a pacifist position, but neither does it accept violence as the only alternative on an *a priori* basis.

Another group of theologians and activists, also well within the mainstream of the movement, advocate a form of active non-violence. Though they are able to understand and to some extent may empathize with limited use of violence, they see this option as contributing to a spiral of violence. Their attitudes are based on the possibility of carrying out a revolution without recourse to violent means, following Christ's footsteps by facing violence with a conscious and willful acceptance of suffering and even martyrdom. This group is not any less vocal in their opposition to repression. However, they see violence as disrupting the moral efficacy of love and as a negative model on which to base a new society.[92]

A third category includes militants who have joined the ranks of rural guerrilla movements in their respective countries as an overt and bold commitment to their faith. Some of them arrive at their decisions as the result of personal reflection within their ecclesiastical basic communities. These groups do not suggest, much less force, their members to join the guerrillas. Each one, when confronted with the liberation objective, decides what course of action to take, given the analysis of the situation and the personal exigencies of his faith.[93] These people see their option for organized violence as a last yet necessary alternative. Their decisions are made within a framework similar to the first category of theologians and activists. They are the hundreds of Nestor Paz's and Camilo Torres's who have remained anonymous in the sense that they have not written about their personal understanding of faith and its relation to liberation and violence. Nonetheless, we may assume that their involvement with the guerrillas reflects deep religious convictions and takes into account certain ethical guidelines.

The previous category should be differentiated from the more radical militants who follow rigid political ideologies and tend to accept violence *a priori* as a means to weaken and demoralize the established system. Some members of these groups are of Catholic extraction. However, they do not function within a liberation theology framework and observe no apparent Christian ethical values.[94]

In liberation theology then, violence plays a secondary, limited, and defensive role. The personal decision leading to that option normally would take place within a religious context, which defines and limits its scope. Here, conscientization prepares the oppressed to resist subjugation. It creates a new type of Christian. Sobrino refers to it — not as the type described by

Marx, resigned and without hope, but as the one who presents a political threat.[95] This approach to violence is similar to the counterpart struggle in Poland, in which the Solidarity movement actively participates and where the Church has played a significant role in creating a liberation awareness among its members. Here too, violence becomes a defensive weapon, though to a much lesser extent, since there repression is better organized.

Perhaps the most radical view in liberation theology is that of presenting violence as a possible expression of love. This may appear somewhat disconcerting, for although the Church has relied on violence before, such means do not usually appear in its doctrine as a manifestation of love. Traditionally, it has been regarded as an evil. Likewise, liberation theology shares the same view. As Girardi states, in a violent conflict between the oppressed and the oppressor one does not choose between a good violence and an evil one, but between two evils.[96] This does not mean that violence cannot be manifested as a means through which love can be expressed. The soldier, for example, may be called to show his love for his country in the battlefield. And, from the standpoint of the Christian exigency, the love of God may demand no less. As Johann Metz shows, there is an ethical balance in the use of violence which in liberation theology mitigates the tension between the love of God and the love of neighbor. He says:

> The love of God may require personal acceptance, resigning oneself to endure the injustice of which one is the victim. But the love of neighbor cannot accept the oppression against others, against the least of our brothers, nor pretend to love God turning one's back on those who suffer.[97]

The conflict in Christian morality arises because the issue of love and violence has been mostly interpreted in a religious culture in terms of opposites, and because the Christian rule to love one's enemy, manifested though the acceptance of injury and forgiveness, has been made the ideal in personal life. However, if one makes an absolute categorical imperative of the ideal, it would limit the ways in which the commandment to love one's neighbor could be actualized in a situation of conflict. From the standpoint of means and ends, the only ways for a person to comply with the commandment would be either to mediate the conflict or to assist the victim while seeking an eventual reconciliation with the oppressor. But defending the victim out of love entails taking sides and participating in the struggle. The dilemma is inescapable. Either one becomes part of the conflict, or else he remains unable to help the person in need.

There is still another decision left: how to join the struggle. We may assume that non-violent means should always be tried first, and they usually are or have been within the liberation movement. As a group of militant Christians in El Salvador once remarked, "the first thing that a just insurrection tells us is that God's patience has reached its limit."[98] But once the oppressor answers non-violent activities with violence or increased repression, the Christian must then opt between martyrdom and violence. And, though the former may be highly commendable and spiritually uplifting from a religious perspective, in Christian morality it still remains an ideal, not a commandment. As we have seen, there are those within the liberation movement who choose martyrdom as part of the praxis, while in the others one does not notice a philosophy of violence per se. Hence, that martyrdom is not the only option available should not lead one to conclude that in liberation theology violence is either a more effective or preferred choice. The issue appears rather as a serious dilemma that once again reveals the eschatological tension in faith.

NOTES

[1]Richard, *La Iglesia Latinoamericana,* p. 23.

[2]Ellacuría, *Freedom Made Flesh,* pp. 150, 153.

[3]José Marins, et al., *Iglesia y Conflictividad Social en América Latina* (Bogotá: Ediciones Paulinas, 1975), p. 12.

[4]Movimiento Sacerdotal ONIS, "Situación del Pueblo y Responsabilidad Cristiana," in *Signos de Lucha y Esperanza,* pp. 36-37.

[5]Organizaciones Laicas de Sao Paulo, "Por Justicia y Liberación," in Ibid., pp. 45-48; Obispos y Misioneros, "El Indio: Aquel Que Debe Morir," in Ibid., pp. 94-97.

[6]Juan Luis Segundo, "De la Sociedad a la Teología," p. 118, quoted in Oliveros, p. 141.

[7]Enrique Dussel, "Historical and Philosophical Presuppositions for Latin American Theology," in Gibellini, p. 198.

[8]Christians for Socialism, "Final Document," in Eagleson, p. 164.

[9]Movimiento Sacerdotal ONIS, "Trabajo Humano y Propiedad Social," in *Signos de Lucha,* p. 170.

[10]Movimiento Sacerdotal ONIS, "Propiedad Privada y Nueva Sociedad," in *Signos de Liberación,* pp. 223-224.

[11]ONIS, "Trabajo Humano," in *Signos de Lucha,* p. 173.

[12]See footnote no. 82 in chapter IV.

[13]Gonzalo Arroyo, "Teoría de la Dependencia," *Christus* 539 (octubre 1980): 15-22.

[14]Ibid.

[15]Klaus Knorr, for example, says that most charges about imperialism and neocolonialism stem from "a genuine sense of grievance," past colonial experiences, and from "malcontent intellectuals" under the influence of Marxism-Leninism. *The Power of Nations* (New York: Basic Books, Inc., 1975), pp. 291-292. A basic problem with this view is that, as he states, imperialism is difficult to prove empirically, evaluations tend to be subjective as a result, and there is a lack of objective criteria concerning neocolonialism. Ibid., p. 307. He adds that "the equation of uneven development and neocolonialism smacks of doctrinal legerdemain." Ibid., p. 308.

[16]As the late Raúl Prebisch, a noted Argentinian economist, points out, "the dynamic of the Center propels development in the periphery insofar as it benefits the interests of the Center's dominant groups." *Capitalismo Periférico — Crisis y Transformaciones* (Mexico, D.F.: Fondo de Cultura Económica, 1981), p. 37.

[17]Ibid., pp. 39-41.

[18]Knorr, p. 255.

[19]See, for example, Robert O. Keohane and Joseph S. Nye, *Power and Interdependence* (Boston: Little, Brown and Co., 1977), and Marshall R. Singer, *Weak States in a World of Power* (New York: The Free Press, 1972).

[20]Along these lines, Prebisch says that although the United States is aware of the social inequalities, it refuses to acknowledge that they are related to the capitalist system. P. 329.

[21]Theotonio Dos Santos, *Dependencia y Cambio Social* (Santiago: CESO, 1970), p. 45.

[22]Arroyo, "Teoría de la Dependencia," pp. 19-22.

[23]J.P. Franco, *La Influencia de los Estados Unidos en América Latina,* quoted in Gutiérrez, *Teología de la Liberación,* p. 120. Prebisch adds the same point some years later:

> "The Center propagates and irradiates in the Periphery its techniques, forms of consumption and way of life, its institutions, ideas, and ideologies. Peripheric capitalism is more and more inspired by the Center, and tends to develop in its image." (p. 39).

[24]P. Renato Poblete, "La Teoría de la Dependencia: Análisis Crítico," in *Diálogos,* p. 210.

[25]Gutiérrez agrees with A. G. Frank, one who has worked in developing the theory of dependence, who says that the term "dependency" is but a euphemism used to speak about oppression, injustice, and alienation. In *Teología de la Liberación,* p. 234 (footnote).

[27]Gutiérrez points out that the one is not separated from the other. It is all one complex process "that finds its profound meaning and its ultimate realization in Christ's salvific task." Ibid., pp. 68-69.

[28]Although after Vatican II the Church no longer considers salvation as an ahistorical process, and has incorporated a socio-political view of liberation, it continues to approach faith primarily in terms of liberation from sin, the personal dimension.

[29]As Boff says, "the present condition calls us to stress the social, economic, and political aspect of liberation because it is in those levels where oppression and social sin is mostly experienced by man, and it is there where Christ's liberation can be experienced most radically, . . ." *Teología Desde el Cautiverio,* pp. 93-94.

[30]*Gaudium et spes,* no. 19. In Vatican II, which was primarily the result of an European and North American mentality and theology, the issues of secularism and atheism strongly influenced its participants, leading to a rediscovery of the essential praxis of evangelization.

[31]John 14:6.

[32]Castro's quote, from a speech to Church representatives in Jamaica in 1977, was cited by Sergio Arce Martinez, "Cristo vivo en Cuba," and quoted by Juan Hernández Pico, S.J., "El Proceso Político en la Nicaragua Liberada," *Christus* 538 (septiembre 1980): 13; the Chilean Cardinal's quote appears in Eagleson, p. 4.

[33]Juan Luis Segundo, "Capitalism Versus Socialism: Crux Theologica," in Gibellini, pp. 240-259; Richard, *La Iglesia,* pp. 76-78; Christians for Socialism, in Eagleson, pp. 3-5; Oliveros, p. 36; Gutiérrez, *Teología de la Liberación,* p. 58; Dom Helder Cámara, "Cristianismo y Socialismo," in *Signos de Liberación,* pp. 213-214; Gonzalo Arroyo, "Socialismo," *Christus* 534 (mayo 1980): 61-63; Episcopado del Peru, "La Justicia en el Mundo," in *Signos de Liberación,* pp. 180-181; Obispos de Nicaragua, "Compromiso Cristiano con una Nueva Nicaragua," *Christus* 531 (febrero 1980): 54-58.

[34]Movimiento Obrero de Acción Católica, "Declaración, " in *Signos de Liberación,* p. 235.

[35]Christians for Socialism, "Chilean National Report," in Eagleson, p. 118. Also, see pp. 168, 174 for references about Marxist alliances, and about Che Guevara.

[36]"El Presente de Chile y el Evangelio," n.a., quoted in Gutiérrez, *Teología de la Liberación,* p. 158.

[37]Ibid.

[38]*The Holy Family,* quoted in Dupre, p. 144.

[39]Alberto Arroyo, "Cambio Estructural," *Christus* 534 (mayo 1980): 18.

[40]Paulo Freire, "Letter to a Young Theology Student," reprinted in LADOC series, no. 1 *Paulo Freire* (Washington, D.C.: United States Catholic Conference, 1980), p. 10.

[41]*Instruction I,* no. 15.

[42]Ibid.

[43]Christians for Socialism, in Eagleson, p. 165.

[44]Gustavo Gutiérrez, "Liberation Praxis and Christian Faith," in Gibellini, p. 11.

[46]*Instruction II,* no. 75.

[47]Juan Carlos Scannone, "Ontología del Proceso Autenticamente Liberador," in Equipo SELADOC — Universidad Catolica de Chile, *Panorama de la Teología Latinoamericana* (Salamanca, España: Ediciones Sígueme, 1975), pp. 253-254.

[48]Ibid. p. 273.

[49]F. Hervé Chaigne, O.F.M. "Son los Pobres los que se Liberan," in "Freres du

Monde," ed., *La Violencia de los Pobres,* trans. from the French edition into Spanish by Juan Estruch (Barcelona, España: Editorial Nova Terra, 1968), pp. 35-37.

[50]"Documento Final del Encuentro Intereclesial de Comunidades de Base," Itaici, Brazil, reprinted in *Christus* 548 (septiembre 1981): 48-49.

[51]Luis del Valle, "Acompañar al Pueblo," *Christus* 547 (agosto 1981): 45-47.

[52]In Brazil, there are millions of participants who act as the government's opposition. They operate under the protection of the Church, and will likely be instrumental in future elections. (From conference by María Herrera Moreira Alves at the Institute for Policy Studies, Washington, D.C. Feb. 18, 1982).

[53]Freire, *Pedagogy,* pp. 51-55.

[54]Freire, "Conscientizing as a Way," pp. 4-6.

[55]*Octogesima Adveniens,* n. 4.

[56]Segundo, "Capitalism," p. 249.

[57]Ibid., p. 255.

[58]Comblin, "Freedom and Liberation," p. 103.

[59]Obispos de Nicaragua, "Compromiso Cristiano," p. 56.

[60]Ibid.

[61]Prebisch, p. 331.

[62]*Instruction I,* no. 10.2.

[63]Pope Pius XI, *Divini redemptoris,* March 19, 1937, 9.

[64]*Instruction I,* no. 8.5-6.

[65]Ibid., nos. 9.2,6; 10.2.5; 11.7.

[66]Ibid., nos. 9.3; 11.7.

[67]López Trujillo, "Las Teologías de la Liberación," pp. 42-45; and in *Hacia Una Sociedad Nueva* (Bogotá: Ediciones Paulinas, 1978), pp. 43-48.

[68]Jules Girardi, pp. 44, 52, 67-69.

[69]Canada, Homily at Namao Airport, Sept. 17, 1984, no. 4.

[70]Karl Marx and Frederick Engels, *Selected Works,* vol. 1 (Moscow: Progress Publishers, 1969), Sec. 1 passim.

[71]See for example, Gutiérrez, in "Liberation Praxis," pp. 9, 17, 28; Christians for Socialism, in Eagleson , pp. 5, 162, 166; Assman, *Theology for a Nomad Church,* pp. 98-99; Dussel, *Ethics,* pp. 88-89; Movimiento Sacerdotal ONIS, "III Encuentro Nacional de ONIS," in *Signos de Liberación,* pp. 249-251.

[72]*Puebla,* nos. 31-40.

[73]*Diálogos,* pp. 52-53.

[74]*Instruction I,* no.1.1.

[75]*Diálogos,* p. 52.

[76]*Instruction I,* no. 1.

[77]*Diálogos,* p. 52.

[78]Pedro Trigo, S.J. ¿"Giro en la Política Religiosa del Partido Comunista Cubano?" in *Christus* 545 (mayo 1981): 36.

[79]Ibid.

[80]These observations are based on a close examination of numerous religious and political educational pamphlets being distributed by militant Christians in Nicaragua.

[81]*Instruction I,* no. 7.8.

[82]Alberto Arroyo, "Clases Sociales," in *Christus* 534 (mayo 1980): 24.

[83]*Instruction I,* no. 4.14.

[84]Ibid., no. 7.12.

[85]Ibid., no. 11.8.

[86]Lucien Pelissier, "La Iglesia y la Lucha de Clases," in *La Violencia,* p. 178.

[87]*Diálogos,* pp. 89-90.

[88]Matthew 12:30.

[89]Girardi, p. 59.

[90]Matthew 23:13-36; Matthew 21:12-13.

[91]Ellacuría, *Freedom,* pp. 62, 183, 193-210; Gutierrez, *Teologia de la Liberación,* p. 150; Nestor Paz, "Al Pueblo de Bolivia," in *Signos de Liberación,* pp. 43-44; Segundo, *Liberation of Theology,* pp. 162-166; Conferencia Episcopal de Nicaragua, "Cristianos en Solidaridad con Nicaragua," in *Servir* 81 (tercer bimestre 1979): 368; Hugo Assman, "El Lugar Propio de una Teología de la Revolución," tran. Javier Medina-Dávila, in *Selecciones de Teología* 38 (1971): 167; Dussel, *Ethics,* pp. 43, 48, 67; Jon Sobrino, "La Esperanza de los Pobres en América Latina," in *Diakonia* 25 (enero-marzo 1983): 20-21; José Miquez-Bonino, "Popular Piety in Latin America," in Geffré, p. 154.

[92]Dom Helder Cámara, "La Violencia en el Mundo Moderno," in *Signos de Renovación,* pp. 72-74; Galilea, "Liberation Theology," pp. 174-177; José Marins, et al., *Iglesia y Conflictividad,* pp. 90-92; Sacerdotes para el Tercer Mundo, "Reflexión Sobre la Violencia," in *Signos de Liberación,* pp. 85-89; Boff, "Christ's Liberation," pp. 120-121.

[93]Clodovis Boff, "Fisionomía de las Comunidades Eclesiales de Base," *Diakonia* 19 (agosto-octubre 1981): 2-9; del Valle, pp. 45-47; Comunidades Eclesiales de Base de Nicaragua, "Carta Abierta a los Obispos, Sacerdotes, Religiosos y demas Laicos del Pueblo de Dios," *ECA* (agosto 1980): 825-830; "Documento Final," pp. 48-49; Arnaldo Zenteno, "Compromiso por la Liberación," *Christus* 548 (septiembre 1981): 41-47.

[94]We refer, primarily, to those who have joined guerrilla groups that tend to use violence indiscriminately against civilian populations.

[95]Sobrino, "La Esperanza. . . ," p. 12.

[96]Girardi, p. 68.

[97]Johannes B. Metz, S.J., "Para una Cultura Política de la Paz," *Christus* 542 (febrero 1981): 26.

[98]Seis Organizaciones Católicas en El Salvador," Sobre la Ofensiva de Enero," *ECA* 36 (enero-febrero 1981): 88.

5. LIBERATION THEOLOGY AND THE CHURCH

The attempt to implement liberation theology is relevant to Latin American politics insofar as the theology becomes part of Church doctrine. This is to say that liberation theology needs the hierarchy's seal of approval to legitimize its work since such a support would make the liberation task more effective. Without Church support, liberation theology would probably become either another religious sect or a political ideology, thereby losing much of its significance. Hence to estimate the political impact that the liberation movement may have in the region, this chapter will seek to find out the extent to which the Catholic Church has accepted its views. In this manner it will be possible to tell whether or not a synthesis between the two theological approaches has taken place. In doing so, this chapter will focus on the Puebla document, which emerged from the bishops' conference that took place in Mexico during January and February 1979, and on Pope John Paul II's speeches during his tours throughout Latin America.

The Church's judgment of liberation theology needs to be understood within the context of what in international politics is known as the national interest. The difference, however, is that while nations often accommodate this concept to their convenience, the Church, although guided by practical considerations like any other human institution, is more uncompromising in its objectives. Fidelity to its mission tends to characterize the

Church's behavior. There are several primary considerations that have guided the Church throughout history. All are interrelated and each has played a more or less primary role in different situations.

First, there is the need in the Church to maintain and assert both its ecclesiastical and its teaching authority, and indicate that these are directly linked to its founder Jesus Christ. We are not referring to unity or to the physical survival of the institution, which are two other important considerations, but to the presence of ecclesiastical authority. Second, largely determining the rationale for authority, is the necessity of safeguarding the doctrine. The Church is the guardian of the dogma and acts as its doctrinal interpreter, and attempts to be faithful to its duty by attempting to prevent errors in orthodoxy. Third, the most essential consideration in maintaining orthodoxy, hence the central nerve in the Church, is the need to affirm the eschatological transcendence of its mission and the divinity of Jesus Christ. In other words, what distinguishes religion from philosophy or science or politics is that, unlike any of them, it has its origin in the belief in a supernatural being. Thus the presence of eschatology is crucial to Church doctrine.

A fourth important objective is for the Church to do as much as possible to seek and to insure its physical presence in every part of the world. This aspect is basic to its duty to evangelize, i.e., to spread the "good news" to all. This is the primary reason for which the Church was founded. This function, however, presents the Church with a dilemma today, in that with visibility comes an involvement with building the earthly city. In many instances in Latin America, silence and lack of involvement in temporal affairs is a prerequisite for Church survival. Thus the institution has to constantly weigh how far it wishes to go in challenging the status quo.

In addition, there are two determining factors that seemingly are the product of modern times. One is the excessive political violence and the constant threat of war throughout different parts of the world. The Church, as witnessed especially in the speeches of popes in this century, contends that present civilization needs an international actor to denounce war as evil and to serve as the symbol of a peacemaking institution. The other one, by far the most conditioning of all, is Marxism, which in Latin America continues to prevent the Church from effectively doing its task out of fear of appearing to support radical objectives and of running the risk of being ideologically co-opted. The political implementation of a radical Marxist-Leninist collectivism would constitute a challenge to each of the Church's interests just mentioned.

Before assessing the extent to which the Church has given its support to liberation theology, a small caveat is in order with regard to Puebla. This conference was the third since CELAM (Latin American bishops conference) was created. The conferences have been held approximately every ten years. The theme at Puebla, *Evangelization in the Present and the Future of Latin America,* points to the way in which the Church will spread the gospel and bear witness to the faith in years to come. Especially since *Evangelii nuntiandi* was published in 1975, the term evangelization has adopted a much broader connotation than in the past, when it referred to priests spreading the gospel and administering the sacraments. Now, not only are the laity involved in these tasks, but a praxis that includes the "wordless" witnessing of the faith, i.e., acting in a "Christian manner" and imbuing the culture with Christian values, would be considered evangelization.[1] Moreover, Pope Paul VI clarified his belief that liberation is an important Church function. He calls on the institution to join in:

> the effort and the struggle to overcome everything which condemns people to remain on the margin of life: famine, chronic disease, illiteracy, poverty, injustices in international relations and especially in commerical exchanges, situations of economic and cultural neo-colonialism sometimes as cruel as the

> old political colonialism. The Church has the duty to proclaim the liberation of millions of human beings, many of whom are her own children — the duty of assisting the birth of this liberation, of giving witness to it, of ensuring that it is complete.[2]

According to the view that Medellín had received papal support, the liberation movement had spread noticeably within the Church, especially among the clergy. However, the continuous identification of a large number of activists with Marxism, and the confusion and rift that the new theology was causing, worried some bishops and the Vatican enough to seek to use the Puebla conference to either slow down or alter the orientation of liberation theology. Through the evangelization criteria, Medellín and its offspring were reevaluated.[3]

Interpreting Puebla is not an easy task, and more than Medellín it needs to be read "between the lines." The document does not represent a compromise in which all involved agreed to approve a common content. Rather it was an exercise in compromise in which the different positions represented were allowed to emerge; thus one hears more than one voice in the document. As a result, in many sections there is no sense of consistency, but chunks of different ideas are interposed next to one another. Under these circumstance, some ambiguity is unavoidable.[4] The document that was initially approved by the bishops was also slightly changed afterward. The modifications do not alter the essence of the document, though according to some they resulted in weakening the original.[5] The changes were primarily the work of former Archbishop López Trujillo who represented the Vatican line and who, depending on the perspective, belongs to either the conservative or the progressive faction at Puebla. For practical purposes the bishop's tendency, as Berryman states, could be considered "to the left of the Democratic party in the United States."[6]

The occurrence of a novel incident regarding the final document's index, along with the discussed changes, sheds some light on the attitude of those who prepared the final version. The index includes not only what *is* in the document but also what *is not*. The entries for "Socialism" and "Theology of Liberation" state that "the expressions do not occur once." Also, in the index the term "Socialism" is identified with "Marxist Collectivism."[7] Thus the implicit message in the document is that the Church is prepared to accept liberation theology but with some basic reservations. The most important of these are that it will not choose violence as a means to redress social conditions and that it will not propagate a Marxist ideology in the name of faith.

Examining liberation theology's main components will provide a more complete picture of liberation which in turn will help to gauge the Church's support for the movement. References to the Puebla document throughout this section appear in parentheses. Other citations will be footnoted.

The Option for the Poor

Without casting aside its traditional value of "spiritual poverty," i.e., the Christian detachment from material trappings and possessions, Puebla has made a firm and decisive choice for the poor by calling attention to the conditions of material poverty in which millions live, denouncing those conditions as sinful and contrary to God's plan (28) and as anti-evangelical (1159). The poor are called the "favorites of God" (1143), and "notwithstanding a deviation from the Medellín spirit" by some, the Church makes a "preferential" option for them (1134).

The bishops, however, have refused to make an exclusive and excluding political option for the poor, as some within liberation theology have wished. To do so would amount to closing the Church doors to some people on the basis of ideological social categories. Aside from committing the institution to a possible Marxist-Leninist class struggle, such an option could lead to a substitution of a political for a religious conversion. Hence, this policy constitutes a refinement of the post-Medellín period, created to deal with a problem not then foreseen. As it is, the Church is committed to the liberation of the poor but with certain limitations that safeguard its praxis from doctrinal deviations. The Church's position subtly weakens any Marxist-Leninist interpretation without detracting from its indictment of those who are responsible for poverty. It constitutes an affirmation of its support for the poor rather than an attack on the rich.

Deprivatization of the Faith

The document emphasizes that the gospel is mutilated when its economic, social, and political aspects are not considered (558). It criticizes those who exclude these issues from the faith, "as if sin, love, prayer, and forgiveness had not any relevance in these areas" (515). Evangelization seeks social transformation (362), and as Pope John Paul II remarked: "evangelization would not be complete unless it took into account the relations existing between the Gospel message and man's personal and social living, between the commandment to love one's suffering and needy neighbor and concrete situations where injustice must be combatted and justice and peace be installed."[8]

Puebla gives faith a political role by deprivatizing it. Further on, the document recognizes the global aspect of politics and holds political activity in high esteem (513-514). Nonetheless, it rejects the notion that everything can and should be reduced to the political realm (483, 513). Though it casts aside political reductionism, the document reflects the political nature of problems in Latin America. Roughly one-half of its content has a strict social and political implication.

Analysis of Reality

The document begins with an exposition of the socio-cultural reality of Latin America (15-71). Its pastoral doctrine is based on considerations of what is perceived as the people's most important social aspirations (126-141). Thus Puebla reveals that the bishops have continued the Medellín and liberation theology tradition of presenting solutions on the basis of an assessment of historical and material reality. Moreover, it acknowledges the need for a concerted effort to discern "the causes and conditionings of social reality" (826). This means that the traditional approach identified with Jacques Maritain's neo-Christendom, in which principles of social action are forced *a priori* into historical reality, is discarded.

Incorporation of the Social Sciences

The document, through the analysis of reality, is a testimony to the extent to which the bishops have depended on the social sciences. One must take into account, however, that it is mainly a theological-pastoral work. The bishops themselves do not feel entirely comfortable using other than their own terminology and methodology. They approach the social sciences with a suspicious eye, for they feel that these can be ideologically manipulated or conditioned.

The bishops also reject a strict scientific vision that reduces truth and humanity to its own empirical standards (315). Nonetheless, among the initiatives suggested under the Church's program of action for a pluralist society in Latin America, there is a surprising paragraph that could prove decisive for future conferences and for theology. It states:

> It is expected of (scientists) especially, research work that leads to the synthesis between science and faith. . . . For this, an interdisciplinary dialogue of theology, philosophy, and science, in search of new syntheses, becomes necessary (1240).

Use of Marxist Analysis

Marxism, both as an ideology and as a social system, is

strongly condemned several times (92, 418, 437, 543, 546). Yet, there is no rejection of its use as a tool for social analysis. The document does show important reservations: it views the Marxist analysis with concern (91), points out the risk to those who use it of politicizing Christian existence (545), and warns of the inherent danger of conditioning the praxis by using it without recognizing its historical ties with class struggle, totalitarianism, and violence (544). This is as far as the bishops could realistically venture in view of what has previously been stated. That is, the Church must leave the doors open to the possibility of a reformulation of Marxism as a philosophy, as a scientific approach, and even as a historical realization. Also, though the document does not make such distinction, those who prepared it were well aware of the historical distinctions between Marxism as a theoretical approach and its various implementations by others who have often given it their own orientation.[9]

Dependence

There seems to be little doubt that Marxism helped to uncover the reality of dependence. Its analysis was not done, however, from a dogmatic Marxist standpoint or even using pure Marxist methodology. In this case Marxism has played more of a heuristic role. Revealing once again its reliance on social science terminology and on instrumental use of Marxist concepts, the Puebla document keeps the term "dependence" and accepts it as one of the conditions responsible for the ills in the region (66). Dependence, furthermore, is related in the document to liberal capitalism (542) and to the world powers which possess high degrees of technology and scientific know-how (417). Though the bishops clearly want to disassociate themselves from any Marxist interpretation, in the end they incorporate the crux of the theory, including the domination/dependence circle. The analysis leads to denunciation of structural dependence and, implicitly, to a commitment in favor of political liberation from those conditions:

> Unfortunately, in many cases . . . our own nations' political and economic institutions, beyond the normal and reciprocal relations, are subjected to more powerful centers that operate at an international level. The situation is worsened by the fact that these centers of power are secretly structured, everywhere present, and they easily elude control by the govenments and even international organizations (501).

Rereading

Giving new meaning to the Scriptures is as necessary as it is problematic. The Church itself has always recognized that while the dogma may remain the same, the Word of God is never static. Pope John Paul II has stated that "the function of theology is to find liberation's true significance within the diverse and concrete contemporary historical contexts."[10] From the standpoint of Puebla, rereading is permissible as long as it is done while safeguarding the integrity of the dogma and without departing from the Church's doctrine. This is one Church principle that clashes with liberation theology, especially since the theologians in the movement have been instrumental in pointing out that while revealed truth may be impervious to cultural conditioning, the doctrine is not. Thus the question is how to keep the doctrine "honest" if Church officials refuse to acknowledge the cultural crust in religion.

Given the freedom that the Church has extended to theologians to pursue their activity, we see the institution using liberation theology as a corrective element. The Church's major objection, however, is that when rereading takes place the tendency is to identify the gospel with a political option, and to interpret the former in light of the latter (559). Rejection of this approach goes to the core of an ideological praxis, be it Marxist or capitalist. In the case of liberation theology, the overall result has been not to discredit the praxis, but to keep it within the parameters of gospel values and, indirectly, under the Church's teaching authority. Depending upon the trust that the Vatican and the bishops develop in liberation theologians and the latitude extended to them, this last issue may prevent a politicized gospel. It appears that the hierarchy is suggesting that the theologians' writings follow the Church's model, in which presentation of the doctrine accompanies the analysis and the conclusions.

Denunciation of Capitalism

Liberation theology has a strong anti-capitalist orientation. In the document, the bishops are as harshly critical of liberal capitalism as they are of Marxist collectivism. This approach is obviously not favored by the socialist wing of liberation theology, primarily because it weakens their attack against the system that prevails over most of Latin America, the one they think is most responsible for the injustices denounced in the document. Some feel that this middle-of-the-road position is ideologically determined. Mikel Munarriz, a Latin American critic of the document, for example, sees an indirect confession by the bishops that the Latin American version of capitalism is more cruel than they portray it, and that they would attack it more persistently if it were not (in the bishops' own words), "for the fear of Marxism that impedes many from facing the oppressive reality of Liberal Capitalism" (92).[11]

The implicit idea in the above argument seems to be that if it were not for the existence of Marxism, the Church itself would adopt a socialist position. This is not necessarily so. What the document implies is that Church denunciations would perhaps be even stronger in the absence of Marxism. The fear of Marxism is only determining the extent and the strategy of confrontation against the capitalist-oriented systems for two basic reasons: one is to avoid giving support to Marxist groups in their attacks against capitalism, thus bolstering their credibility; second, to prevent "rightist" governments from using the Marxist infiltration argument as an excuse to persecute the Church.[12]

Moreover, this third position by the Church is at least theoretically aligned with its doctrinal stand of not identifying itself with any political system.

Thus Puebla's denunciation of capitalism is almost identical to that in liberation theology, but without some of the Marxist concepts. Both the capitalist and the Marxist collectivist systems are marked by sin (92). Both violate principles of human dignity (550) and inspire structures that generate injustices (437). Both are atheist, capitalism given its value orientation and Marxism because of its atheistic militance (546). And finally, both systems give way to institutionalized violence and injustice (509, 531, 532).

Condemnation of the National Security Ideology

The bishops agreed that it was necessary to make the important distinction between the capitalist and the national security ideologies. Though often they go together, the latter finds its own justification in the attacks by the opposition against capitalism, which present a threat to the political culture and the status quo that protects the economic system. According to Puebla, national security systems in Latin America have been repressive and abusive of their powers. They have been characterized by violations of numerous human rights, including torture, disappearance, and arbitrary detentions (42). They have led to totalitarian or authoritarian uses of power, in many instances "under the pretext of defending Western civilization and Christianity," all the while "professing a Christian faith" (49, 547).

The Role of the Church

Liberation theology stresses the need for the Church to participate actively in the liberation process, specifically in its political aspects. Medellín committed the bishops to involvement with political issues, and from then on many priests and other members of religious orders began taking part in social protests and community organization. A few, along with many more from the laity, either openly supported or actually participated in the guerrilla movement. Also, many within the clergy were becoming identified with versions of Marxist socialism.

Puebla was supposed to have been a restraining force on liberation theology, and to some extent it was. To begin with, priests and the religious orders were advised not to become involved in partisan politics or work in an official capacity for any government, "unless under concrete and exceptional circumstances the well-being of the community requires it," and then only with the consent of the bishops. The reason for imposing such limitations was that as official representatives of the Kingdom of God, the clergy might create the false impression that the kingdom is identified with a specific political system. The Church cannot support a determined political program any more than a political party, "no matter how inspired it may be by the Church's doctrine, may arrogate the representation of all the faithful, since its concrete programme will never be able to have an absolute value for all" (523, 527). To the bishops, partisan politics exercises a conditioning effect that is detrimental to the desired unity within the Church. Free of ideologies, the bishops think that the clergy can authentically evangelize the political realm as Christ did (526).

Many within liberation theology were probably disappointed with this position, even though for the Church to have done the opposite would have fulfilled the liberation theologians' own warning against Church collusion with government. Liberation theology, of course, would not have minded, since in this case the Church would then be supporting liberation-oriented governments. In their understandable desire to be effective while helping the poor, liberation theologians do not realize the value of a critical Church on the side of the poor, involved in political issues but not in a partisan manner. From the moment the Church aligns itself with either a political party or a system of government, it compromises its credibility by associating with groups that are not under its authority and upon whom it cannot exert direct influence. In short, the Church would be justifying a system for which it will not have any responsibility.

These limitations have been interpreted by the public at large to mean that the Church has forbidden the clergy from becoming involved in politics. This rule, however, although traditional in the Church, is only applicable to partisan politics. Politics, defined in its broader context which seeks the common good of the society, is of great interest and importance to the Church. From this angle, it seeks to balance the traditional issues in politics: internal stability with national security, equality with freedom, governmental authority with legitimate autonomy and participation of groups and individuals, national sovereignty with international solidarity, and, we may add, the social duties with individual rights (521).

In this area both the pope and the bishops have embraced an extensive praxis of denunciation and political involvement. Along with deprivatization, and because of it, this aspect of liberation theology has been among the most significant changes in the Latin American Church, especially when viewed against the background of its traditional pre-Vatican II mentality. It has transformed the institution from a spiritualized and evasive Church into a prophetic one, committed to the human race. Upon his return from the conference, while discussing the role of liberation theology, Pope John Paul II remarked:

> In the service of truth and of Christ's prophetic role it is the duty of the Church to call by its name injustice, man's exploitation by man, or the exploitation of man by the State, by Institutions, by economic mechanisms and systems, and by regimes that often act without sensitivity. We have to call by its name every social injustice, discrimination, violence inflicted against man, his body, and his spirit, against

his conscience, and against his convictions.[13]

Puebla has demanded of governments the right to give witness, and to denounce the "false images of society which are incompatible with a Christian vision" (1213). It assumes the struggle for justice, just as it did in Medellín (87-90, 92, 562), and has made the defense of human rights the platform for socio-political liberation (90, 146, 318, 337, 338).

Basic Ecclesiastical Communities

The document has recognized the positive results that grassroots evangelization has brought about through basic ecclesiastical communities (CEBs) (96-97). Despite attempts by political groups to manipulate these communities for other than religious purposes (98), the CEBs have received the hierarchy's support (156). A negative review would have given the liberation movement a fatal blow, mainly because this approach has proven to be the most effective and least expensive means of evangelization. With the approval of such an organizational approach, liberation theology may well spread even more among the poor classes. CEBs may constitute the best indicator of the direction and the intensity of the movement in the next few years.

The New Man

The document's model for the "new man" compares in some degree with the one proposed by liberation theology. Both include "a moral conscience, a gospel-like critical attitude vis-á-vis reality, a communitarian spirit, and a social commitment" (308). Both present the figure of Jesus Christ as a role model. In Puebla, however, Christ and Mary are the only concrete examples given, and are continually stressed throughout the work (197, 298, 333, 1296). The document rejects the reduction of Christ's image to a political revolutionary or liberator (178). Instead he appears as the one who summons all people to an integral liberation, one that includes liberation from sin as well as from oppression (1183).

As in the case of liberation theology, the new man is someone who is converted to the poor (1134, 1140), to justice and love (1206). His conversion must lead to a commitment to liberation, which entails the "swift and far-reaching transformation of structures" (438). At the same time this new man is peaceful, rejects violent methods, and in the end holds no grudges against his enemies. He would oppose egoism and unjust structures, and as a result would take a stand against those who resist changes by denouncing them, but would not take part in a Marxist-Leninist type class struggle based on hatred (486). In summary, the new man, according to the document, is not so much a socially conditioned individual (largely the product of social structures). In Puebla the ideal is best described as a converted socially-oriented being. This implies that the person's individuality is not absorbed or lost in the socialization process, while his social dimension is mainly inspired by gospel values (349).

The People's Church

The bishops appear to be in favor of a Church that is no longer in collusion with governments or with the rich and the powerful. While rejecting accusations of being alienating, the hierarchy has moved from an elitist position to a people-oriented Church. This is reflected in the document by its support for CEBs and its choice for an institution that, while open to all, identifies primarily with the poor. Nonetheless, the pope and the bishops object to the creation of a "parallel church" that, while alluding to the need to find its true significance among the poor, sets itself up against the authority of the institutional Church (263). They see this tendency as the result of ideological conditioning. In particular, in a public letter addressed to the Nicaraguan bishops, but clearly intended for those who favor a dilution of hierarchical authority, John Paul II made reference to the "deadly attacks" by those who operate from within the institution and called upon priests and religious to maintain unity with their bishops.[14] This attitude should not be interpreted only in light of the Church's concern for Marxism. The Vatican would not hesitate to reprimand an extremely conservative group who, in opposition to ecclesiastical authority, would try to establish a separate Church.[16]

The Praxis of Liberation

The fundamental objective that a revised liberation theology seeks as it is being incorporated into the mainstream of the Latin American Church still needs to be assessed. For this we need to focus on the praxis. We must bear in mind that in the document the term "praxis" is seldom used. Instead, the bishops discuss this concept in terms of liberation. In turn, they view liberation (synonymous with structural changes in the theology of liberation) from the standpoint of an integral approach and evangelization.

Liberation theology, because of its omissions and its emphasis on the political, gives the impression that reality dictates the praxis, with no criteria to evaluate its action other than effectiveness in attaining the liberation goal. The bishops have objected to this presentation because it misrepresents Christian orthopraxis by rejecting values that are in line with the gospel and going against orthodoxy when essential truths are omitted. The document acknowledges that individual praxis cannot be deduced *a priori,* but adds that it is incorrect to affirm that the entire road ahead needs to be discovered (265). In other words, there are certain truths and principles that are given, on which there is no compromise. In line with liberation theology, the document sees the praxis itself, i.e., the concern and the commitment to the poor, as the starting point (1136), but it must be elaborated while departing from a sense of biblical history in which the person responds to the original call of God (279). To prevent a secularized praxis, one divested of any religious tradition and based only on human truth, Pope John Paul II established orthodoxy as the measure of an authentic Christian liberation. Thus the praxis needs to be in agreement with the truths of the faith and cannot be reduced to temporal politics only.[16]

Such doctrinal reservations do not nullify the praxis; however, they condition it. The praxis takes place within certain dogmatic boundaries that will determine in some form the scope of its action. The alternative would have resulted in an erosion of Church identity. But in the Church, though pragmatism has its place, its practice has always been understood within the context of maintaining the purity of its dogma. The significant issue from the perspective of liberation is whether these limitations on the praxis may sufficiently prevent the ideological conditioning of the doctrine. We recall that the Church's doctrine is the application of the Scriptures to particular temporal issues. Hence, it was the rereading of the gospel from a different historical perspective, along with the incorporation of the human sciences and a rudimentary praxis, that led to a commitment to the poor and the birth of liberation theology.

The praxis aids in the elaboration of theology and in liberation, but by itself it is not a safeguard against ideological conditioning. On the contrary, the praxis alone, without any self-criticism and without remaining itself open to external feedback, is vulnerable to cultural and ideological conditioning. A Christian version of the praxis, according to the Church, can enjoy a relative but not an absolute freedom. There is ample room to revise the doctrine, as the Church has done in Puebla, but only insofar as it does not contravene the dogma or its principles.

On another point, we remember that as a reaction to traditional and modern European theology, liberation theology has insisted primarily on the radical change of social structures, often downgrading and omitting (though not necessarily rejecting) the need for internal personal conversion. The Church, on the other hand, has persisted in stressing that conversion is not only necessary but should be the guiding consideration in establishing new social relationships.[17] The Puebla document represents a clarification of the Medellín position on this issue. In Puebla the bishops come forth with an ambivalent and uneasy synthesis of the two postures.

The injustices that characterize Latin America and the structures that generate them are denounced as sinful (1258) and violence-prone (509, 1259). Since these structures are linked to present systems, particularly of the liberal capitalist orientation (437), the bishops have called for "swift and far-reaching changes" within the systems themselves (30, 1250). At the same time, the Church's traditional doctrine is stated. That is, the evil in structures is caused by human attitudes, "selfishness, pride, ambition, and envy, which generate injustices, domination, violence at all levels" (328). Thus the document calls for a conversion in which the person becomes liberated from personal sin, ultimately through a conversion to Jesus Christ (329).

The bishops' objective at Puebla was to incorporate liberation while preventing its praxis from being reduced to any single level: "neither to a verticalist unincarnated spiritual union with God, nor to simple existential personalist bonds among individuals or small groups, nor much less to a socio-economic and political horizontalism" (329). They accomplish this through the use of the concept "integral liberation," in which they bring together the human person's three basic dimensions: his relationship to the world, to his fellow human beings, and to God (322).

Integral liberation entails two separate but necessary levels: personal liberation from one's own sins and liberation from the sins of others (socio-political liberation). The latter can be approached in two ways: liberating oneself from oppressive conditions and participating in the liberation of others. This clarification is important because the Church criticizes liberation theology for equating personal liberation from one's sins with one's own socio-political liberation. It is in this context that John Paul II says that it is a mistake to state that socio-political liberation coincides with salvation in Jesus Christ.[18] If the pope had omitted this statement, it would signify that salvation comes about through a conversion to a political ideology that promises to lead to political liberation. The Church would appear to be supporting the identification of a political system with the Kingdom of God, a reduction that is not theologically permissible. Moreover, from a political standpoint it could give way to a messianism and inject a powerful socio-religious element into politics, similar to the Shiite version of the Muslim religion or the spirit that prevailed during the Crusades. Nevertheless, what is not stated in the document, but undoubtedly is considered traditional doctrine, is that participating in the liberation of others may coincide with the path to salvation insofar as the praxis implies the giving of oneself to the other who is in need. Throughout the document, however, while referring to liberation, to praxis, or to evangelization, the Church tries to convey the message that both structural changes and conversion are necessary (30, 193, 329, 362, 388, 394, 534, 1155, 1206, 1221).

The ideal Church praxis is that integral liberation should come as a result of conversion. By this the bishops refer to a free internal change of attitudes, the result of an awareness of a new vision of reality that encompasses Christian values. The process entails "affecting and as it were upsetting, through the power of the Gospel, mankind's criteria of judgment, determining values, points of interest, lines of thought, sources of inspiration and models of life, which are in contrast with the Word of God and the plan of salvation."[19] The two aspects of integral liberation — personal and socio-political — are interrelated. From the standpoint of salvation, personal liberation from sin is more important than one's own liberation from oppressive conditions. Here the Church's point is that salvation is individually attained primarily not by avoiding temporal afflictions but by eradicating the evil in oneself and choosing instead what is morally right. Both personal liberation from sin and salvation, however, have a basic social dimension that ties them in with the socio-political liberation of others. Rightful moral behavior is nearly always understood to be in relation to other people. Thus someone who refuses to manifest his conversion at the social level, neglecting his temporal duties toward his neighbor, "jeopardizes his eternal salvation."[20] That is why the bishops have insisted that conversion becomes authentic only if and when it leads to social changes (329, 395). We notice that the document, in line with liberation theology, calls for a conversion of "hearts and minds" toward the poor, and toward justice and love (1135, 1206).

Meanwhile, the Church's criticism of liberation theology on this issue deals with evangelization, or the spreading of the gospel. For example, the Pope objects to an evangelization by the Church that does not show the eschatological dimension of salvation in Jesus Christ. In other words, any presentation of gospel matter carried on in the name of faith cannot simply be reduced to a conversion to socio-political liberation attitudes. That would reduce salvation to a temporal project. Hence "the need to restate clearly the specifically religious finality of evangelization."[21]

The Process of Change

So far, we have seen that the Puebla document incorporates socio-political liberation by making a bid for structural changes. Also, that conversion by itself, without leading to and without calling for social transformation, is not acceptable. At the same time, the Church seems to indicate that liberation should be understood primarily in terms of a Christian personal conversion and that structural changes should come about only as a result of such conversion. For example, Pope John Paul II states:

> Liberation signifies man's internal transformation, which is a consequence of knowing the Truth. Such transformation is then a spiritual process in which man grows in justice and in true holiness. Man,

> maturing internally, transforms himself into the representative and advocate of that justice. . . .[22]

Roger Heckel, S.J., CELAM's Secretary of the Pontifical Commission on Justice and Peace, maintains the position that the Pope purposely distinguishes between liberation (from sin) and the human efforts to attain social changes, which he refers to with the terms development, justice, human promotion, and the defense of human rights. The reason, according to Heckel, is that John Paul II wants to avoid the ambiguities of the term, particularly that of identifying liberation in Christ with political liberations. Also, his intention is to allow the religious liberation brought about by Christ to be the one that promotes political liberations.[23]

At times the Puebla document reiterates the same point: structural changes should come about as the product of internal liberation or conversion (388, 395, 1206, 1221). But there are two other variations. One states that social transformations should be inspired by an evangelical spirit (199, 438), while the other stresses that social changes are not completed without a change of "hearts and minds" at the personal and collective levels (534, 1155). What does it all mean?

Most in liberation theology follow the structural changes approach more closely because they see an urgent need to remove that which they perceive as oppressive, violent, and sinful. Their decision to pursue social change through variations of Marxist socialism does not suggest a rejection or negation of conversion. It implies a recognition of unchristian aspects within the historical realization of capitalism, of the human being's imperfection in this world, and the difficulty or unwillingness of some people to accept conversion. Hence the need to use the State to deter social wrongdoing and establish new social relations.

The Church's position originates from the other end. Since people are ultimately responsible for fashioning social structures, the natural and effective way of implementing lasting structural transformations is through a change of hearts and minds. Its decision to stress conversion is not only the result of its eschatological orientation. It also constitutes its sociological theory: "the Church is conscious that the best structures and the most idealized systems soon become inhuman if people's inclinations are not rectified, if there is no conversion of hearts and minds on the part of those who either inhabit those structures or who rule them" (534). The Church accepts that structures may condition attitudes and behavior only to a certain extent. Sheer coercive power would then have to be used to transform the remaining evil tendencies in people in order to transform them into social moral beings. That, however, would not be in line with the Church's concept of the human being who is free and has dignity. By stressing conversion, the institution is above all asserting personal freedom, dignity, and accountability to oneself, to others, and to God. Thus the institution cannot force conversion.

Liberation theology uses a similar argument to account for its approach. God calls us to freedom, and gives us a special dignity by making us in his image. Society and government cannot allow those who do not wish to be converted to violate other people's freedom and dignity through oppression; hence the liberation tendency among many to centralize power. Through this approach certain social evils will be deterred, some unjust structures will be replaced by just ones, and these changes in turn will condition social behavior to some extent. The only problem that this version of liberation faces is that while accomplishing its objectives it runs the risk of violating the principles and the foundation on which it bases its approach. Historically speaking, such systems end up trespassing people's freedom and their rights, thereby giving way to repression.

The Church's approach does not fare any better. The institution is aware of the obstacles involved in liberation through personal conversion due to the forces of sin in the hearts of people and in the structures (281). The changes it proposes, though swift and far-reaching, should not be abrupt or violent (534). The whole approach depends, then, on the willingness of the oppressors to change. If the oppressors remain indifferent or refuse to accept conversion, and do not feel the least pressed to implement reforms, then the social change process comes to an end or becomes radicalized when patience wears thin and frustration sets in. The alternatives are to endure systemic oppression or to set in motion the spiral of violence and revolution.

The Puebla document recognizes this dilemma. Pope Paul VI was aware of the possibility of violence in Latin America,[24] as John Paul II is today. The Pope, speaking to members of the ruling classes in Brazil, said: "the realization of justice on this continent faces a clear dilemma: either it will come through profound and courageous reforms . . . or it will come . . . through the forces of violence."[25] Thus the Church, in keeping with its mission and its doctrine, prefers to push for social changes from within through conversion. Nevertheless, it leaves the door open to the possibility that structural changes may precede conversion on some occasions, in which case it warns and recommends that if lasting transformations are desired a personal change of attitude is still needed.

Its repeated calls for structural changes, and its acceptance that these could have priority over conversion, give the Church more credibility in the short run. Now the praxis for change is consistent with its praxis of denunciation. Such a response is based on the liberation theology premise, the emphasis on the love of neighbor, and the option for the poor. At this stage, the Church is closer to integrating the crux of liberation theology while disavowing historical Marxism.

A Single History and Political Liberation

The Church at Puebla seems to have narrowed the gap in the separation of planes between the sacred and the profane, but still finds itself at odds over the issue. We may recall that liberation theology, by postulating the concept of one history of salvation, gives socio-political liberation more credence as a religious movement. In Vatican II the Church took the first step, which served as the point of departure for liberation theology. In *Gaudium et spes* it said:

> Earthly progress must be carefully distinguished from the growth of Christ's kingdom. Nevertheless, to the extent that the former can contribute to the better ordering of human society, it is of vital concern to the Kingdom of God.[26]

The emphasis of the above citation is on the significance of earthly progress, insofar as it contributes to establish a more livable society. Socio-political liberations, even secular ones, when undertaken with justice and charity, make such contributions. Hence they are of importance to the kingdom. Liberation theology goes further than this. If God's kingdom is already present on earth, and it is neither completed nor static, then its progress and its growth are, in part, reflected whenever the changes that occur approximate God's designs and wishes. Thus, in effect, political liberations from oppression contribute to the growth of the kingdom. The bishops at Puebla would have no quarrel with such an approach, as long as the transcendent dimension of such liberations is included in the message. But the ten years that followed Medellín witnessed an excessive (but perhaps necessary) preoccupation with the political component by liberation theologians. Also taking place was an uncritical identification and association with Marxism, understandable we think, yet unjustified in light of liberation theology's own premise of critical consciousness. Moreover, there was an outgrowth of violence in the region, in some instances related to clerical activities.

Puebla had to come to grips with such reality in order to preserve orthodoxy, prevent the spreading of Marxist ideology, and attempt to put an end to violence. The document, in one instance, presents two parallel histories, one temporal and the other eschatological (267), i.e., the history of God's kingdom as it progresses within human history. There is also another citation that appears to be saying the opposite: "There is, then, one human history that, although it has its own consistency and autonomy, is called to be consecrated to God by man" (491). A third one points toward one history saying, "we cannot disfigure, partialize, or ideologize the person of Jesus Christ, . . . who is the Lord of History" (178). And yet, there is a fourth version that seems to move Vatican II a step backward: "the objective of the Church's social doctrine . . . is always the promotion of the human person's integral liberation . . . contributing in that manner to the building of the ultimate and definite kingdom, without confusing, nonetheless, earthly progress with the growth of Christ's kingdom" (475). Here, the Vatican II quotation is reversed. The emphasis is on the distinction that exists between earthly progress and the kingdom. Socio-political liberation now appears to be less vital to the kingdom.

More than anything else, these variations show the lack of consensus among the participants with regard to a complex issue. It must be understood that acceptance of the one history concept has its benefits as well as its risks, one of which is facing up to the secularization process in the world. Pope John Paul II appears to lean closer to the one history aspect. Already in his first encyclical he alluded to this when speaking about the act of redemption:

> This act of redemption marked the high point of the history of man (sic) within God's loving plan. God entered the history of humanity and, as a man, became an actor in that history. . . .

And more recently, writing within the context of a temporal issue, human work, again he seems to close the gap between the two planes. He is concerned about joining the person's work dimension with redemption, or as he puts it, temporality and immortality, and says:

> These two dimensions, that of work and that of faith, are not divided, as neither are the dimension of the world and that of the kingdom of God. Both have been united in the eternal thought and the eternal will of the Creator.[28]

Violent Revolution or Civil Disobedience?

The most significant difference between the Medellín and the Puebla documents concerns the issue of violence. The brunt of Medellín's denunciation, we may recall, was upon the institutionalized violence on the part of governments. The post-Medellín period greatly concerned the bishops, especially the clergy speaking about political liberations, their increased persecution, and the possible links between the preaching of a liberation theology and the incidence of guerrilla activity in some parts of Latin America.[29]

The Puebla document stresses in different ways the Church's opposition to all kinds of violence. The peculiarity, though, is the way it does it. Rather than undertaking a systematic analysis of the "spiral of violence" that would highlight both oppressive and repressive violence by government authorities, the emphasis is on revolutionary and guerrilla action. The spiral is presented, but in a very subtle and almost imperceptible manner, by the order of its criticism. Twice the document denounces first government-related violence, then guerrilla activity (42-43, 531-532). Also, on one occasion it links violence with the ideology that causes it, in the order in which they occur: liberal capitalism, Marxism, national security (542-549).

The bishops, however, appear to have given up the Church's doctrine on just insurrection. It is not included in the document as it was in Medellín. Even more surprising, in one instance the document appears to find such a doctrine to be incompatible with the gospel and with the Church, for it identifies guerrilla violence with terrorism and labels both as criminal (531, 486).[30] In another passage it makes no distinction between subversive and repressive violence, placing them both on equal footing (1259). Moreover, there is no mention of the violence that ensues following a refusal to implement needed reforms, as was the case in Medellín.[31] And gone, too, is part of Pope Paul VI's quotation in the Medellín document, in which after he states that violence is neither Christian nor evangelical, he adds (and this is omitted), that "Christians, while preferring peace, are not afraid to fight" (534).

Pope John Paul II followed a similar format throughout his trips to Latin America. While he denounced unjust conditions, he condemned all forms of violence. But, as liberation theologian Ignacio Ellacuría points out, the pontiff is more critical of revolutionary violence, particularly that which is inspired by Marxist ideology and class struggle. While lauding John Paul II for his message of peace, Ellacuría laments that the presentation of the violence issue was onesided, for the Pope did not speak specifically about repressive violence, which in Central America, he says, is responsible for more killings than the leftist guerrilla movements. Furthermore, he notes the Pope omitted references to the traditional Church doctrine on just defense or insurrection.[32]

The Pope's words, on the other hand, do not reflect an attempt on his part to downgrade structural injustices or to minimize the level of violence caused by public authorities. In Guatemala he recognized the presence of systemic violence: "let us remember that one's neighbor can be made to die slowly, day by day, when he is denied the access to the material resources that God created for the benefit of all, not for their use by a few."[33] And upon his return from Central America, he commented again on the conflictive situation: "the tensions have their origin . . . in the unjust structures which permit the accumulation of the greater part of the wealth in the hands of an elite few. . . ."[34] The problem lies in that the Church is caught in a "no-win" situation. Its objectives in Latin America are to bring to an end both injustice and violence; however, these two are interrelated. Against this background John Paul II's message is to insist that as much as he abhors unjust structures and the human suffering they cause, revolutionary violence is not the means to effect lasting social changes.[35]

One may ask why the Pope chose not to invoke the just insurrection doctrine. Not only is it a legitimate part of the Church's doctrine, but in some instances a violent revolution may prove to be the only viable alternative that can put an end to both an unjust regime and the circle of violence. Between Medellín and Puebla the Church made an appeal on two occasions to insurrection based on its own doctrine, once by Archbishop Oscar Romero of San Salvador, who was assassinated only a few months later, and later by the Nicaraguan Episcopal Conference during the struggle against the Somoza regime.[36] Certainly, the reason is not because the Pope finds violence "repugnant to the Christian condition," and "contrary to God's love."[37] None of this is new. The Church has never regarded violence as Christian or evangelical. These views are in line with John Paul II's predecessors, who always had seen violence as evil. Accordingly, when it becomes necessary to use violence it is done as a "last resort," as the "lesser of two evils," and along with conditions that call either for a just self-defense, a just war, or a just insurrection.[38] As one who has studied the Church's doctrine on revolution has remarked, the way to interpret it is to regard violence as a greater evil, and thus inadmissible, "save in the case of an evident and prolonged tyranny." As such, it is always an anomaly within the norm of evolution.[39]

The bishops' and John Paul II's omission of a just defense is best understood in light of the present Latin American reality as perceived by a concerned Church mentality. They have realized that many people in the region have chosen the violent path to social change. Hence one intention is to avoid adding fuel to an already explosive situation. The other reason is that the Pope and the bishops see a different type of violence taking hold of Christians, one that is being conditioned by Marxist-Leninist ideology. In other words, they are not rejecting an approach that takes into consideration the conditions and follows the principles of a just insurrection, but one that is guided by class hatred and which proceeds from an *a priori* belief that the existing conflict leaves no room for reconciliation through the political process.

The Church's endorsement of insurrection in a document that is addressed to many countries at the same time would result in a situation with unforeseen consequences, a condition that could hardly justify violent revolutions from the standpoint of its doctrine. Moreover, the Church fears that its intention would be co-opted by Marxist-Leninist movements, giving the impression that the institution is supportive of class violence. The Pope made clear the effects of such an alternative. He told a group of rural workers in Panama:

> You cannot allow yourselves to be dragged by the temptation of violence, of armed guerrilla action, or the selfish class struggle. . . . Where will such a path lead? Hatred and the gap between social classes will increase, the social crisis will deepen. . . .[40]

And, in referring specifically to class hatred, he said in Brazil:

> The class struggle is not the path leading to a just social order, because it carries with it the risk of raising the unfavored up to becoming the privileged, thereby creating a fresh situation of unjustice against those who have so far had advantages. One cannot build with hatred on the destruction of others.[41]

The bishops also fear that a Marxist-Leninist revolution

would not insure a satisfactory solution if class hatred, repression, and statism replace the old unjust structures. Furthermore, they are apprehensive of the threat that such regimes pose to the institution. They have realized that historical Marxism will not give the Church the necessary freedom to perform its mission.[42] On the other hand, most of the persecution against the Church in Latin America has come from "rightist" regimes that do not need the Church to rely on just insurrections to rationalize their repressive measures. The bishops, as early as Medellín, recognized that dominant groups "tend to characterize all attempts to change a social system that favors their privileges as subversive action."[43]

Thus, facing a real potential for violence that would deteriorate rather than improve conditions, the Church opted for a radical approach that it hopes will "break the chain of hatred and violence that produces hatred and violence."[44] Social reforms will have to be implemented through non-violent means. The Puebla document proposes the use of "defensive means, that are within the reach of the weak" (533), referring probably to Gandhian tactics of civil disobedience. These means are in line with the document's allusions to martyrdom, calling for an "authentic heroism" in the struggle against sin and misery (281), liberating "suffering through suffering, that is, assuming the Cross" (278). Also, evangelical values should characterize the liberation process, values that include "reconciliation and forgiveness."[45]

The liberation praxis that the Church suggests operates at both the grassroots and the elite levels, while aiming at the entire culture. It consists of conscientization through evanglization, critical denunciation, protest, opposition through civil disobedience, overt Church support for causes, and martyrdom. Hence, the Church assumes a non-violent path as a challenge to all parties involved.

It is unfortunate that being so opposed to violence, the bishops were not more explicit in the implementation of a non-violent praxis. Very little is known about this approach as a suggested means by the Church, other perhaps than its political efficacy. To gain a religious perspective, we have to rely on a document drawn up by a group of bishops, priests, and lay persons that outlines the approach's main characteristics, its intentions and attitudes, and its plan of action.[46] Briefly summarized, evangelical non-violence is an act of freedom identified with the figure of Jesus. It is not confused with either passivity, fear, or tolerance for injustice. It does not ignore institutionalized violence. Rather, it denounces it firmly and clearly.[47] It departs from the conviction that conflict does not imply the futility of reconciliation but the challenge to overcome it through dialogue. Its strategy consists of exercising an active moral pressure that would allow the oppressor to become aware of his injustice.

Evangelical non-violence requires a personal conversion that would overcome selfishness, comfort, and fear. It seeks to end not only oppression, but violence too. Thus attitudes of hatred and vengeance also have to be buried: "The spirit of reconciliation does not arise out of cowardice or weakness; Christian forgiveness is the fruit of love; it is an act of freedom. . . ."[48] As such, it distinguishes between oppression and the oppressor; it combats the former, but tries to love the latter. It does not rely on offensive language, avoids domination of people, and eliminates all elements of discrimination and superiority. Its action does not stop at the personal level. Its main target is to bring new changes to society, thus it incorporates social analysis.[49]

Citing the method's accomplishments by Gandhi, Martin Luther King, Jr., Danilo Dolci, and César Chavez, the authors point out that nonviolence is not mere idealism but a practical ideal with concrete applications to a political situation. Overall, we see the approach as taking more time to implement, and it is definitely more difficult to consolidate. It requires a special kind of charismatic leadership that is harder to obtain than skillful guerrilla leadership. On the other hand, it presents two great advantages. Since the method does not depend militarily or economically on other nations, which could attach strings or hinder the process because of political considerations, autonomy is achieved. And any national Church could probably count on the support of the largest transnational organization in the world, the Church, which could mobilize public opinion within other nations. This is an aspect which the institution has not yet used effectively.

Whether the non-violent approach will spread or not depends largely on the Church itself. It is not enough to say that liberation should be integral, Christ-inspired, and non-violent. It is up to each bishop and each national episcopal conference to draw up their own programs of action and implement them. Insofar as they do not take the initiative, offering activists a means to channel their aspirations and ideals of social change, one may expect radicalized violent groups to fill the praxis vacuum.

The New Society

In accordance with Vatican II, the Latin American bishops understand that it is not the Church's function to provide specific social, economic, and political solutions (1211).[50] The institution's role in the political realm is to "interpellate, relativize, and criticize" society and its ideologies (539), with the end in view of establishing "the human community according to the divine law."[51] This is not an attempt on the part of the Church to extend the power of the clergy into politics, but rather part of its mission to permeate the culture with Christian values. It is not clericalism but evangelization. In light of this function, the Church is claiming the same opportunity and freedom accorded to other ideologies to spread its message. It seeks competition within the "free market of ideas."

Hence it becomes necessary for the institution to be present in every nation, working for the betterment of society at large. Its policy vis-á-vis the State and the political community is one of "active peaceful coexistence."[52] This means that the Church coexists with all political systems. Not being bound to any one in particular, however, it will seek "to give testimony of its message, and to use its prophetic mission to announce and denounce, . . . to correct the false images of society which are incompatible with the Christian vision" (1213).

Though it is not clearly stated in any of the Church documents, one is able to trace a configuration of the ideal society proposed by the bishops. As such, it represents a goal and identifies a path to it. The Church's guiding consideration in its review of public policy and political objectives is the extent to which these approximate the goal, or lead to its progressive attainment. These characteristics of the new society are deduced from the Church's critique of political systems and of conditions in Latin America, and its description of human rights and the uses of power, as well as from its omissions.

To begin with, a rigid type of "free market" system that, while placing capital before work and giving priority to economics over social needs, is responsible for "widening the gap between the rich and the poor" throughout Latin America is strongly condemned (47, 92, 437, 550). Also rejected is a materialist version of society that is mainly expressed through "consumerism." This view, according to the document, values material acquisition, power, status, and pleasure in a way that detracts from spiritual values. A distorted profit motive then becomes a primary consideration in society (311). We would think that although this aspect is mainly encountered in capitalist societies, the bishops would also reject the consumerism tendency that has become the trademark within some nations in the Eastern bloc. Finally, Puebla is highly opposed to an economic liberalism that presents an individualistic version of the person; particularly, one in which economic efficacy and individual freedom, along "with an individualistic concept of religious salvation, becomes blind to the requirements of a social justice and subordinates itself to the international imperialism of money . . ." (312). This attitude often creates illegitimate privileges due to its consideration of private property as an absolute right (542).

The conditions of inhuman poverty, high child mortality rate, lack of adequate housing, health problems, "hunger wages," unemployment and sub-employment, malnutrition, labor unrest, and forced massive migrations, call for changes that "either have not taken place or have been too slow" (29-30). In addition, the document denounces systematic repression, tortures, exiles, disappearances, insecurity due to illegal arrests, repressive measures against labor, farm workers, and popular organizations, general dependence, private and public corruption, and others (42, 44, 51-70), all of which represent the "cry of a people who suffer and who demand justice, . . . asking their pastors for a liberation that never reaches them" (87-88).

If the document appears to make a strong point, it is that the Church's version of the new society will not be in accordance with the liberal capitalist ideology, at least as it is manifested throughout Latin America today. The reforms that are called for would transform the system beyond recognition by American standards — not only in terms of ending poverty and injustice, but in the way in which a society would prevent their recurrence. The content of evangelization and its social priorities presuppose a rearrangement of society in accordance with a new set of social criteria.

Another significant issue is the type of system the document refers to as capitalist. Michael Novak, a Catholic theologian noted for his criticism of the American Church's social doctrine, has insisted that there are significant differences between the socio-economic and political systems in Latin America and in the United States.[53] To be sure, many capitalist practices in the region have been standardized due to the influence of Western values through academic training and the work of major corporations. But there is in Latin America a tradition of exploitation that goes back to the Colonial period and in some cases to the Indian culture. This combination of "feudo-capitalism" results in many instances in attitudes and behavior that are the product of cultural practices, social castes, and religious views that antecede capitalist development.

Are the bishops taking these differences into account in their criticism? We think so. They do not say that all of the problems we have just mentioned are due only to economic capitalism. However, according to the document capitalist influence does not take place only through economic structures. The bishops point out to "imported values and life styles which are alienating" (53). Properly speaking, in Latin America these refer primarily to an individualistic materialism, which in their words has "subverted" social values and attempted to erect barriers against "communion and participation," terms they use to indicate the religious basis on which the person's social and political involvement should be elaborated. The communion among persons — solidarity — is not only desired by God, but it is achieved insofar as men and women maintain a close relationship with Him (55, 215-216). Other sources of problems, viz., consumerism, deterioration of family life and public honesty, and public vices, are linked to a liberal culture in which secularism has had an accompanying hand (83, 435-436). So it is important to bear in mind that the document denounces not just the economic aspect or its ideology, but an entire cultural system that includes feudal-type and capitalist structures, liberal cultural values, a national security ideology, and the corresponding effects and conditions that have resulted from them.

The new society includes a human rights platform that has an original approach in that individual rights, traditionally identified with Western democracies, are linked to the social rights with which socialism is associated. Moreover, the Church is espousing new "emerging rights" that would safeguard the self-image of the person, one's reputation, individual privacy, objective information, and the right to a conscientious objection (1271-1273). Along with these, the document presents a concept of private property based on a "social mortgage," in which its use is subordinated to the common good. It defends the right of private property upon the condition that access to it be extended so that more people may participate in its use (492). The bishops proclaim a "new international order," that should include statutes to regulate the activities of transnational enterprises, new rules for international cooperation, and political, social, and economic self-determination (1276-1282). Their commitment to a "new humanism" entails the human person's liberation from the "idolatry of wealth" with the goal in mind of "an economy which is at the service of people and not people at the service of the economy, as happens in the two forms of idolatry, the capitalist and collectivist" (497).

The bishops also have made clear that any restructuring of society should not take place along the guidelines of historical Marxist ideology. Their objections are with the manifestations of Marxism, mainly its materialist orientation, its militant atheism, its tendency toward systematic hatred and violence as political strategies, and its invariable totalitarian realization (48, 313, 544). These aspects are linked to the rigid stances of Marxism's philosophical and political premises. Historical materialism postulates that material conditions and social reality are the prime movers in one's life, thus allowing little or no autonomy to the spirit. Religion is found to be alienating for the human condition and is rejected as the creation of false consciousness. Class conflict is assumed to be irreconcilable; thus the dominant class will not give up power without violent struggle. Hatred, as the product of the egoism and exploitation on the part of the dominant class, is used as a strategy to foster unity and class consciousness among the exploited. Authoritarianism is called for by the dictatorship of the proletariat, by the need to repress anti-revolutionary elements, and by the urgency to "educate" society without critical thinking. Hence, seeking the meaning of human existence within the production process, a rigid Marxism ends up reducing the human person to external structures (313).

The issue, then, is how to achieve the desired changes without violence yet at an accelerated pace, and which model offers the best guarantees of attaining them. The document appears to be somewhat flexible on these aspects. Along the political continuum, the boundaries of the new society would appear to range from versions of neo-socialism, without the objections raised by the bishops against the historical Marxist model, to a socially-oriented capitalism, entailing the traditional combination of capital and labor but in which the profit motive, private property, and market forces are subordinated to the needs of the person and the common good.

Pope John Paul II has made some definite indications concerning the use of governmental power toward this purpose. The Church's social doctrine has traditionally reaffirmed the principle of subsidiarity, in which the individual and private groups and associations are primarily responsible for the activities and the initiatives in a society. Government would intervene only when the private sector appears ill-equipped to provide for the common good and for those activities that require more comprehensive planning. The Pope, however, has recognized that today's profound and complex problems require a more active participation by the government. During his trip to Brazil, in his address to the Brazilian president, he referred to the need for social changes and said: "all of society is coresponsible (for the task), but initiatives and the human direction and logic of the processes depend in large part on those who are invested with positions of government and leadership."[54] And in an address to the Diplomatic Corps, he sided with the social, rather than the liberal, interpretation of power (which plays a more limited role in government), mainly in the protection of individual freedom. Again, speaking about social reforms, he said:

> It is a particular responsibility of those who exercise power, because theirs is a service of social justice. Power has the right to show itself strong vis-á-vis those who cultivate an egoism of one group to the detriment of the whole. It must in any case demonstrate

> it is at the service of men and women, . . . especially those who need sustenance.[55]

The bishops, on their part, despite strong condemnation of historical Marxism, do not speak in favor of a specific type of government. Still, they leave the door open to some forms of socialism. They are well aware that Marxism is not the only type of socialism, nor is Leninism the only version of Marxist socialism.[56] The document does not reject all forms of collectivism but only the historical concretions of Marxist-Leninist collectivism. It denounces the totalitarian practices that accompany nationalization, along with the other objections already mentioned. Given the way in which socialist thought has evolved throughout the years, Church and Socialist leaders admit that nationalization does not necessarily lead to socialism and that socialism does not necessarily imply totalitarianism.[57]

The document calls for "the commitment of Christians in the implementation of historical projects in accordance with the needs of the moment and of each culture" (553). So, ultimately, it is up to Christians themselves to decide how to proceed, within the parameters established by the Church. Then, with Marxist socialism in the back of their minds, the bishops add:

> The Christian owes special attention and discernment to one's eventual commitment in historical movements that arose out of different ideologies, and which are distinct from them. . . . One cannot identify the false philosophical theories with the historical movements that have originated in them, to the extent that these historical movements can be influenced in their evolution (554).[58]

Thus, provided that human rights safeguards are built into the system and that the basic religious concepts on which Christian ethics are based — free will and Divine Law — are not denied and the primary interests of the Church are not attacked, socialism, not being condemned, remains an alternative historical realization. It is against this background that one may understand Pope John Paul II's remarks that "the unjust system" needs to be changed, and that change should come without violence and in accordance "with the principles of Social Democracy."[59] A democratic electoral process is the only road to power that promises the possibility to minimize violence and uphold human rights while it implements social changes. Although the bishops do not mention the democratic approach to government, it appears from their criticism of the abuses of power that only through the electoral process and a system based on laws and institutions may political power be kept from becoming absolutized (42, 49, 500). Moreover, among the characteristics of "the new man," the bishops point to "a free person, capable of making one's own choices and exercising one's responsibilities individually and collectively" (491). Overall, the political system must offer equal participation to all citizens, with the same rights and duties and without legal privileges. Also, the system must be based on political and legal institutions that would insure self-determination and social justice (503-506). Moreover, it is within this framework that the realization of some sort of social democratic capitalism is also possible.

In the end, the Church seems to elaborate an ideal synthesis out of liberal capitalism and Marxist collectivism. But does not this position contradict the initial statement at the beginning of this section, namely, that it would be improper for the Church to advocate a specific political system? In a way it is a contradiction, so a clarification is required. In first place, Puebla has not identified itself with, or extended its support to, a specific political party or movement. Second, although the Pope chose the term "social democracy" on one occasion, he was not alluding to the ideological political movement, to which he may have some particular objections, but to the general orientation of a political alternative as it is realized today.

Still, it is crucial that we read accurately the Church's intentions. The institution's object is to focus on desirable values, conditions, and situations rather than on the particular political ideologies or movements that may attain them. This is why the document lacks a systematic political approach. Viewed with a religious eye, it is the product of the Church's socio-political function "to interpellate, relativize, and criticize" society and its ideologies (539). Thus the institution gives no support to nor recommends specific systems. What it does is to announce, i.e., to identify, the ideal political environment, reserving for the laity its realization through the political process.

We also said that the Church's pronouncements have a realistic flexibility. Munarriz overreads Puebla when, dissappointedly, he sees the bishops supporting a reformed capitalism instead of a "Socialism with a human face, . . . capable of overcoming the actual historical concretions of Marxist Collectivism."[60] Indeed, the document allows for that interpretation, as well as for the socialist, if it is read from a political ideological standpoint. However, Munarriz implies something else, namely that the Church is identifying itself with a political option, the neo-capitalist. Aside from the indiscretions that were committed, including the changes that softened the extent, not the high pitch, of the capitalist critique, and aside from the fact that the majority of bishops are not of the Marxist persuasion, the document does not reflect Munarriz' version any more than it attempts to save neo-socialism.

Because the document does not speak with a single voice, but different ones, it has no definite political orientation. It is true that things would have been easier for the Church if it had to struggle only against present systems and conditions throughout Latin America. But the threat of Marxism, competing with the Church for the social conscience of the region, threw the institutions into turmoil. Its identity having been questioned, the Church could have opted for a defensive reaction as it had done in the past. Instead, it chose to confront the issue. The bishops' accomplishment consisted in that they decided to meet the challenge; and, despite the precarious situation, in the end they have been able to preserve the institution's religious identity and integrity. In doing so they have faced the social question, at least in theory, in a more profound way than either the European or the North American Church.

The Church's posture does not appear as being "middle of the road" or a compromise position. Puebla signifies a Church in search of a posture that identifies it with its mission. That the fundamental affirmations of liberation theology have been kept throughout the document, there is no doubt. Pope John Paul II summarized the Church's position while speaking to the Ecumenical Council of Churches. Quoting Pope Paul VI, this time he used the term liberation in the liberation theology context:

> We recognize that it is impossible to accept that in evangelization one could or should ignore the importance of the problems so much discussed today, concerning justice, liberation, development and peace in the world. This would be to forget the lesson which comes to us from the Gospel concerning love of our neighbor who is suffering and in need.[61]

NOTES

[1]Pope Paul VI, *Evangelii nuntiandi* (henceforth *EN*), 8 December 1975, nos. 17- 22.

[2]Ibid., n. 30.

[3]During his speech inagurating the Puebla conference Pope John Paul II alluded to the task ahead:

> "Ten years have passed (since Medellín). And there have been interpretations at times in contradiction, not always correct, not always beneficial to the Church. For this reason, the Church seeks to find the ways that would allow her to understand more deeply and comply with greater desire with Christ's mission." (Inagural address, *Puebla,* no. 15.)

[4]Mikel Munarriz, "Los Cambios Introducidos en el Documento", *SIC* 422 (febrero, 1980): 77. Also, see Berryman's article "What Happened at Puebla" for another view.

[5]Prior to the conference, it was stipulated by Vatican officials and the Puebla Preparatory Commission that the document was to be considered provisional until signed by the Pope. In the interim, it would be corrected by CELAM commissions. Beyond providing explanations for changes in style, few others were given for modifications to approximately 340 paragraphs, or 26% of the text (Munarriz, pp. 77-78). Also, see his other article on the same topic, "Los Cambios Introducidos en el Documento (II)", *SIC* 423 (marzo 1980): 113-116.

[6]Berryman, p. 57.

[7]*Puebla,* p. 279. This observation is pointed out in Munarriz, "Los Cambios. . .(II)", p. 113.

[8]Address to Workers in Morumbi Stadium, Sao Paulo, Brazil, July 3, 1980, no. 9.

[9]See Pope Paul VI. *Octogesima adveniens,* no. 32-33. On one occasion Pope John Paul II stated that Christian liberation does not use Marxist praxis or analysis (Address to the Bishops of CELAM, Rio de Janeiro, July 2, 1980, no. 8).

[10]General Audience Address, Vatican City, Feb. 21, 1979.

[11]Munarriz, "Los Cambios . . .", 423, p. 114.

[12]Whether or not the Church has shown its wisdom in this respect is an issue open for discussion. Ironically, the two fears are becoming a reality in some parts of Latin America.

[13]General Audience Address, Feb. 21, 1979.

[14]Letter to the Nicaraguan Bishops, Vatican City, June 29, 1982.

[15]Well known is the celebrated case of conservative Archbishop Marcel Lefevre, who after continuous disobedience to Church directives was finally suspended from religious duties by the Vatican.

[16]Inagural Address, *Puebla,* nos. 1.1-1.4.

[17]*EN,* no. 18.

[18]Inagural Address, *Puebla,* no. 1.8.

[19]*EN,* no. 19.

[20]*Gaudium et spes,* no. 43.

[21]*EN,* no. 32.

[22]General Audience, Feb. 21, 1979.

[23]Roger Heckel, S.J., "El Tema de la Liberación en Juan Pablo II," *Medellín* (journal), 27 (septiembre 1981): 435.

[24]*Populorum Progressio,* no. 30.

[25]Address in Salvador, Brazil, July 6, 1980, no. 9.

[26]*Gaudium et spes,* no. 39.

[27]John Paul II, *Redemptor hominis,* March 4, 1979, 1.

[28]Homily on occasion of the Workers Jubilee, Vatican City, March 25, 1984. This quote seems to be in accordance with the view he expressed, while still a Cardinal, at the 1974 Synod of Bishops. There, he said, in the words of Fr. Bonaventura Kloppenburg O.F.M.: "Eternal salvation and human advancement cannot be separated in the action of the Church, nor in the actions of any Christians since they are intimately linked in the same work of creation and redemption." (in *Christian Salvation and Human Temporal Progress,* Trans. Paul Burns [Chicago: Franciscan Herald Press, 1979], p. 42)

[29]Galilea remarked that these concerns were very much in the minds of the bishops, and were reflected at Puebla. (Lecture given by Segundo Galilea at St. Joseph Seminary, Washington, D.C., June 1981.)

[30]The index explicitly states that the Gospel "prohibits" violence, p. 280.

[31]The following two quotes appear in the *Medellín* document:

> "We should not be surprised to see the temptation to use violence in Latin America. One should not abuse the patience of a people who for years endure a situation that those who have a greater conscience of human rights would hardly accept for themselves." (Medellín, no. 2.16)
>
> "We make an urgent call [to those who have a major participation in wealth, culture, and power], not to rely on the Church's peaceful posture to become opposed to the far-reaching transformations that are required. If their privileges are jealously kept and if they are defended through violent means, they become accountable to history for provoking 'the explosive revolutions of desperation.' " (Medellín, no. 2.17)

[32]Ignacio Ellacuría, "Mensaje Etico-Político de Juan Pablo II al Puebla Centroamericano," *ECA* (1983): 268.

[33]Homily at Campo di Marte, Guatemala, March 7, 1983, no. 6.

[34]General Audience, Vatican City, March 16, 1983, no. 3.

[35]Address to Women Religious, Costa Rica, March 3, 1983, no. 4; Homily at the Metro Centre, El Salvador, March 6, 1983, no. 2; University Message, Guatemala, March 7, 1983, no. 7; Homily at the Airport, Haiti, March 9, 1983, no. 4.

[36]Archbishop Romero alluded to the right of a violent insurrection in one of

his Pastoral Letters: *Iglesia y Organizaciones Políticas Populares,* Aug. 6, 1978. The Episcopal Conference of Nicaragua, in a Pastoral Letter dated June 2, 1979, describes the conditions that justify recourse to insurrection: "The extremes of revolutionary insurrection hurt and affect us all, but its moral and juridical legitimacy cannot be denied 'in the case of an evident and prolonged tyranny . (Cristianos en Solidaridad con Nicaragua," *Servir* 81 (tercer bimestre 1979): 367-68.

[37]First quote taken from Address to Bishops, Costa Rica, March 2, 1983, no. 7; second quote taken from Address to Farmworkers, Panama, March 5, 1983, no. 6.

[38]In addition to the two principles mentioned, the others are: a legitimate defensive action; violence is not sought as an end in itself; consideration for popular sovereignty; recourse to less violent alternatives first; avoidance of inherently evil acts, e.g., terrorism, murder, etc.; the harm that present conditions are causing must be asssessed as very grave; the expected results are thought to be better than the harm that violence may bring. (Taken from Higuera Udias, pp. 221-222)

[39]Ibid., p. 224. Pope Paul VI, three months prior to the publication of his *Populorum progressio,* told the Diplomatic Corp, in January 1967:

> "Revolutionary action ordinarily engenders a whole series of injustices and suffering, for violence, once unchained, becomes difficult to control, having its effects on people and on the structures at the same time. In the eyes of the Church, this is not the adequate solution to cure social ills." (Ibid., pp. 223-224)

[40]Address to Farmworkers, Panama, no. 6.

[41]Address to Workers, Sao Paulo, Brazil, no. 4.

[42]One may safely assume that the present Nicaraguan experience, in which several priests have been harrassed and/or expelled by a Marxist-influenced government, will drive the hierarchy into a more conservative posture, much to the delight of governments on the "Right."

[43]*Medellín,* no. 2.5.

[44]Address to the Youth, Costa Rica, March 3, 1983, no. 5.

[45]Inaugural Address, *Puebla,* no. 3.6.

[46]Encuentro internacional de Obispos de América Latina, "La No-Violencia Evangélica, Fuerza de Liberación, *Nueva Sociedad* 36 (mayo-junio, 1978): 127-38.

[47]Ibid., p. 133.

[48]Ibid., p. 132.

[49]Ibid., p. 133.

[50]*Gaudium et spes,* no. 42.

[51]Ibid.

[52]Ibid., nos. 42, 76. The characterization of "peaceful coexistence" is found in Abbott, S.J., footnote 134. However, we thought it was important to distinguish between an active and a passive approach, both of which are possible.

[53]Michael Novak, "Liberation Theology and the Pope," in Quade, pp. 80-3.

[54]Address to the President, June 30, 1980, parentheses mine.

[55]Address to Diplomatic Corps, June 30, 1980.

[56]Former Archbishop López Trujillo, who was mainly responsible for the drafting of the Puebla document, acknowledges a variety of Socialisms, in *Hacia una Sociedad Nueva,* pp. 37-43.

[57]Ibid., pp. 42-43. Also, Enrique Obregón Valverde, "Principios de la Social Democracia," in *Nueva Sociedad,* 36 (mayo-junio 1978): 147. Also, see Harrington, *Socialism,* pp. 2-8, 41-46.

[58]This section in the document pertains to the scrutiny that Christians should make when dealing with Socialism, or any other ideology, as suggested by Pope Paul VI in *Octogesima adveniens,* no. 4. In it, the Pope points out that one solution may not be equally applicable to all nations. Thus each community is called to "analyze with objectivity the situation which is proper to their own country," and make their discernment in light of Gospel values.

[59]General Audience, March 16, 1983, no. 3.

[60]Munarriz, "Los Cambios . . . (II)," p. 113.

[61]The quote is from *EN,* no. 31, in Address to the Ecumenical Council of Churches, Geneva, June 12, 1984.

6.
CONCLUSIONS

Toward an Evaluative Critique

During the years before Puebla, many bishops had become apprehensive about liberation theology. The new theology was seeking no less than to redefine most aspects within the Church. Indeed, it was becoming a threat to the unity of the ecclesiastical community, to its authority, and to the orthodoxy of the faith. The Puebla conference has not allayed those fears entirely, but it has established clear guidelines for the Church and provided common ground that can be used to discuss deviations and excesses. From another standpoint, some governments see liberation theology's promotion of its blueprint for restructuring society as a menace to social and political stability. Since after Puebla the Church intended to be actively involved in preaching its version of liberation, the intensity of the social conflict in the region may increase. That will depend, however, on the prospects for the implementation of the Puebla conference. The implications that liberation theology poses for Latin American politics depend on the bishops' readiness, willingness, and ability to pursue their own recommendations.

Today, a struggle is going on between moderate and liberal forces, both among the Latin American bishops and within the Vatican, over the kind of liberation theology that will be preached: whether it will be a "European" version of Puebla, more spiritualized and insisting primarily on conversion, or its Latin American counterpart that calls first for structural changes, or a combination of both. In this respect, the full impact of liberation theology has not been seen yet. The Church's task in this respect, as distinguished from the state's, is mainly educational: it seeks to teach believers the proper Christian attitudes, values, and orientation in life. Hence, a document as important as Puebla takes years to implement, and it takes even more time to observe its results. One only has to note that after twenty years the bulk of Vatican II still has not been assimilated by the laity.

Liberation theology was originally inspired and guided by religious, not political, values. One may ask if the distinction has any significance in this analysis. The question is relevant for, both as a movement and as a current of thought, liberation theology has often been discredited and rejected as being politically motivated and for subordinating theology and religion to politics. In this context politics is understood as an activity which due to its temporal nature tends to relativize Christianity by reducing it to a historical phenomenon. Also, liberation theology's association with Marxism creates concern and anger among those who see the faith as being used by an atheist doctrine that opposes religion and ultimately wishes to subvert the values of Western liberal civilization — namely, religion, individual freedom, free enterprise, and private property.

Such rejection of liberation theology takes place within a cultural context that often is permeated by a traditionally-minded and spiritualistic-oriented religious framework, and by liberal capitalist values. From this perspective, it appears that God and Christianity are being manipulated, and that faith is reduced to an alien ideology — all for political reasons. In fact, seldom have the critics of liberation theology spoken of any contributions that either the movement or the theology have made. While they accuse the theologians of being subjective in their criticism of the established order, the critics act in the same manner with respect to liberation. At a political level, liberation becomes a partisan issue. This had led to a lack of objectivity in the analysis. In this sense, the critics, for the most part, have reacted similarly to the way the Church responded to past historical movements — defensively and apologetically. Latin American governments have reacted even more strongly to liberation theology, many of them openly persecuting and harassing supporters of the movement, to the extent of torture and killings.[1]

Criticism and rejection of liberation from a culturally conditioned posture does not always invalidate the critique, nor does it imply that those who criticize it always do so only as a reaction based on their cultural values.[2] It is important to bear this point in mimd, for too often, when dealing with partisan issues, critics on one side will automatically reject those of the opposition on the grounds that their views are expectedly partial. Nevertheless, because of its excessive emphasis on a political praxis, its stress of the political dimension of the gospel, and the uncritical use of Marxism by a large part of the movement — all without a corresponding presentation of dogmatic truths, of the eschatological aspect of Christianity — along with a casual disregard for Church authority, the liberation theology movement has been perceived by its critics as a separate entity, working more against than for the institution. It is in this context that liberation theology is accused of subordinating theology and religion to politics.

It is quite possible that the intentions and attitudes of many within the liberation movement are similar to that of Christians for Socialism, now dispersed all over Latin America following the fall of the Allende government. They claimed that doing a critical social analysis of the situation without a corresponding presentation of the "theological truths" does not mean that they are in any way denying or rejecting those aspects.[3] Although their argument is logical — focusing on one aspect does not necessarily imply rejection of the others — that does not mean that reductionism is not taking place by default when the same method is used over and over again. Thus perhaps without any intention on their part, they contribute to a distortion of evangelization. This is the great concern of the Latin American hierarchy and the Vatican.[4]

In effect, conscious or unconscious reductionism detracts from the liberation movement's religious roots and its theological basis. It was not accidental that liberation theology did not arise from the laity but from within the ranks of the clergy, who are more knowledgeable about theology and who because of their socialization process would have a more religious attitude. It would be difficult to deny in them the presence of a religious vocation, religious feelings, and a special sensitivity to serve God and others under conditions that few would choose for themselves. Many within the clergy enjoy a great deal of credibility in caring and struggling for the poor, with whom they tend to be closely associated. Indeed, Marxism may have played an intellectual role in the development of the liberation movement, but it was a Christian sensitivity that drew these men and women closer to those in need. And it was their faith that originally led them to question the status quo.

The whole purpose of liberation theology espousing the concept of "one history" and advocating erasing the separation of planes is not to relativize Christianity, or part of a subversive conspiracy. Rejecting the separation can be undertaken either to foster a non-eschatological naturalism, or to stress its opposite — the supernatural and transcending nature of human history. In the case of liberation theology, the overall message is to affirm that the world, in its essence, is sacred and not profane; that it has its end in God.[5] The objective is to create the awareness that Christian faith has a socio-political and material dimension, in addition to the interpersonal and spiritual, and that salvation, like the kingdom, is not only ahistorical but, being based on one's actions throughout life, it has its roots on earth. As a group of Brazilian bishops and religious superiors wrote in a document:

> The world is the location where God's salvation begins to take place. . . . Salvation cannot be perceived as a reality beyond the world, that is reached only in transhistory, in the life of the world to come. It begins to take place here. . . . Such salvation that irrupts in humanity, in a historical context reveals itself progressively through the long and complex process of man's liberation.[6]

By affirming the historical roots of salvation, the liberation process acquires a logical religious significance. Thus liberation theology presents itself as a theological answer to a situation that is as political as it is religious, and for which political action is required. Liberation theology suffers from an image problem because the nature of issues in Latin America is political, and many simply do not consider politics, or any other secular temporal activity for that matter, as truly religious. That is why deprivatization of the faith has played such an important role in liberation. As a theology, it deals with the issue of justice (a Christian virtue) and love of neighbor ("the kernel of the Gospel"). It perceives social conditions in Latin America as being such that they violate the person's God-given dignity. It sees material poverty and injustices as contrary to God's design and the product of sinful structures and practices. Hence the human condition, in light of God's aspirations for us, reflects the call to liberation, a call that previously has been made by Jesus Christ. The response, to commit oneself to the liberation of others, is an affirmation of the Christian faith.[7]

The Church has been hesitant to accept this view, out of fear of temporalizing its own mission. However, this is the same risk the laity face constantly while being engaged in temporal affairs. The Church is not the only one called to observe eschatology. The tendency now is toward the realization that closing the separation of planes may enhance religion even more. Many of today's problems persist, in part, precisely because some aspects of the temporal world are still considered profane, and thus inferior. Erasing the separation, while maintaining a healthy distinction, would go a long way toward giving a sacred meaning to many of our tasks on earth and a religious significance to human activities.

A thorough reading of the works and documents of liberation shows what appears to be a constant preoccupation with the poor. The commitment of those who have joined the liberation process, judging by their self-abnegation — lack of material rewards and the personal risks they take — reflects the extent of their convictions. There is a sense of spirituality in these people, indeed, an angry one; a spirituality that is not evasive, but anchored and affected by the social conditions that surround their lives. As Jon Sobrino, one of the best known liberation theologians, says, spirituality must point to the relationship between the person and historical reality "to avoid the temptation of it being described in purely spiritualistic terms, thereby avoiding historical reality." Such distortion, he adds, was rejected by Jesus in the parable of the Samaritan, where He implies that "a person cannot attain one's spiritual identity while ignoring the reality that is imposed on one."[8]

Having said that liberation theology is religiously motivated should not in any way obscure its political intentions, its revolutionary or radical character, or even its ideological bent on some issues by some of its participants. The movement appears as a praxis, i.e., as an action geared to change social reality, on the basis of which a theory (the theology) is being elaborated. By making people aware of their conditions through conscientization, by denouncing the system they see as unjust, by relating the political commitment to an expression of faith, and by making liberation from oppression accessible to all, without religious distinctions, liberation theology establishes, from a political perspective, an attitudinal criterion — the liberative one — as the fundamental basis of what it means to be a Christian. When presented without its eschatological context, it loses its religious orientation. Nevertheless, the extraordinary appeal of the movement comes from its fusion of theology and politics, first at the individual, then at the social level (the masses), through the element of religious feelings. That is, the spirituality of liberation theology allows social conditions to be more than just analyzed. Through "compassion" and love for the poor, reality is now internalized and can be felt. The masses do not need to understand the complexity of reality in scientific terms, since religious terminology simplifies it. In the process, the religious person becomes more politically aware, while those who are not that religious but are politically conscious encounter the possibility of developing a sensitivity for religious values. In this sense liberation theology appears as a Christian political ideology.

The ideological bent of liberation is definitely anti-capitalist. Some have chosen a variety of socialisms as alternative solutions, including Marxist-Leninist socialism. Others opt for sweeping changes within the present structures, in the form of a blend of capitalist and socialist practices. Some within the movement rely partially and with reservations on the Marxist analysis, while others become self-avowed "Christian Marxists."

The Marxist option must be seen within the context of what Marxism represents to those who have opted for it. They find in it a strong emphasis on the praxis, and the interest and motivation to change reality to more just conditions. They see traditional spirituality and modern European theology as not being responsive enough to the needed changes in Latin America, and as lacking such perspective. Marxism, on the other hand, provides them with a more or less precise and concrete approach that allows them to understand and change reality.

Their posture is dictated by socio-political conditions, but also it is affected by frustration and their own sense of political impotence in bringing about social reforms through less radical means. In this sense, becoming Marxist in the name of the faith appears as a rationalization amid the desperate struggle against capitalism. This attitude should not be surprising. The same occurs with those who may be labeled "Christian capitalists," who either accommodate or attempt to justify their "capitalist" values and defend them in the light of faith and the gospel.[9]

The issue of Christian Marxists illustrates a problem which the Church has realized for some time now, but which liberation theology has brought to the surface again. Xavier Alegre, another liberation writer, pinpoints it with clarity when he states that the gospel "does not provide the political, economic, sociological, or historical elements, on which today depends a political option or a concrete form of political action"; and without this, he adds, it is impossible to deduce what the Scriptures demand of a Christian.[10]

From a liberation standpoint a socialist option may be dictated by the praxis (Assman), may be the product of a reflection on the faith (Gutiérrez and Segundo), or may be the result of a personal identification of Marxist and Christian values (Ernesto Cardenal and Bishop Sergio Mendez Arceo). Nonetheless, the common denominator is basically the same: the need to find a concrete political ideology through which the Christian faith can be mediated and which at the same time opposes capitalism.

An adequate explanation of the liberation phenomenon can be presented from the standpoint of the heaven/earth dilemma posed in chapter one. Up to the Puebla conference, liberation theology can be interpreted as a reaction against a spirituality and a theology that were seen as alienating for not being sensitive enough to the conditions of the poor, for not inspiring the necessary social transformations, and for not being able to provide either the ideas or the means to attain such changes. Describing liberation theology as a reaction does not imply that it is an irrational or an impulsive movement lacking premeditation and reflection. It is impossible, however, to deny the presence of emotions and passions. After all, liberation theologians do not approach their theme in a cold and detached manner. In their own words, their theology is a "reflection on the praxis," the result of an active involvement in the liberation process.

The use of two perspectives may help to understand the liberation theology phenomenon. One way of comprehending it is through the explanation of scientific revolutions proposed by Thomas Kuhn.[11] According to this view, there comes a point in time when a present theory (theology) in use ceases to provide adequate explanations or, in this case, fails to deal effectively with the problem at hand. When scientists (theologians) notice that the approach has outlived its usefulness, their discontent takes them to search for new "paradigms," which usually involves "discarding some previously standard beliefs or procedures and, simultaneously, replacing those components of the previous paradigm with others."[12] Kuhn summarizes this process as follows: "The proliferation of competing articulations, the willingness to try anything, the expression of explicit discontent, the recourse to philosophy and to debate over fundamentals, all these are symptoms of a transition from normal to extraordinary research."[13]

The above example is useful from a socio-political angle. Here liberation theology appears as the alternative approach, which is how the theologians and the activists see themselves at present.[14] Nonetheless, this view presents its limitations when liberation is seen from the perspective of eschatology. In this case the process is not yet completed.

Through a second explanation liberation theology may be seen historically, in dialectical terms, as the antithesis of traditional spirituality and modern European theology, caused by the irruption of a social phenomenon, secularism, and the values that accompany it, namely, humanism, materialism, existentialism, and the human sciences. Along these lines, secularism began to force a shift of focus from God to people and from heaven to earth. From then on, religion was seen more and more from an anthropological perspective.

Liberation theology perceives the traditional view as hindering present goals: liberation and human advancement. As an antithesis, the new theology implies a swift change of methodology. It interprets Christ's commandment to love one's neighbor in eschatological terms by means of its intra-historical orientation. That is, God is reached through the love of the poor. While the thesis stresses the kingdom and salvation, the antithesis focuses more on justice and liberation; the one is moved more by the love of God, and the other more by the love of people; the former spiritualizes the gospel and seeks liberation from personal sin, while the later politicizes the Scriptures and pursues a socio-political liberation from the sins of others; the primary intention of the one is to adapt personal life to historical reality — it is personally active though socially passive, while the other's intention is to motivate the person to change reality — it is revolutionary. In the one, capitalism has been its socio-economic and cultural manifestation; in the other, Marxism becomes the opposing force to capitalism.

Traditional spirituality and European theology have the Church's seal of approval and present themselves as expressing the true faith. Liberation theology has had to struggle to gain credibility and acceptance by claiming that its interpretation is religiously based, and that Christianity is ultimately defined not only by the Church's standards, dogmas and beliefs (orthodoxy) but also by proper attitudes and commitments to liberation (orthopraxis). Through the rejection of its counterpart, liberation theology has committed the Church, including the Vatican, to provide a more definite answer to the heaven/earth dilemma. In part through *Evangelii nuntiandi,* and lately through the Puebla document, the universal and the Latin American churches are moving toward a new synthesis of the two poles.

The Future of Liberation Theology Within the Church

Can it be safely assumed that, having been integrated into the mainstream of Catholic doctrine, liberation theology will spread throughout Latin America? It would be difficult to provide a definite answer. To begin with, the bishops, who will be primarily responsible for the implementation of the Puebla document, enjoy a great latitude and autonomy from the Vatican. Quite a few of them who had supported liberation theology from the start will rely on Puebla to push evangelization along the liberation path. Others will pay more attention to the political situation in their countries, the degree of support they may find among their colleagues, considerations to safeguard the institution and its members, and, on a personal level, the beliefs and individual attitudes of each bishop.[15]

Moreover, it does not suffice that the content of liberation theology be incorporated into the Church's doctrine. Attitudes on both sides may determine even more the way in which liberation will be perceived. The intra-ecclesiastical conflict may be seen in terms of an original reaction against the institution and its praxis, and a counter reaction by liberation theology's critics. In an atmosphere reminiscent of past experiences, of which the Church should be more aware, each side has tended to close ranks and trade accusations. It is ironic that Pope Paul VI had suggested years before an attitude of dialogue on the part of the Church as a means to communicate truths and attempt common solutions to problems.[16] Today, when that attitude is most needed, it has been practically ignored by both sides.

The possibility of a rift within the Church cannot be ignored. Nor can liberation activists afford this any more than the Church. So far liberation theology enjoys appeal and influence because it operates as part of the institution. Divorced from it, and without any religious legitimacy whatsoever, the liberation movement would probably be co-opted by secular political ideologies. The question then is whether the institution will be driven to a point where Puebla will become only a piece for historical archives. In this case the bishops will have to ask themselves who will promote social change in Latin America.

Hence the Church appears to be in a quandary. Its main task is to evangelize, to lead its people through a kingdom that is now present but one that finds its fulfillment at the end of history. Yet it knows that leadership requires credibility, and the dynamics of a credible leadership are found in the element of caring. That is, the leader will not have many followers unless he is sensitive enough to attend to the needs and aspirations of his people. And, while at one time these needs and aspirations were perceived as being mostly spiritual, today in Latin America they are also highly social, economic, and political.[17]

To compound the dilemma, one may notice that the bishops themselves continue to have problems with the separation of planes. The tension is still present, and it might be added that it will always be so; such is the nature of eschatology. Nonetheless, some bishops may be reluctant to emphasize a socio-political praxis for fear that to do so may reflect more concern for temporal affairs than for eternal ones and that the Church's image may become too politicized. Though it is clear that in Christianity the spirit is superior to matter, as Pope John Paul II has stated[18] this is often understood as meaning that human care detracts from religious truths. And though "love for man" is the prime value in the temporal order,[19] a prevailing neo-dualism within the Church makes it appear as secondary in importance.

Thus there appears in the Puebla document an assertion that the truths about Jesus Christ are essential to evangelization (351) while liberation is only an integral part of it (355). The implications that may be derived from this interpretation are crucial to the way the bishops will approach socio-political liberation, especially when faced with a multitude of problems. For example, Fr. Bonaventura Kloppenburg, Dean of the Pastoral Theological Institute of CELAM, who is highly responsible for interpreting Puebla, has stated within the context of present Latin American conditions that "action on behalf of justice, human development, the economic, social, and cultural liberation of the poor and the oppressed, are certainly important for Christians, *but they are not essential constitutive elements of evangelization itself.*"[20] One wonders how many would fail to interpret him as saying, "from the standpoint of the Church's evangelizing mission, the love of the poor and the oppressed is important but not essential to being a Christian."

This issue merits enough consideration to make a caveat at this point. Kloppenburg alludes to the "central truths" in the document (166) that make up the essential content of evangelization, and points to paragraphs n. 170 (about Jesus Christ), n. 220 (about the Church), and n. 304 (about man). He omits, however, what Puebla said in n. 166 and n. 169. These paragraphs say: "We propose to announce the central truths of evangelization: Christ, our hope . . . , sent by the Father . . . , offering man his life to lead him to his integral liberation" (166). After stating two other "central truths," about the Church and about Mary, the document adds a fourth one, saying: "Man, because of his dignity in the image of God, deserves our commitment in favor of his liberation and total realization in Christ Jesus" (169).

Puebla bases its interpretation of central truths on Pope Paul VI's *Evangelii nuntiandi (EN),* so it is important that we go to that document itself. In the work Paul VI dealt with a conflictive issue, socio-political liberation, from the standpoint of the Church's main task, evangelization. It reflects his way of handling a topic whose discussions during the 1974 Special Synod of Bishops were anything but conclusive.[21] The Pope needed to measure his words carefully, and distinguish between essential and secondary elements. He refers to the essential content as "the living substance, which cannot be modified or ignored without seriously diluting the nature of evangelization itself" (*EN,* n. 25).

The content of evangelization, in order of presentation, is as follows: the preaching of Jesus Christ, Son of God, and of a transcendent and eschatological salvation (*EN,* n. 27); the preaching of God's promises, of God's love for the person and the person's love for God; brotherly love (called the "kernel of the Gospel"); the mystery of evil; the preaching of the mystery of prayer, of the Church, and of the Sacraments (*EN*, n. 28); and a message of liberation (*EN*, nn. 29-37). Kloppenburg somehow sees clearly what the essential content is, and implies that it does not include liberation.[22] The document, however, does not state that liberation should be considered secondary or even integral. Its relation to evangelization is, indeed, ambiguous. Liberation appears within the context of "completing evangelization," not being foreign to it, and having "profound links" with it (*EN*, nn. 29, 30, 31). And, there follows the already quoted citation that it is impossible to accept that evangelization could or should ignore the importance of justice and liberation (*EN*, n. 31).

Evangelii nuntiandi seems to imply that socio-political liberation, by itself, is not an essential part of evangelization. But it would become essential if it is presented "without reduction or ambiguity" (*EN*, n. 32), if it opens itself to God (*EN*, n. 33), if it is centered on the Kingdom of God (*EN*, n. 34), as long as it is not identified, or associated, with salvation (*EN*, n. 35), if it involves conversion (*EN*, n. 36), and if it excludes violence (*EN*, n. 37). Even Kloppenburg himself points out that "full liberation," i.e., integral, emerges as the final consensus at the 1974 Synod.[23] What this means is that the Church may preach the need for socio-political liberation within the context of the above requirements as an essential part of its message.

The problem lies in that evangelization is seen from at least two perspectives, both of which are reflected in the Puebla document. From the standpoint of human advancement, the terms temporal progress, social reforms, or any other impersonal terminology, do not reflect the serious plight of the human condition. Also, if the issue is approached from the standpoint of people who do not find themselves in conditions which the Church describes as sinful, inhuman, and as a cry for liberation, it may very well be that temporal progress is integral, though not essential to evangelization. This is not, however, the way that liberation theology sees reality. And, quite possibly, neither do Popes Paul VI and John Paul II.

A socio-political liberation is more like a theology geared to rescue the children of God from wretchedness. It needs to be seen in terms of the global dimension of the Samaritan action that Pope Paul VI spoke about in *Populorum progressio.*[24] It is possible then, that the socio-political aspect needs to be considered "essential" for as long as people are not fully liberated *from* oppression and not yet ready to be liberated *to* become more as human beings. Only when viewed from that central truth, "the preaching of brotherly love for all people — the capacity of giving and forgiving, of self-denial, of helping one's brother and sister" (*EN,* n. 28), may liberation be understood from a religious standpoint. It would be difficult to see how the liberation of people from the conditions described by Paul VI and John Paul II — famine, chronic disease, illiteracy, poverty, and injustice (*EN,* n. 30) — and those described by the bishops at Puebla (Puebla, nn. 27-70) may not be considered essential. That is, how can such a task be "modified or ignored without seriously diluting the nature of evangelization itself" (*EN,* n. 25)?

The other view is more in line with the neo-dualist interpretation, in which socio-political liberation is important but not essential to evangelization. From this perspective liberation theology is mostly a political program. This opinion, though narrow, has some validity in the sense that for faith to be realized in the political realm, it needs to be mediated through politics. Its socio-political dimension will need to have political manifestations, though in the case of the Church not partisan ones. It is understandable, however, that people may gather only a political impression of liberation theology. After all, many of those involved in the movement have contributed to create that image. The impression is even greater for people with a more traditional view of religion, who are not accustomed to religious involvement in politics. For them, liberation theology will cause an uproar.

Human liberation, as reflected in liberation theology, has suffered from serious excesses, deviations, omissions, and ambiguities. That is why the Puebla corrective became necessary. Still, the Church's implementation of the document is not certain. Much will depend on whether the bishops see the sociopolitical aspects of liberation from a religious perspective that includes its social feature, or from a narrow political angle.

A most important indicator will be how the Vatican deals with the issue, since many bishops will take their cues from Rome. In this regard,the Vatican's *Instructions* on liberation theology may deal a serious blow to the implementation of the socio-political aspects of the Puebla document. The first *Instruction* presents a description of conditions in Latin America that corresponds with liberation theology's own. The document accepts the term "theology of liberation" as a valid one, and anchors it on a biblical foundation, both in the Old and New Testaments. Moreover, in its criticism it correctly points out the reductionist tendency in some theologians and the risks involved. And in what appears to be the motivating factor behind the document, it calls attention to the use of Marxist concepts "in an insufficiently critical manner," when their ideological aspects are accepted as scientific analysis, leading many to embrace Marxism in its totality.[25] Nevertheless, instead of demanding that the theologians be more rigorous in their conceptualization of the terms, and more specific on the relationship between socio-political liberation and the theological bases, the document attempts to evaluate "some liberation theologies" from the standpoint of the historical realization of Marxism and a dogmatic interpretation of its theory, which it opposes.

Much of its criticism is based on aspects of liberation theology that appear to have been taken out of their proper context, such as the class struggle, the concept of one history, the role of Christ in history, social change, and eschatology. A dogmatic Marxism is attributed to the theologies that, frankly, is not there in most instances. On the contrary, it is a lack of precision in the use of the praxis and its relationship to Marxism, and not a concrete formulation, that one notices in liberation writings. Since liberation theology has a Marxist component, as do aspects of the Church's social doctrine (though to a lesser extent), one may not properly speak of "some liberation theologies" that do and others that do not. The document does not indicate on what it bases its views, or on which authors, so it becomes difficult to substantiate the charges attributed to the theology. As a result it gives the impression that the Latin American version of liberation theology is being condemned.

The critique of liberation theology has been undertaken outside the Marxist framework, and without giving proper consideration to the historical context in which the theme of liberation arose. It appears that certain groups within the Church are attempting to shape a liberation doctrine devoid of Marxist elements. That is why the document states that it is not possible to separate parts of Marxism, including aspects of its epistemology, without accepting the entire ideology, or that it is "perhaps impossible to purify" its concepts.[26] The document does not say, however, that in the past, as we have seen, the Church has done precisely what it now says cannot be done. What is even more important, the Church needs precisely to "purify" Marxist concepts by systematically conceptualizing them in accordance with a Christian perspective. The alternative would be to give added strength to Marxism by presenting an alienating and supposedly reactionary Church as its opponent.

The way to accomplish this is indirectly suggested by Cardinal Joseph Ratzinger, supposedly the one responsible for issuing the *Instruction*.[27] His approach, which appeared in an in-house version of the document that was leaked to the press, is intended to deal with liberation theology, though it applies to Marxism as well. He says:

> An error cannot subsist without lacking a nucleus of truth in it. Hence, when dealing openly with the error, . . . a question must undoubtedly always be kept present: what truth is hidden beneath the error and how can it be recovered fully from the error?[28]

There are implicit risks involved in such an attempt, especially the Church's fear of being manipulated and co-opted by Marxism. At the same time, however, ideas do not vanish or become less effective merely by opposing them, any more than Marxism can be made spiritual simply by rejecting its materialist foundations. Also, the document cannot oppose materialist Marxism by resorting to a spiritualist Christianity and then adopting a caricature of materialism in the name of its social doctrine without falling into terrible contradictions.

A theology that is forced to rely on an abstract spiritualism due to a fearful vision of modern society's tendency to set aside Christ and religion is harmful to people. Marxism's arbitrary rejection of the spiritual does not necessarily have to lead to the latter's rejection of materialism's positive insights. In the first *Instruction,* however, we see again a good-bad valuation assigned to the spirit-flesh dichotomy, and a failure to recognize adequately the conditioning effect of "sinful" structures and values in a culture. This last point is related to what may be Christianity's greatest religious problem today: people who commit evil without knowing or without caring, due to a lack of a religious conscience and education and to the pressure imposed by a culture that sanctions its own morality. The Church's answer is to respond with abstraction. Thus, we see statements in the document such as "God, and not man, has the power to change the situations of suffering," and "God is the defender and the liberator of the poor."[29]

Millions of believers and non-Christian Marxists not well-versed in the Church's theological jargon will interpret the above passage in a passive and alienating way: one has only to wait for

God to physically liberate His people and change conditions. Even conversion appears to be secondary. Yet if "God is the Lord of history" and guides liberation, as the Church affirms, He does so by making the call. Nevertheless, the response is up to us ourselves, and whatever praxis takes place on earth is not executed by God but by us. If a person refuses to respond to God's call for liberation, and we can, liberation simply will not take place. Failure to acknowledge our role in history, which does not exclude God's action, takes all the responsibility from one's actions and makes salvation look like a puppet theater.

As Segundo shows, this argument leads unavoidably to a separation and not just a distinction of planes, and to the existence of two histories.[30] A Catholic theology is not incompatible with a well-understood materialism. In it, when the individual responds to the liberation call, one does not do it of one's own intitiative but at God's urging. It is here where a statement from the *Instruction* becomes clear by affirming that "the Christian cannot forget that it is only the Holy Spirit. . . . who is the source of every true renewal."[31] And, it may be added once more, a Holy Spirit that blows on whomever it wants to.

From a political standpoint, the Vatican's view at the time the first *Instruction* was issued reflected a legitimate anxiety over the political panorama in the region. This is seen in the document's approach to social change, in which it insists on making an appeal for personal conversion as the only means to bring about structural transformation.[32]

Given the present political situation in the region, especially in the aftermath of the Nicaraguan revolution, Pope John Paul II's task is even more difficult than that faced by Pope Paul VI at the time of Medellín. Today, the Pope is attempting to steer the Church and its people in Latin America through liberation while avoiding the creation of Marxist governments and the use of violence. The problem with liberation theology arises out of its ambiguous treatment of Marxist terms such as class struggle and socialism, its reductionist tendencies, and some of the theologians' and activists' lack of historical awareness in suggesting alliances with Marxist revolutionaries. For the Church not to stress personal conversion in these conditions could be interpreted as favoring a narrow Marxist approach that entails those negative aspects that the institution wants to avoid. In effect, an emphasis on the transformation of structures would most likely result in a tacit support of a revolutionary praxis that may easily be co-opted by Marxist guerrillas.

Today the Church is undergoing an experience similar to the one it went through a century ago. At that time the institution reacted strongly against civil and individual human rights for fear that espousing them could lead to the demise of the mythical Catholic State, and to acceptance of their sources: naturalism, liberalism, and secularization. In condemning these philosophical currents, the Church opposed those rights which it now defends so strongly. Likewise, in Latin America the Church may not escape its present dilemma without paying a heavy price. Ronaldo Muñoz, another liberation theologian, notices the conflict. According to the biblical faith, he argues, the practice of justice and the option for the poor constitute the fundamental exigency of the commandment to love one's neighbor, which is inseparable from the love of God and the crux of authentic religion. Given the concrete situation of injustice and oppression in the region, the same fundamental exigency of love leads one to the struggle on behalf of those in need. The struggle will have to be an active and efficient praxis requiring the conscientization and mobilization of the masses, since the opposition is strongly organized in its resistance. The basic premise, the one rooted in the faith, needs to be operationalized through the mediation of minor premises which are based on a concrete analysis of socio-economic and political conditions. Hence, Christians cannot fall back on one approach — which by itself may not be considered effective to overcome the conditions that affect the poor on the basis of dogmatic attitudes, without ignoring the basic or major premise or, as Munoz says, "without rendering the Gospel sterile."[33] In other words, its concern over

Marxism and violence will drive the Church to a position which precludes the operationalization of Christianity's major commandment.

The Vatican's failure to deal with these problems caused a deep dissatisfaction among liberation theologians and progressive members of the Latin American hierarchy. In the first *Instruction,* the Vatican had reverted to a subtle separation of planes, backing away from the open-ended position on social change that the bishops approved at Puebla. The critical tone in the document, and the shift it indicated, must have taken many of the bishops who follow Rome closely by surprise.

At the time the first document was issued, the Vatican had stated that a second document dealing with Christian freedom and liberation would be forthcoming. This one, issued seventeen months after, purports to establish the theoretical basis of freedom and liberation. In this document there are subtle changes from the first, although there exists, according to the Vatican, an "organic relationship" between the two documents, which means that they should be read "in the light of each other."[34]

The second *Instruction* appears to extend an olive branch to liberation theology. Its tone is not as harsh or as critical as the first document. Some of the changes indicate that the Vatican has reflected on its earlier views and has incorporated the liberation line. The changes show a desire to close ranks in order to mend fences with the liberation theology movement, without compromising doctrinal orthodoxy. There is even a humble, though positive, recognition of the Church's members' "failings and their delays" in the quest for liberation.[35] Moreover, there is a firm determination on the part of the Vatican "to respond to the anxiety of contemporary man," which evolves around freedom and liberation, and which the Church accepts as "among the principal signs of the times in the modern world."[36]

Nowhere, however, are the changes so significant as in the approach to social change. The document affirms the intimate relation between salvation and liberation by indissolubly linking the former "to the task of improving and raising the conditions of human life" in the world.[37] It stresses that in promoting social change the appeal to conversion should take precedence over structural changes. Nonetheless, this time the Vatican seeks a more realistic and balanced position by stating that it is "perfectly legitimate that those who suffer oppression on the part of the wealthy or the politically powerful should take action, through morally licit means, in order to secure structures and institutions in which their rights will be truly respected."[38] Hence, the new position of the Vatican is that conversion of hearts and structural changes should take place simultaneously.[39] Moreover, in a bold statement, the document admits recourse to armed struggle as a last resort — a traditional doctrine within the Church, but one that had not been enunciated by the institution since the days of Pope Paul VI.[40] Also, calling it "a way more conformable to the moral principles and having no less prospects for success," the document calls for 'passive resistance' as a tactic of political opposition that implies less use of violence.[41]

Days after the second *Instruction* was issued, the Pope sent a personal letter to the Brazilian bishops, many of whom are among the most ardent supporters of the liberation movement, in which he is said to have offered his support and endorsed their work.[42] It remains to be seen if these two events signal a decision by this Pope to override the fear that otherwise may prevent the Church's will from matching its desires and good intentions.

Puebla and Its Political Implications

Today, the Puebla document represents one of the most progressive approaches to social change in the region. If the Church does not spearhead social transformations other groups, probably more violent ones, will move in to fill the vacuum. Given the level of radicalization in Latin America, Puebla represents a more restrained and controllable approach to change.[43]

As social conditions deteriorate or fail to improve in the region, a situation of rising expectations and high levels of frustration will lead to popular discontent. Without political freedoms to vocalize their anger and channels to implement changes, many will resort to subversive violence. Responding to these actions, governments will increase political repression. It is repression, more than anything else, that contributes to the political strength and the radicalization of Marxist guerrilla groups. Some within the Church in Latin America have realized that much. In their struggle against what is perceived as a communist threat, governments too often rely on the same means for which they criticize their enemies. Thus they lose moral and legal legitimacy. By resorting to torture, imprisonment, and killings they confer the prestige of martyrdom on communist groups.[44]

Even more significant is the way in which the guerrillas gather military strength. Lacking military skills and capability, many non-Marxist Christian-turned-revolutionaries, as well as others who oppose present conditions, will find in a diminutive guerrilla group an established channel of revolution. The types of revolutions that non-Marxists have in mind, naturally, are not Marxist. However, these revolutions will be led by those who possess military expertise, the Marxist minority, who will receive manpower and political support from the non-Marxists. If the revolution is successful, those who have the weapons, the organization, and the military leadership will claim the right to rule. Thus a very small, yet militarily prepared, Marxist guerrilla can become the nucleus around which an opposition may consolidate.

It would be naive to expect the kind of bold reforms that are required in Latin America to take place without some sort of political pressure. Without any negative feedback from the populace, governments will tend to support the status quo. Hence the question of how peaceful social changes may be, will be determined by numerous variables. One has to assess the degree of change the people seek and its political orientation; how badly do they want these changes; how many want the changes; how organized they are; their potential for mobilization; the means they are willing to use. On the other side, one has to gauge the responsiveness capability of change on the part of a government; how far is it willing to go with a minimum of political pressure; the way in which it perceives change; the values that condition such perceptions; the alternatives, or lack of them, to cope with political or military pressure, including domestic and foreign support.

There is no single general rule to determine the possibility of violence across the region. Each nation has its own peculiar situation. Thus in Argentina, the military, facing a decline in popular support and lack of credibility, opted for popular elections and averted greater political unrest. In Chile, meanwhile, the government has met stiff yet unorganized opposition with a minimum of concessions, and has been able to continue its authoritarian rule. In El Salvador, it took external persuasion before the government consented to a form of popular elections (although too late to avoid violence). The one aspect that remains unknown is the extent to which the Church praxis, as outlined in Puebla, will result in more or less violence. For the reasons stated in the previous chapter, but mostly to avoid further bloodshed, the bishops have opted for non-violence in a most emphatic manner. The crucial question is whether their approach will work, and if it does not, whether the Church will pull back from its objectives. Again, the institution faces another serious dilemma.

Possibly, the type of changes that the bishops in Puebla have in mind may not come about as peacefully as they wish. Ironically, as much as the document advocates the use of non-violence, it would be difficult for the bishops not to realize that their own commitment to the poor and to their liberation will result in an intensification of the struggle in which the violence and repression will likely increase. For example, let us say that to fulfill its religious mission, and to prevent Marxism from being at the head of social transformations, which could result in military involvement by foreign powers, the national Church decides to implement Puebla. Some of the obstacles that so far have prevented a high level of activism and militancy by the masses in Latin America include lack of awareness of the situation, indifference, indecisiveness, fear, and lack of organization. It is in these aspects that a religious oriented liberation praxis will be most effective. A Church committed to social justice will engage in religious education that includes formation of a critical social consciousness and political and civic awareness. The masses will be sensitized about oppression and material deprivation. They will be told that God does not accept such conditions and neither should they, that they have it within their power, while trusting God to be on their side, to forge their own liberation. All this leads to conscientization, the basis of a political praxis.

At the same time, the Church, through prophetic denunciation and its advocacy of human rights, will bring pressure on the government from above and below. The clergy, for example, without becoming involved in partisan politics, may follow the practice set by Pope John Paul II during his trips throughout the continent and have an extrordinary impact on the masses. The major difference is that the clergy's actions can represent an ongoing process with more lasting effects than the Pope's visits, though at higher personal risk. Undertaken by local clergy, John Paul II's denunciations and annunciations would be regarded as subversive by many governments, mainly because of the close relationship that exists between the priest and his people. He preaches to them, attends their needs, shares their conditions, and instructs them in their faith.

The Church's praxis does not need to rely on a Marxist-type class struggle as a strategy to bring about social changes. Nonetheless, conscientization and denunciation, no matter how spiritual the tone, if they are to be effective, invariably result in some degree of antagonism against those who impede liberation. Moreover, those on the other side, if they are less predisposed to non-violence, see themselves as being on the defensive and protecting the status quo, and as the indirect target of denunciations are likely to become more prone to hostility.

Furthermore, even the absence of violent Marxist ideology may not necessarily prevent an outbreak of violence. There are psychological and sociological elements that often neutralize a non-violent ethic. The previous chapter pointed out the great internal discipline that non-violence requires. This discipline is constantly being put to a test in many parts of Latin America. Watching, as Pope John Paul II remarked, how a human being can be forced to die a slow death when one is deprived of basic necessities can, indeed, tire the patience of a people. These conditions give way to frustration and despair, which in turn often lead to violence. Repressive measures, too, result in anger and vengeance on the part of relatives and friends of victims. The majority of those involved in violence, either as a result of these attitudes or out of support for the cause of others, most probably do not know much about the intricacies of Marxism or communism, its premises or its philosophical basis. A former seminarian, whose brother was a priest killed by government forces in a Central American country, said when told about the historical experience with Communist regimes: "Maybe I am substituting one form of hell for another; I do not know, but I am willing to take the risk."[45]

The Puebla approach is not geared toward a quick mobilization of grassroots support. It involves long-term, comprehensive but unsystematic action. The effectiveness of the Church's praxis lies in not being narrowly political, but in projecting the moral strength that is derived from religious credibility. It can lose such a credibility if it is perceived that instead of contributing to the better ordering of society it begins to pursue partisan political objectives. Moreover, the institution will not end its critical function even after new changes take place, as long as it sees that human rights, both individual and social, are still violated.[46]

There is a strong possibility that the Church's praxis may lead first to stronger systematic repression by governments of the Right and the Left. It is quite realistic, however, that the Church's praxis may weaken the government's repressive system, opening the way for political parties to struggle for power, but without the conversion of attitudes that Puebla seeks. As a result, conditions in the short run may definitely improve with the elimination of repressive measures. But politics will probably return to the usual ideological fights, which most likely will retard social changes. In countries where the electoral process has been instituted, the Puebla approach is oriented toward some forms of social pluralist democracies. In all, the policies of the United States could be crucial in determining what may happen within a particular country. Within the last fifteen years, as is publicly known, the United States has persuaded El Salvador to hold elections and the Dominican Republic to abide by its results; conspired to bring down the Allende government; probably influenced the Bolivian and Panamanian governments to respect the electoral process; allowed the downfall of the Somoza regime in Nicaragua and is presently putting pressure on the Sandinistas to introduce a more pluralistic and open political process; was instrumental in shortening the war between Argentina and Great Britain; brought down the Marxist-influenced government in Grenada; and continues to extend its support to Right-wing dictatorships. Thus it would not be an exaggeration to say that the United States can, if it wants to, affect the destinies of many of the Latin American nations.

The United States and Puebla

What may the United States expect from a Puebla theology? In the past, American administrations have shown a genuine lack of empathy with regard to the social problems in Latin

American countries. American foreign policy objectives, mainly based on self-interest, have sought to assert political, economic, and military supremacy in the region, avoid the establishment of communist regimes, support and defend American investments, and preserve access to sources of raw materials. Its policies have vaccillated from benign neglect, to demonstrations of political and economic interest when faced with the communist threat, to paternalism and some authentic social concern.

It will be difficult for the United States to understand the level of political radicalization in Latin America, probably because of an ethnocentric tendency on our part to expect other societies to be similar to ours. We often find it difficult to comprehend how others can reject our way of life, our customs, and our values. In this respect we are still a rather closed-minded society.

Furthermore, it is difficult for us to understand Puebla. We often overlook the extremely high levels of individual participation in the political, economic, and cultural life in the United States, in contrast to the low levels of opportunity and conditions of poverty that characterize many parts of Latin America. The civil rights that we often take for granted in the United States are routinely ignored abroad. Thus our everyday political activities, such as demonstrations, petitions, freedom of the press, labor strikes, political campaigns, and social action on behalf of the poor, are in many instances looked upon as subversive in Latin America. Inequalities in the region are greater, and basic needs often go unmet. In addition, popular representation, respect for the law and for political institutions, a strongly diversified economic base, innumerable political and legal processes in the United States, are largely responsible for making the American capitalist system more responsive to human needs and aspirations, in contrast to the Latin American systems. Hence, whatever is won via the ballot and the courts in the United States is too often earned with the bullet and violent social revolution in Latin America. Popular discontent in the region is greater, and given the lack of authorized channels it will be expressed through unlawful and unconventional means. It happens, then, that a traditional law-and-order society such as ours will tend to frown on radical political behavior when it fails to comprehend such differences.

Our policies aside, some of the actions of our multinational corporations do not enhance the United States' image abroad. Because of their sophisticated technology, centralized management, secretive decision-making process, lack of public accountability, and enormous financial holdings, these economic entities wield great political and economic power. Their primary interest is to insure a political climate in which they can operate with little or no governmental interference. Their function is, above all, to safeguard investments and to seek higher returns. These priorities, though understandable from a capitalist standpoint, too often give way to policies and to conditions that are insensitive to the needs and problems in Latin American countries. Blind to this fact, private corporations often collude with governments and ruling classes in order to establish themselves firmly. With little or no sense of social responsibility, some of these corporations fail to notice that in the long run, they help to create an adverse environment for American business.

Even though the Puebla theology does not preach nationalism, one should not be surprised to see strong nationalist tendencies emanating from the Church as means to assert national cultural independence. The bishops themselves set the tone early in the Puebla document. They stated:

> We refuse the condition of becoming satellites of any country in the world, or of their ideologies. . . . It is time that Latin America warns the developed nations not to render us stagnant . . . ; not to exploit us. . . .[47]

Thus the United States, because of the role it has played in supporting unjust political and economic systems, will likely suffer antagonism from priests and the laity.[48] From a Puebla perspective one sees past American administrations feeling proud of the country's political heritage, its democratic values, and its highly advanced economic system. At the same time, while focusing mainly on the national interest and conditioned by an inordinate fear of communism, they have supported political systems and economic structures that are inimical to our own domestic political tradition. The United States has regarded Latin America as its own backyard, but without much concern for how well it is kept. Indifference and condescending policies provoke the reactions that a liberation theology has echoed.

Nevertheless, in the Church's case, Puebla goes beyond anti-Americanism. The bishops see in the American culture the model of a consumerist society exporting a way of life that does not respond to Latin American priorities, and one they find incompatible with Christian values. They see a fetishism with regard to material possession taking hold of the society, making people insensitive to the plight of millions around the world who struggle to meet their most basic needs.

Out of this picture there emerges a desire to follow a path of development different from the one the United States has taken. This means that policies often will not be in accordance with American interests. In the past the United States has reacted defensively against claims of insensitivity and criticism of its way of life, failing to notice the role of our past attitudes and policies in determining and cementing anti-American sentiments. Though diversity and pluralism characterize American culture, we still have difficulty projecting and upholding these values in our foreign policy. This may present problems for the United States, as nations, moving away from a bipolar world to one characterized by interdependence, assert themselves more.

The United States would err if it were to interpret Puebla from a political or ideological standpoint, while overlooking its religious basis, on which we could find common ground, given our Judeo-Christian tradition. It would be a mistake to regard the document as subversive or radical, when from a wider perspective it can lead to a sincere and legitimate examination of our own values and priorities. In this regard, opening ourselves to other perspectives and options, and granting other nations a more ample margin for self-determination and governance, may perhaps be more effective in the long run.

A Final Word

A well integrated liberation theology, one that without being devoid of religious transcendence focuses on a religious praxis of social justice, may well revitalize Latin American Christianity in ways not foreseen by the Church. The task of building the earthly city would not contradict one's faithful adherence to God's kingdom. In the early 1960s, for example, French social scientist F. Houtart wisely observed that "development needs a system of (religious) values that would integrate it as the temporal task of Christians."[49] This is precisely what Puebla has attempted to accomplish. In its synthesis, it has sought to harmonize spiritual and material values, individual and social consciousness, theory and praxis, into a flexible socio-political doctrine.

Its praxis, more than its theoretical formulations, may pose interesting philosophical and political questions for communism. Just as Marxism forced Christianity to take a hard look at itself, a liberation praxis may lead to the eventual reformulation of the communist praxis. Otherwise, it risks exposing even more the moral bankruptcy of its totalitarian aspect, thereby making itself unappealing to its followers in Latin America.

The point is dialectically implied in a reflection made by poor villagers at Solentiname, off the Nicaraguan coast. They remarked that there would have been no need for communism if Catholics had preached a true gospel.[50] The remark is somewhat exaggerated, for preaching a true gospel still does not insure an automatic conversion. However, it is far from being off target. The Church itself has indirectly admitted as much in Vatican II, while dealing with the problem of atheism. First, it stated: "To the extent that they (believers) neglect their training in the faith, or teach erroneous doctrine, or are deficient in their religious, moral, or social life, they must be said to conceal rather than reveal the authentic face of God and religion."[51] It then adds:

> The remedy which must be applied to atheism, is to be sought in a proper presentation of the Church's teaching as well as in the integral life of the Church and her members. . . . Faith needs to prove its fruitfulness (its praxis) by penetrating the believer's entire life, including its worldly dimensions, and by activating him toward justice and love, especially regarding the needy.[52]

This insight becomes particularly important today. Marxism is not so much philosophically as it is historically atheist. Marx's social critique of the State entailed the religious critique, since religion and the State were identified with each other. Marx realized that religion was used to support the political status quo, thus a critique of religion would weaken the State's ideological basis.[53] Milan Machoveč, "a self-avowed Marxist," adds to the point:

> Atheism has meaning only as a critique, limited in place and in time, of certain dominant models used in contemporary religious faith. Marx developed his 'atheism' as a critique of the conventional nineteenth-century representations of God, and

> should these change, then the genuine Marxist would have to revise his critique.[54]

As Machoveč adds, the Marxist problem is not with the ideals of Jesus, but with the way in which Christians present them.[55] Their distorted image has allowed Marxism to become the bearer of justice in today's world, while the Marxist historical manifestation continues to appear as the only alternative to a crude individualism.

The same argument applies to liberal capitalism. Marxism was not elaborated in a historical vacuum. It grew as a protest against conditions that were the product of the liberal bourgeois wing of the French Revolution, from which modern capitalism, supported by classical liberalism, emerged. Thus, Marxism, too, has been conditioned by a religious, economic, and political culture. The crux of its critique of capitalism retains its validity to the extent that the system continues to operate in a traditional fashion. Some of the Marxist predictions, namely, a class struggle revolution in the most advanced societies, have failed to materialize in Western developed countries, in part because the system has shown some flexibility in incorporating social demands. Capitalism has within itself the possibility of weakening the Marxist praxis. In the long run, this can be one of liberation theology's unintended consequences, to cause the reformulation of historical capitalism.

NOTES

[1]On this point see Penny Lernoux, *Cry of the People* (New York: Penguin Books, 1980). Also, the Annual Reports of Amnesty International on Human Rights Violations.

[2]To evaluate a position from its opposite stand does not necessarily mean that a distorted evaluation will result. That will depend on the extent to which the presence of one's values is consciously or unconsciously allowed to play a role, and on whether a common criterion is used to evaluate the position.

[3]"Response of the Coordinating Committee to Cardinal Silva," March, 1972, in Eagleson, p. 57.

[4]*Puebla,* nos. 535-559.

[5]Gustavo Gutiérrez, *Teología de la Liberación,* pp. 193-203. In this line, Enrique Dussel, the Liberation historian states: "Christians assert that there is an eschatological order and a historical order; working toward the historical future which they know is not absolute, they witness to the eschatological kingdom." In *Ethics,* p. 51.

[6]"He Escuchado el Clamor de mi Pueblo," June, 1973, in *Signos de Liberación,* p. 132.

[7]Boff, *Teología desde el Cautiverio,* pp. 58-60.

[8]Jon Sobrino, "Espiritualidad de Jesús y Espiritualidad de la Liberación," *Espiritualidad de la Liberación,* n.a. (Lima: Centro de Estudios y Publicaciones, 1980), p. 67.

[9]See, for example, Michael Novak, *The Spirit of Democratic Capitalism* (New York: Simon and Schuster, 1982).

[10]Xavier Alegre, "Mi Reino No Es De Este Mundo," *Diakonia* 21 (enero-abril 1982): 81.

[11]Thomas S. Kuhn, *The Structure of Scientific Revolutions,* 2nd edition enlarged (Chicago: The University of Chicago Press, 1970).

[12]Ibid., p. 66.

[13]Ibid., p. 91.

[14]Galilea, for example, who by no means is among the radicals in the movement, sees liberation theology as compensating for European theology's excessive tendency to look at itself, and not at the third World. For him, it is a complement that the Church presently lacks. (From interview with Segundo Galilea) Inasmuch as this may be correct, we are mindful that up to Puebla the integration of the two aspects had not been accomplished, and there are questions as to whether both sides will accept it in practice.

[15]One may notice the enormous contrast between Archbishop Rivera y Damas from San Salvador, not a liberation theology supporter in the strict sense, who opposes external military involvement and supports a dialogue between the guerrillas and the government, and his colleague, bishop Pedro Arnoldo Aparicio of San Vicente, El Salvador, who not only rejects a dialogue (he thought John Paul II would not call for one — he did) but favors American military involvement to combat the Communist threat.

[16]See Pope Paul VI, *Ecclesiam Suam,* Aug. 6, 1964, nos. 58-118.

[17]Christ himself tied the concept of leadership with that of service to others (Matthew 20:24-27). Also, we must notice that in the Gospel Christ treats both spiritual and material needs as important, when "the other" comes into view. In several instances spiritual gifts are provided along with material ones, and even material ones by themselves, so that the person may either accept faith and God's love, or learn the meaning of faith. (Matthew 9:1-8; Matthew 14:13-21;

Luke 10:30-37). This does not mean that Christ wanted to convey the message that individual health is more important than eternal salvation, but that the way of faith is through care and love for the needy — compassion.

[18]*Redemptor hominis,* no. 16.

[19]Pope Paul VI, *Octogesima adveniens,* no. 23.

[20]"La Eclesiología Militante de Leonardo Boff," in *Medellín* 30 (junio 1982): 282. Italicizing mine.

[21]Fr. Bonaventura Kloppenburg has an excellent work in which he describes the different views on liberation by the world's bishops, in *Christian Salvation,* pp. 31-57.

[22]Ibid., p. 60.

[23]Ibid., p. 56.

[24]*Populorum progressio,* nos. 43-49.

[25]*Instruction I,* no. 8.

[26]Ibid., first quote is found in no. 7.6, and second quote in Introduction.

[27]Although Cardinal Ratzinger signed the document, which came for the congregation he oversees, many of the arguments and the terminology in it resemble those used in the past by Cardinal López Trujillo, who has been waging for years a personal ideological war against liberation theologians.

[28]The text appeared originally in the Italian magazine *30 Giorni,* March, 1984; the quote is found on pp. 48-49.

[29]*Instruction I,* nos. 4.5; 6.

[30]Segundo, *Liberation of Theology,* pp. 138-149.

[31]*Instruction I,* no. 11.10.

[32]Ibid., no. 11.8.

[33]Ronaldo Muñoz, "Lucha de Clases y Evangelio," in *Panorama de la Teología,* pp. 292-93.

[34]*Instruction II,* no.2.

[35]Ibid., no. 57.

[36]Ibid., no. 44.

[37]Ibid., no. 80.

[38]Ibid., no. 75.

[39]Ibid.

[40]Ibid., no. 79.

[41]Ibid.

[42]*National Catholic Reporter,* 25 April 1986, p. 1.

[43]This is not to say that a sincere implementation of the Puebla document will not exacerbate tensions at times, but that being the action of an established credible institution, it can play a moderating role, as it has done in El Salvador and Chile, for example.

[44]"La No-Violencia Evangélica. . . .," pp. 135-136.

[45]Conversation with the former seminarian took place in Washington, D.C. in June, 1982. He requested that his name be kept anonymous.

[46]Hence we see how the Nicaraguan Church joined the struggle against the Somoza regime, and now remains critical of the Sandinista government's actions against its members and of its increasingly authoritarian policies. In a statement made public, it called on the government to stop abusing the Church. *L'Osservatore Romano,* Aug. 5, 1984, Daily edition, p. 2.

[47]CELAM, "Mensaje a los Pueblos de América Latina." *Puebla,* no. 8.

[48]The following is excerpted from a talk by Fr. Jose Alemán, S.J. to American Jesuits in 1972:

> "The U.S. image in Latin America is very bad at this moment. You will find, for example, some Jesuits in my house who really hate North Americans. The students are another thing. You cannot imagine the anti-American feeling among students. . . . It is too easy to say that you alone are responsible for our problems. If you are responsible it is because there are people in Latin America who have been willing to betray their own people and support you and your politics against the common good. . . . The poor people, the masses, . . . even they are anti-American, perhaps because it is in the air. Every day there is propaganda against the U.S.A., for instance from news commentators, so even the poor are likely to be anti-American." (Alemán, p. 19) Nothing tells us that these attitudes have changed. On the contrary, we suspect that they have grown worse.

[49]"Les effets du changement social sur la religion Catholique en Amerique Latine," ARchSR. 12 (1962). p. 72, quoted in Eugenio Recio, "Responsabilidad de la Iglesia en el Subdesarrollo," p. 130 in Garcia, S.J., ed.

[50]Ernesto Cardenal, S.J., *El Evangelio en Solentiname* (Salamanca, España: Ediciones Sígueme, 1975), p. 131. (Reference to English translation.)

[51]*Gaudium et spes,* no. 19. Parentheses mine.

[52]Ibid., no. 21. Parentheses mine.

[53]See George Lichteim, *Marxism: An Historical & Critical Study* (New York: Praeger Publishers, 1965), pp. 3-20.

[54]*A Marxist Looks at Jesus,* trans. Kreuz Verlag, with an Introduction by Peter Hebblethwaite (Philadelphia: Fortress Press, 1976), p. 21.

[55]Ibid., p. 194.

BIBLIOGRAPHY

Abbott, S.J., Walter M., gen. ed. *The Documents of Vatican II*. Introduction by Lawrence Cardinal Shehan. Translation ed., Very Rev. Msgr. Joseph Gallagher. New York: The America Press, 1966.

Alegre, Xavier. "Mi Reino no es de este Mundo." *Diakonia* 21 (enero-abril 1982): 68-82.

Alemán, S.J., José A. "How U.S. Jesuits can Help Us." In *Priests and Sisters for Latin America*. LADOC Keyhole Series N. 4. Washington, D.C.: U.S. Catholic Conference.

Antoncich, S.J., Ricardo. *Los Cristianos Ante La Injusticia*. Bogotá: Indo-American Press, 1980.

Arroyo, S.J., Alberto. "Cambio Estructural." *Christus* 534 (mayo 1980): 18-20.

______. "Clases Sociales." *Christus* 534 (mayo 1980): 20-4.

Arroyo, S.J., Gonzalo. "Socialismo." *Christus* 534 (mayo 1980): 61-3.

______. "Teoría de la Dependencia." *Christus* 548 (septiembre 1981): 15-22.

Assman, Hugo, "El Lugar Propio de una Teología de la Revolución." Translated by Javier Medina-Dávila. *Selecciones de Teología* 38 (1971); 157-71.

______. *Theology for a Nomad Church*. Introduction by Frederick Herzog. Translated by Paul Burns. Maryknoll: Orbis Books, 1975.

Augustine, Saint. *The City of God*. Translated by Marcus Dods, D.D. Introduction by Thomas Merton. New York: The Modern Library, 1950.

______. *The Confessions*. Books I-X. Translated by F.J. Sheed. New York: Sheed and Ward, 1942.

Bandera, Armando, *La Iglesia Ante el Proceso de Liberación Cristiana*. Madrid: Biblioteca de Autores Cristianos, 1975.

Benedict XIV, Pope. *Vix pervenit*. 1 November 1745.

Berryman, Phillip. "What Happened at Puebla." In *Churches and Politics in Latin America*, pp. 55-86. Edited by Daniel H. Levine. Preface by John P. Harrison. Beverly Hills: SAGE Publications, Inc. 1979.

Bigó, S.J., P. Pierre. "El 'Instrumental Científico' Marxista." In *Liberación: Diálogos en el CELAM*, pp. 247-51. Edited by Celam. Bogotá: CELAM, 1974.

Bluhm, William T. *Theories of the Political System*. New Jersey: Prentice-Hall, Inc., 1965.

Boff, Clodovis. "Fisionomía de las Comunidades Eclesiales de Base." *Diakonia*

19 (agosto-octobre 1981): 2-9.

Boff, Leonardo. "Christ's Liberation via Oppression." (In Gibellini below).

______. ¿"Que es hacer Teología desde América Latina"? (In Encuentro Latinoamericano below).

______. *Teología Desde el Cautiverio*. Bogotá: Indo-American Press, 1975.

Brown, Robert McAfee. *Theology in a New Key: Responding to Liberation Themes*. Philadelphia: The Westminster Press, 1978.

Bruneau, Thomas C. *The Political Transformation of the Brazilian Church*. London: Cambridge University Press, 1974.

Cámara, Dom Helder. "Cristianismo y Socialismo." (21 julio 1972). (In Centro de Estudios y Publicaciones. *Signos de Liberación* below).

______. "La Violencia en el Mundo Moderno." (25 abril 1968). (In Comisión Episcopal de Acción Social below).

Cardenal, S.J., Ernesto. *El Evangelio en Solentiname*. (English translation) Salamanca: Ediciones Sígueme, 1975.

Cardoso, Fernando H. and Faletto, Enzo. *Dependencia y Desarrollo en América Latina: Ensayo de Interpretación*. 7th ed. Buenos Aires: Editores Síglo 21, 1973.

Catherine of Siena, Saint. "The Attainment of Perfect Love." (In de Jaegher, below).

CELAM. *La Evangelización en el Presente y en el Futuro de América Latina*. 2da ed. Bogotá: Editora L. Canal y Asociados, 1979.

______. *La Iglesia en la Actual Transformación de América Latina a la Luz del Concilio*. Vol. 2: Conclusiones. 5ta ed. Bogotá: Indo-American Press, 1970.

______. *Liberación: Diálogos en el CELAM*. Bogotá: CELAM, 1974.

Centro de Estudios y Publicaciones, ed. *Signos de Liberación*. Lima: Centro de Estudios y Publicaciones, 1973.

______. *Signos de Lucha y Esperanza*. Lima: Centro de Estudios y Publicaciones, 1978.

Chaigne, O.F.M., F. Hervé. "Son los Pobres los que se Liberan." In *La Violencia de los Pobres*, pp. 13-37. Edited by "Frères du Monde." Translated by Juan Estruch. Barcelona: Editorial Nova Terra, 1968.

Comblin, Joseph. "Freedom and Liberation as Theological Concepts." (In Geffré and Gutiérrez below).

Comisión Episcopal de Acción Social. ed. *Signos de Renovación*. Lima: Editorial

Universitaria, 1969.

Comunidades Eclesiales de Base de Nicaragua. "Carta Abierta a los Obispos, Sacerdotes, Religiosos y demas Laicos del Pueblo de Dios." *ECA* (agosto 1981): 825-30.

Conferencia Episcopal de Nicaragua. "Cristianos en Solidaridad con Nicaragua." *Servir* 81 (3er bimestre 1979): 367-70.

Convención del Escorial — 1972. *Fe Cristiana y Cambio Social en América Latina.* Salamanca: Ediciones Sígueme, 1973.

Danielou, Jean. *Oración y Política.* Translated by O.L.M.S. Barcelona: Editorial Pomaire, S.A., 1966.

de Chardin, Pierre Teilhard. *The Divine Milieu.* General editor of the English edition, Bernard Wall. New York: Harper and Brothers, Publishers, 1960.

de Egaña, S.J., Antonio. *Historia de la Iglesia en la América Española - Hemisferio Sur.* Madrid: Biblioteca de Autores Cristianos, 1966.

de Jaegher, Paul, ed. *An Anthology of Christian Mysticism.* Translation by Donald Attwater. Springfield: Templegate Publishers, 1977.

de Valle, Luis. "Acompañar al Pueblo." *Christus* 547 (agosto 1981): 45-47.

Deutsch, Karl. *The Nerves of Government.* New York: The Free Press, 1966.

"Documento Final del Encuentro Intereclesial de Comunidades de Base." *Christus* 548 (Septiembre 1981): 48-9.

Dos Santos, Theotonio. *Dependencia y Cambio Social.* Santiago: CESO, 1970.

______. *Dependencia Economica y Cambio Revolucionario en América Latina.* Caracas: Editorial Nueva Izquierda, 1970.

Dupre, Louis. *The Philosophical Foundations of Marxism.* New York: Harcourt, Brace and World, Inc., 1966.

Durant, Will. *The Story of Civilization.* Vol.3: *Caesar and Christ.* New York: Simon and Schuster, 1944.

______. *The Story of Civilization.* Vol. 4: *The Age of Faith.* New York: Simon and Schuster, 1950.

Durant, Will and Ariel. *The Story of Civilization.* Vol. 9: *The Age of Voltaire.* New York: Simon and Schuster, 1965.

Dussel, Enrique. "Domination-Liberation: A New Approach. " Translated by J.D. Mitchell. (In Geffré and Gutiérrez below).

______. *Ethics and the Theology of Liberation.* Translated by Bernard F. McWilliams, C.SS.R. Maryknoll: Orbis Books, 1978.

______. "Historical and Philosophical Presuppositions for Latin American

Theology." (In Gibellini below).

Eagleson, John, ed. *Christians and Socialism.* Translated by John Drury. Maryknoll: Orbis Books, 1975.

Easton, David. *A Framework for Political Analysis.* Englewood Cliffs: Prentice-Hall, Inc., 1965.

Ellacuría, Ignacio. "El Auténtico Lugar Social de la Iglesia." *Diakonia* 25 (enero-marzo 1983): 24-36.

_____. *Freedom Made Flesh.* Translated by John Drury. Maryknoll: Orbis Books, 1976.

_____. "Hacia un Fundamentación Filosófica del Método Teológico Latinoamericano." (In Encuentro Latinoamericano de Teologia below).

_____. "Mensaje Etico-Político de Juan Pablo II al Pueblo Centroamericano." *ECA* (marzo-abril 1983): 255-72.

Encuentro Internacional de Obispos de América Latina. "La No-Violencia Evangélica, Fuerza de Liberación." *Nueva Sociedad* 36 (mayo-junio 1978): 127-38.

Encuentro Latinoamericano de Teología, ed. *Liberación y Cautiverio.* Mexico, D.F.: n.p. 1975.

Episcopado del Perú. "La Justicia en el Mundo." (agosto 1971). Reprinted in *Signos de Liberación,* pp. 178-85. Edited by Centro de Estudios y Publicaciones. Lima: Centro de Estudios y Publicaciones, 1973.

Evans, M. Stanton. *The Liberal Establishment.* New York: The Devin-Adair Company, 1965.

Fierro, Alfredo. *The Militant Gospel: A Critical Introduction to Political Theologies.* Translated by John Drury. Maryknoll: Orbis Books, 1977.

Freire, Paulo. "Conscientizing as a Way of Liberating." In *Paulo Freire,* pp. 3-10. LADOC Keyhole Series, n.1. Washington, D.C.: U.S. Catholic Conference, 1980.

_____. "Letter to a Young Theology Student." In *Paulo Freire,* pp. 10-14. LADOC Keyhole Series n.1. Washington, D.C.: U.S. Catholic Conference, 1980.

_____. *Pedagogy of the Oppressed.* Translated by Myra Bergman Ramos. New York: Herder and Herder, 1970.

Furtado, Celso. *La Economía Latinoamericana Desde la Conquista Ibérica Hasta la Revolución Cubana.* 3a ed. Translated by Angelica Gimpel Smith. Santiago: Editorial Universitaria, 1973.

Galilea, Segundo y Vidales, Raúl. *Cristología y Pastoral Popular.* Bogotá: Ediciones Sígueme, 1973.

Galilea, Segundo. New York, New York. Interview, 18 July 1979.

———. Lecture at St. Joseph Seminary. Washington, D.C. June 1981.

———. "Liberation Theology and New Tasks Facing Christians." Translated by John Drury. (In Gibellini below).

———. *Teología de la Liberación Después de Puebla*. 2da ed. Bogotá: Indo-American Press, 1979.

Geffré, Claude and Gutiérrez, Gustavo, eds. *The Mystical and Political Dimension of the Christian Faith. Concilium* New York: Herder and Herder, 1974.

Gibellini, Rosino, ed. *Frontiers of Theology in Latin America*. Translated by John Drury. Maryknoll: Orbis Books, 1979.

Gil, Victor. "Ateismo y Marxismos Occidentales de Hoy." *Vida Pastoral* 101 c (órgano oficial de la Conferencia Episcopal Uruguaya). (enero-febrero 1984): 43-64.

Girardi, Jules. *Amor Cristiano y Lucha de Clases*. Salamanca: Ediciones Sígueme, 1975.

Gomez Caffarena, S.J., José. *Hacia el Verdadero Cristianismo*. Madrid: Editorial Razón y Fe S.A., 1966.

Gudorf, Christine E. *Catholic Social Teaching on Liberation Themes*. Lanham, Maryland: University Press of America, Inc., 1980.

Gunder Frank, André. *Capitalism and Underdevelopment in Latin America*. New York: Monthly Review Press, 1969.

Gutiérrez, Gustavo. "Comunidades Cristianas de Base: Perspectivas Eclesiológicas." *Diakonia* 19 (agosto-octobre 1981): 24-42.

———. "Liberation Praxis and Christian Faith." (In Gibellini above).

———. "Liberation, Theology and Proclamation." Translated by J. P. Donnelly. (In Geffré and Gutiérrez above).

———. *Teología de la Liberación*. 8va ed. Salamanca: Ediciones Sígueme, 1972.

Häring, C.SS.R., Bernard. *Faith and Morality in the Secular Age*. Garden City: Doubleday and Company, Inc., 1973.

Harrington, Michael. *Socialism*. New York: Saturday Review Press, 1972; Bantam Books, 1973.

Heckel, S.J., Roger. "El Tema de la Liberación en Juan Pablo II." *Medellín* 27 (septiembre 1981): 424-37.

Hennelly, Alfred T. *Theologies in Conflict: the Challenge of Juan Luis Segundo*. Maryknoll: Orbis Books, 1979.

Hernández Pico, S.J., Juan. "Método Teológico Latinoamericano y Normatividad del Jesús Histórico para la Praxis Política Mediada por el

Análisis de la Realidad." (In Encuentro Latinoamericano de Teología above).

_____. "El Proceso Político en la Nicaragua Liberada." *Christus* 538 (septiembre 1980): 11-22.

Higuera Udías, Gonzalo. ¿"Evolución o Revolucion"? *In Teología y Sociología del Desarrollo,* pp. 209-26. Edited by Matías García, S.J. Madrid: Editorial Razón y Fe, S.A., 1968.

Hofinger, S.J., Johannes. *Evangelization and Catechesis.* New York: Paulist Press, 1976.

Hook, Sidney, *From Hegel to Marx.* With a new Introduction. Ann Arbor: The University of Michigan Press, 1971.

Houtart, Francois and Pin, Emile. *The Church and the Latin American Revolution.* Translation by Gilbert Barth. New York: Sheed and Ward, 1966.

Jaguaribe, Helio. *La Dependencia Política-Economica de América Latina.* Mexico, D.F.: Editories Síglo 21, 1969.

Jedin, Hubert and Dolan, John, gen. eds. *History of the Church.* 10 vols. New York: The Crossroads Publishing Co., 1965-1981. Vol. 8: *The Church in the Age of Liberalism,* by Roger Aubert. Translated by Peter Becker.

The Jerusalem Bible. General Editor, Alexander Jones, L.S.S., S.T.L., I.C.B. Garden City: Doubleday and Company, Inc., 1966.

John of the Cross, Saint. "Complete Mortification Necessary for Wisdom." (In De Jaegher above).

John Paul II, Pope. Address to the Bishops. Costa Rica. 2 March 1983.

_____. Address to the Bishops of CELAM. Rio de Janeiro, Brazil: 2 July 1980.

_____. Address to Diplomatic Corps. Brazilia, Brazil. 30 June 1980.

_____. Address to the Ecumenical Council of Churches. Geneva, Switzerland. 12 June 1984.

_____. Address to Farmworkers. Panama. 5 March 1983.

_____. Address to the President of Brazil. Brazilia. 30 June 1980.

_____. Address in Salvador, Brazil. 6 July 1980.

_____. Address to Women Religious. Costa Rica. 3 March 1983.

_____. Address to Workers in Morumbi Stadium. Sao Paulo, Brazil. 3 July 1980.

_____. Address to the Youth. Costa Rica. 3 March 1983.

_____. General Audience Address, Vatican City. 21 February 1979.

_____. General Audience Address, Vatican City. 16 March 1983.

———. Homily at the Airport. Haiti. 9 March 1983.

———. Homily at Campo di Marte. Guatemala. 7 March 1983.

———. Homily at Metro Centre. El Salvador. 6 March 1983.

———. Homily at Namao Airport. Canada. 17 September 1984, 4.

———. Homily on Occasion of the Workers Jubilee. Vatican City. 25 March 1984.

———. Letter to the Nicaraguan Bishops. Vatican City. 29 June 1982.

———. *Redemptor hominis*. 4 March 1979.

———. University Message. Guatemala. 7 March 1983.

Keohane, Robert O. and Nye, Joseph S. *Power and Interdependence*. Boston: Little, Brown and Co., 1977.

Kloppenburg, O.F.M., Bonaventura. *Christian Salvation and Human Temporal Progress*. Translated by Paul Burns. Chicago: Franciscan Herald Press, 1979.

———. "La Eclesiología Militante de Leonardo Boff." *Medellín* 30 (junio 1982): 267-86.

Knorr, Klaus. *The Power of Nations*. New York: Basic Books, Inc. 1975.

Kuhn, Thomas S. *The Structure of Scientific Revolutions*. 2nd ed. Chicago: The University of Chicago Press, 1970.

Le Bras, Gabriel, "The Sociology of the Church in the Early Middle Ages." In *Early Medieval Society*, pp. 47-57. Edited by Sylvia L. Thrupp. New York: Appleton-Century-Crofts, 1967.

Leo XIII, Pope. *Immortale Dei*. November 1, 1985.

———. *Inscrutabili Dei*. April 21, 1878.

———. *Libertas praestantissimum*. June 20, 1888.

———. *Rerum novarum*. 15 May 1891.

Lernoux, Penny. *Cry of the People*. New York: Penguin Books, 1980.

Lichteim, George. *Marxism, An Historical and Critical Study*. New York: Praeger Publishers, 1965.

Liss, Sheldon B., and Peggy K., eds. *Man, State, and Society in Latin American History*. New York: Praeger Publishers, 1972.

López Trujillo, Alfonso. *Hacia Una Sociedad Nueva*. Bogotá: Ediciones Paulinas, 1978.

———. *Liberación Marxista y Liberación Cristiana*. Madrid: Biblioteca de Autores Cristianos, 1974.

_____. "Las Teologías de la Liberación en América Latina," in *Liberación: Diálogos en el CELAM,* pp. 27-67. Edited by CELAM. Bogotá: CELAM, 1974.

Machoveč, Milan. *A Marxist Looks at Jesus.* Translated by Kreuz Verlag. Introduction by Peter Hebblethwaite. Philadelphia: Fortress Press, 1976.

Marins, José; Trevisan, Teolide, M.; and Jensen, Daniel. *Iglesia y Conflictividad Social en América Latina.* Bogotá: Ediciones Paulinas, 1975.

McLellan, David. *The Thought of Karl Marx: An Introduction.* New York: Harper and Row, Publishers, 1971.

Marx, Karl. "Contribution to the Critique of Hegel's Philosophy of Right." In *Karl Marx - Early Writings,* pp. 43-59. Edited and translated by T.B. Bottomore. Foreword by Erich Fromm. New York: McGraw-Hill Book Co., 1963.

Marx, Karl and Engels, Frederick. *The German Ideology.* Translated and edited by S. Ryazanskaya. Moscow: Progress Publishers, 1968.

_____. *Manifesto of the Communist Party.* In *Selected Works.* Vol. 1. Moscow: Progress Publishers, 1969.

Meunier, A. Dauphin. *La Iglesia Ante el Capitalismo.* Translated by Francisco Sabate. Valencia: Ediciones Fomento de Cultura, 1956.

Metz, S.J., Johannes B. "Para una Cultura Política de la Paz." *Christus* 542 (febrero 1981): 25-7.

_____. "Teología Política." Translated by Javier Medina-Dávila. *Selecciones de Teología* 38 (abril-junio 1971): 98-103.

Miguez-Bonino, José. "Popular Piety in Latin America." (In Geffré and Gutiérrez above).

Miranda, José P. *Marx and the Bible.* Maryknoll: Orbis Books, 1974.

Moreira Alves, María. Conference at the Institute for Policy Studies, Washington, D.C. 18 February 1982.

Morse, Richard M. "Political Foundations." Excerpt reprinted in *Man, State, and Society in Latin American History,* pp. 73-8. Edited by Liss, Sheldon B., and Peggy K. New York: Praeger Publishers, 1972.

Movimiento Obrero de Acción Católica (Chile). "Declaración." (septiembre 1970. (In Centro de Estudios y Publicaciones above).

Movimiento Sacerdotal ONIS. "Propiedad Privada y Nueva Sociedad." (17 agosto 1970). (In Centro e Estudios y Publicaciones above).

_____. "Situación del Pueblo y Responsibilidad Cristiana." (17 enero 1977). (In *Signos de Lucha y Esperanza,* Centro de Estudios y Publicaciones above).

_____. "Trabajo Humano y Propiedad Social." (27 octubre 1973). (In *Signos de Lucha y Esperanza,* Centro de Estudios y Publicaciones above).

Munarriz, Mikel. "Los Cambios Introducidos en el Documento." *SIC* 422 (febrero 1980): 76-9.

———. "Los Cambios Introducidos en el Documento (II)." *SIC* 423 (marzo 1980): 113-16.

Muñoz, Ronaldo. "Lucha de Clases y Evangelio." In *Panorama de la Teología Latinoamericana*, pp. 289-99. Edited by Equipo SELADOC -Universidad Católica de Chile. Salamanca: Ediciones Sígueme, 1975.

———. *Solidaridad Liberadora - Misión Eclesial*. Bogotá: Indo-American Press, 1977.

Northeastern Bishops in Brazil. "He Escuchado el Clamor de mi Pueblo." (6 mayo 1973). (Centro de Estudios y Publicaciones above).

Novak, Michael. "Liberation Theology and the Pope." In *The Pope and Revolution*, pp. 73-85. Edited by Quentin L. Quade. Foreward by Richard John Neuhaus. Washington, D.C.: Ethics and Public Policy Center, 1982.

———. *The Spirit of Democratic Capitalism*. New York: Simon and Schuster, 1982.

Oakely, Francis. *The Medieval Experience: Foundations of Western Cultural Singularity*. New York: Charles Scribner's Sons, 1974.

Obispos y Misioneros del Brasil. "El Indio: Aquel Que Debe Morir." (julio-agosto 1974). (In *Signos de Lucha y Esperanza*, Centro de Estudios y Publicaciones above).

Obispos de Nicaragua. "Compromiso Cristiano con una Nueva Nicaragua." *Christus* 536 (octubre 1980): 54-8.

Obregón Valverde, Enrique. "Principios de la Social Democracia." *Nueva Sociedad* 36 (mayo-junio 1978): 143-48.

Oliveros, S.J., Roberto. *Liberación y Teología*. Lima: Centro de Estudios y Publicaciones, 1977.

Organizaciones Laicas de Sao Paulo. "Por Justicia y Liberación." (18 septiembre 1977). (In *Signos de Lucha y Esperanza*, Centro de Estudios y Publicaciones above).

Paul VI, Pope. *Ecclesiam suam*. 6 August 1964.

———. *Evangelii nuntiandi*. 8 December 1975.

———. *Octogesima adveniens*. 14 May 1971.

———. *Populorum progression*. 26 March 1967.

Paz, Nestor. "Al Pueblo de Bolivia." (1970). (In Centro de Estudios y Publicaciones above).

Pelissier, Lucien. "La Iglesia y la Lucha de Clases." In *La Violencia de los Pobres*, pp. 148-85. Edited by "Freres du Monde." Translated by Jan Estruch. Barcelona: Editorial Nova Tierra, 1968.

Pike, Frederick B. *The Conflict Between Church and State in Latin America*. Except reprinted in *Man, State, and Society in Latin American History*, pp. 205-20. Edited by Liss, Sheldon B., and Peggy K. New York: Praeger Publishers, 1972.

Pius IX, Pope. *Syllabus*. December 8, 1864.

_____. *Quanta cura*. December 8, 1864.

_____. *Divini redemptoris*. 19 March 1937.

Poblete, P. Renato. "La Teoría de la Dependencia: Análisis Crítico." In *Liberación: Diálogos en el CELAM*. pp. 201-20. Edited by CELAM. Bogotá: CELAM, 1974.

Poradowski, Miguel. "Puebla y la Revolución Marxista." *Verbo* 179-180 (noviembre-diciembre 1979): 1149-73.

Powell, S.J., John. *Fully Human, Fully Alive: A New Life Through a New Vision*. Niles, Illinois: Argus Communications, 1976.

Prebisch, Raúl. *Capitalismo Periférico - Crisis y Transformaciones*. Mexico, D.F.: Fondo de Cultura Económica, 1981.

Ratzinger, Cardinal Joseph. *Instruction on Certain Aspects of the "Theology of Liberation."* Translation by the Vatican. 6 August 1984.

"Ratzinger: Vi Spiego la Teología della Liberazione." *30 Giorni* (March 1984): 48-55.

Rauschenbusch, Walter. *Christianity and the Social Crisis*. Edited by Robert D. Cross. New York: Harper and Row, Inc., 1964.

Recio, Eugenio. "Responsibilidad de la Iglesia en el Subdesarrollo." In *Teología del Desarrollo,* pp. 125-50. Edited by Matías García, S.J. Madrid: Editorial Razón y Fe, S.A., 1968.

Richard, Pablo. *La Iglesia Latinoamericana Entre el Temor y la Esperanza*. Bogotá: Indo-American Press, 1981.

_____. "El Rol Político e Histórico de la Iglesia," *Nueva Sociedad 36* (mayo-junio 1978): 14-23.

Rodriquez, Federico, ed. *Doctrina Pontificia - Documentos Sociales*. Madrid: Biblioteca de Autores Cristianos, 1959.

Rodriquez de Yurre, Gregorio. *El Marxismo*. Vol. 2. Madrid: Biblioteca de Autores Cristianos, 1976.

Rogier, Louis J., gen. ed. *The Christian Centuries: A New History of the Catholic Church*. 5 vols. New York: Paulist Press, 1963-1978. Vol. 5: *The Church in a Secularized Society,* by Roger Aubert. Translated by Janet Sondheimer.

Romero, Msgr. Oscar Arnulfo. *Iglesia y Organizaciones Políticas Populares*. 6 agosto 1978.

Sacerdotes Para el Tercer Mundo. "Reflexión Sobre la Violencia." (4 octubre 1970). (In Centro de Estudios y Publicaciones above).

Scannone, Juan Carlos. "Ontología del Proceso Autenticamente Liberador." In *Panorama de la Teología Latinoamericana,* pp. 246-87. Edited by Equip-oSELADOC - Universidad Católica de Chile. Salamanca: Ediciones Síqueme, 1975.

Second Vatican Council. "Gaudium et spes." (In Abbott above).

______. "Lumen gentium." (In Abbott above).

Seis Organizaciones Católicas en El Salvador. "Sobre la Ofensiva de Enero." *ECA* 36 (enero-febrero 1981): 85-9.

Segundo, S.J., Juan Luis. "Capitalism Versus Socialism: Crux Theologica." (In Gibellini above).

______. "Condicionamientos Actuales de la Reflexión Teológica Latinoamericana." (In Encuentro Latinoamericano de Teología above).

______. *Masas y Minorías en la Dialéctica Divina de la Liberación*. Buenos Aires: La Aurora, 1973. Quoted in Hennelly, above.

______. *The Liberation of Theology*. Translated by John Drury. Maryknoll: Orbis Books, 1979.

Singer, Marshall R. *Weak States in a World of Power*. New York: The Free Press, 1972.

Sobrino, Jon. "El Conocimiento Teológico en la Teología Europea y Latinoamericana." (In Encuentro Latinoamericano de Teología above).

______."La Esperanza de los Pobres en América Latina." *Diakonia* 25 (enero-marzo 1983): 3-23.

______. "Espiritualidad de Jesús y Espiritualidad de la Liberación." In *Espiritualidad de la Liberación,* pp. 53-70. Lima: Centro de Estudios y Publicaciones, (1980).

______. "Persecución a la Iglesia en Centro América," *ECA* (julio 1981): 645-64.

Southern, R.W. *Western Society and the Church in the Middle Ages*. The Pelican History of the Church. General Editor, Owen Chadwick. Middlesex, England: Penquin Books Ltd., 1970.

"Statement by the Nicaraguan Bishops." *L'Osservatore Romano,* 5 August 1984, daily edition, p. 2.

Stein, Stanley J., and Barbara H. *The Colonial Heritage of Latin America: Essays on Economic Dependence in Perspective*. Excerpt reprinted in Liss above.

Sunkel, Osvaldo. *El Subdesarrollo Latinoamericano y la Teoría del Desarrollo.* Mexico, D.F.: Editores Siglo 21, 1970.

Suso, Blessed Henry. "The Worth of Temporal Trials." (In De Jaegher above).

Tellenbach, Gerd. *Church, State and Christian Society at the Time of the Investiture Contest.* Translation and Introduction by R.F. Bennett. New York: Harper Torchbooks, 1970.

Trigo, S.J., Pedro. ¿"Doctrina Social de la Iglesia"? *Nueva Sociedad* 36 (mayo-junio 1978): 35-44.

_____. ¿"Giro en la Politica Religiosa del P.C. Cubano"? *Christus* 545 (mayo 1981): 34-38.

Turner, Frederick C. *Catholicism and Political Development in Latin America.* Chapel Hill: University of North Carolina Press, 1971.

Ullman, Walter. *Papal Government in the Middle Ages.* London: Methuen and Co., Ltd., 1955.

Vidales, Raúl. "Acotaciones a la Problemática Sobre el Método en la Teología de la Liberación." (In Encuentro Latinoamericano de Teología above).

_____. "Methodological Issues in Liberation Theology." (In Gibellini above).

Watkins, Frederick. *The Political Tradition of the West.* Cambridge: Harvard University Press, 1948.

Winter, Derek. *Hope in Capitivity: The Prophetic Church in Latin America.* London: Epworth Press, 1977.

Wolff, Robert Paul. *The Poverty of Liberalism.* Boston: Beacon Press, 1968.

Zenteno, S.J., Arnaldo. "Compromiso por la Liberación." *Christus* 548 (septiembre 1981): 41-7.

APPENDIX

Biographical Data on the Best Known Liberation Theologians

Hugo Assman

He studied philosophy and sociology in Brazil, and pursued a degree in theology in Rome. He was director of the Sao Paulo Institute of Philosophy and Theology (Brazil); Visiting Professor on the theology faculty of the University of Munster (Germany); lately, University Professor of communications in San José, Costa Rica. He uses Marxism on global terms, perhaps more than any other liberation theologian. He has been forced out of Brazil, Uruguay, Bolivia, and Chile.

Leonardo Boff

Born in Brazil. He was ordained into the Franciscan Order in 1964. Studied philosophy and theology in Brazil, and in Munich under Karl Rahner. He is Professor of systematic theology at the Petropolis Institute for Philosophy and Theology in Rio de Janeiro, Brazil. Well known for his studies on Christology, he was called to Rome in 1984 to testify before the Vatican Congregation for the Doctrine of the Faith about his writings.

Joseph Comblin

Born in Brussels, Belgium. Holds a doctorate degree in theology from the University of Louvain. Ordained to the priesthood in 1947. Also, expelled from Brazil, where he taught theology at the Campinas Catholic University in São Paulo. He is a contributor to the theme of the theology of revolution, which was in vogue in Europe years before liberation theology appeared.

Enrique Dussel

An Argentinian Catholic layman, he holds a doctorate in

philosophy from the University of Madrid, a doctorate in history from the Sorbonne, and a licentiate in theology from the Catholic Institute of Paris. He is President of the Historical Commission of the Church in Latin America, and considered an expert in Latin American Church History. He was expelled from his country for his political views during the military regime.

Ignacio Ellacuría

Born in Spain. Has lived and worked in Central America for over twenty years. He became a Jesuit and studied under Karl Rahner. He holds a licentiate in theology and a doctorate in philosophy. He is Professor at the Universidad Centroamericana Jose Simeon Canas in El Salvador, and is actively involved in religious grassroots organizations.

Paulo Freire

Born in Brazil. Though he holds a licentiate in law, he became a specialist in pedagogy. He is mostly known for establishing an educational method to teach literacy to the poor, which leads to the creation of a critical consciousness through consciousness raising. This method forms one of the theoretical bases of liberation theology and leads to "conscientization," one of the prime objectives in the praxis of liberation.

Segundo Galilea

Born in Chile. Ordained a priest in 1956. His work focuses mainly on pastoral theology and the spirituality of liberation. Occasionally, he lectures in the United States. He has held posts at CELAM, and has been director of the Latin American Pastoral Institute.

Gustavo Gutiérrez

Considered the pioneer in liberation theology in the sense that he was the first one to articulate in a systematic fashion the main themes of the theology. Born in Lima, Peru, he pursued studies in philosophy and psychology at the University of Louvain. Holds a degree in theology from the University of Lyon, France. He was ordained to the priesthood in 1959. He teaches theology and Marxist philosophy at the Catholic University in Lima, and acts as advisor to Christian Ecclesiastical Base Communities in Peru. He is member of the National Secretariat of the priests movement known as ONIS.

Ronaldo Muñoz

He was born in Chile, where he pursued studies in philosophy and theology. Ordained a priest in 1961. In 1972 he obtained his doctorate in theology from the University of Regensburg, West Germany. He is a former advisor for the Latin American Confederation of Religious (CLAR).

Pablo Richard

Chilian theologian. Active participant in Christians for Socialism Movement in Chile along with one of its co-founders, Gonzalo Arroyo, S.J.

Juan Carlos Scannone

A Jesuit priest since 1962, Scannone was born in Buenos Aires, Argentina. He received his doctorate degree in philosophy from the University of Munich, and a licentiate in theology from the University of Innsbruck, Austria. At present, he is Dean of the Philosphy Faculty at the University of Salvador (Argentina).

Juan Luis Segundo

Probably the most prolific writer in the liberation movement. Born in Uruguay, he was ordained a Jesuit in 1955. Studied theology at Louvain, and received his Doctorate of Letters from the University of Paris. He is associated with the Peter Faber

Center in Montevideo, doing research in the sociology of religion. He has taught at Harvard University.

Raúl Vidales

Born in Mexico and ordained to the priesthood in 1967. Holds a licentiate in theology and sociology. Actively involved in grassroots organizations and evangelization along liberation lines. Presently, he works with Gustavo Gutiérrez at the Bartolomé de las Casas Research Center in Lima, Perú.